LEMONS, LIMES & ORANGES
150 CITRUS RECIPES

LEMONS, LIMES & ORANGES
150 CITRUS RECIPES

A guide to zesty fruits and how to cook
with them, shown in 600 photographs

CORALIE DORMAN

southwater

This edition is published by Southwater,
an imprint of Anness Publishing Ltd,
108 Great Russell Street, London WC1B 3NA;
info@anness.com

www.southwaterbooks.com; www.annesspublishing.com;
twitter: @Anness_Books

If you like the images in this book and would like to investigate
using them for publishing, promotions or advertising, please visit
our website www.practicalpictures.com for more information.

Publisher: Joanna Lorenz
Senior Editor: Margaret Malone
Photographer: Nicki Dowey
Home Economist: Carol Tennant
Stylist: Helen Trent
Designer: Nigel Partridge
Additional Photography: Edward Allwright, Steve Baxter, Nicki Dowey,
    James Duncan, Gus Filgate, Ian Garlick, Michelle Garrett, Amanda
    Heywood, Janine Hosegood, David Jordan, Dave King, Don Last,
    William Lingwood, Thomas Odulate, Craig Robertson and Sam Stowell
Additional Recipes: Catherine Atkinson, Alex Barker, Angela Boggiano,
    Jacqueline Clark, Carole Clements, Trish Davies, Roz Denny, Matthew
    Drennan, Joanna Farrow, Christine France, Yasuko Fukuoka, Brian
    Glover, Nicola Graimes, Christine Ingram, Lucy Knox, Sue Maggs,
    Sally Mansfield, Maggie Mayhew, Norma Miller, Sallie Morris, Jenni
    Shapter, Anne Sheasby, Hilaire Walden, Kate Whiteman, Elizabeth
    Wolf-Cohen and Jeni Wright
Production Controller: Stephanie Moe

PUBLISHER'S NOTE
Although the advice and information in this book are believed to be
accurate and true at the time of going to press, neither the authors
nor the publisher can accept any legal responsibility or liability
for any errors or omissions that may have been made nor for any
inaccuracies nor for any loss, harm or injury that comes about from
following instructions or advice in this book.

COOK'S NOTES
Bracketed terms are intended for American readers.
For all recipes, quantities are given in both metric and imperial measures
and, where appropriate, in standard cups and spoons. Follow one set of
measures, but not a mixture, because they are not interchangeable.
Standard spoon and cup measures are level. 1 tsp = 5ml, 1 tbsp = 15ml,
1 cup = 250ml/8fl oz.
Australian standard tablespoons are 20ml. Australian readers should
use 3 tsp in place of 1 tbsp for measuring small quantities.
American pints are 16fl oz/2 cups. American readers should use
20fl oz/2.5 cups in place of 1 pint when measuring liquids.
Electric oven temperatures in this book are for conventional ovens. When
using a fan oven, the temperature will probably need to be reduced by
about 10–20°C/20–40°F. Since ovens vary, you should check with your
manufacturer's instruction book for guidance.
Medium (US large) eggs are used unless otherwise stated.

CONTENTS

INTRODUCTION

From their cultivation in China and India, thousands of years ago, citrus fruits have been highly valued by people all around the world. They have inspired much art and architecture, been a source of scientific fascination and study, and have constituted an important trade commodity. Not least, however, they offer something unique to food and drinks, be it the fresh taste of an orange or the bittersweet bite of a grapefruit.

The citrus family has grown rapidly over the last few decades, so that today varieties differing enormously in size, shape, colour and taste are grown worldwide in over 100 countries. Each fruit has something special to offer, whether it is the quality of the juice, the sweetness of the segments, the aromatic essential oils in the skin or the way in which even just a small quantity of grated peel or dried rind can add a burst of flavour to any number of savoury and sweet dishes.

All kinds of fruit

Though rare and exciting new varieties of citrus are constantly appearing, this introduction focuses on the most widely cultivated ones. There are the "oranges and lemons" of the nursery rhyme; grapefruit that appear in shades of white, pink and ruby; new varieties of citrus such as fragrant citron, used in Jewish festivals; and the ungainly looking but sweet-tasting Ugli fruit.

Modern cross-breeding has resulted in many successful and delicious new specimens though, sometimes, the original is still the best. From the early bitter orange, for instance, which grew wild in China thousands of years ago, there are now almost 50 different varieties growing today, including juicy, seedless sweet oranges as well as the bitter Seville (Temple) oranges. Despite this wide choice, Seville oranges are still considered by experts – and seasoned marmalade makers – to be the only orange to use for marmalade.

Above: Citrus medica, *citron, has been used in the Jewish festival of Sukkot or Tabernacles for centuries.*

First fruit

From its early history, citrus fruits have developed into an important source of trade throughout the world. Often initially viewed as marvellous botanical curiosities, scientific innovation has led to the breeding and exporting of many new varieties of citrus fruit.

In the ancient world, oranges and mandarins first grew in China, where the word "mandarin" also meant a powerful official. Traders carried fruit to India and Arabia, and on to Greece and the shores of the Mediterranean. The Golden Apples of the Hesperides, stolen by the Greek hero Heracles, may have been bitter oranges. Lemons and limes originally grew in India or Malaysia and, through trade, were introduced into Assyria. From there, the soldiers of Alexander the Great took them to Greece. In ancient Athens and Sparta, lemons were used as a flavouring for food, and for medicinal and cosmetic purposes. Roman gardeners planted orange groves in Italy and they may have taken them to Spain. Other historians believe that Muslim invaders

Left: Citrus fruit has long been a source of inspiration to artists, as shown in this still life of grapes, oranges and a lemon by J Gillemans (1618–75).

Above: Two well-dressed ladies buy sweet oranges from a street vendor, engraving by L Schiavonetti, 1794.

were responsible for first introducing them to Spain. Oranges were known as *narayam* or "perfume within" in India 3,000 years ago, and to the Arabs as *narandj*. The Italians softened it to *arancia*, and with a shift of sound, and because the medieval town of Orange was a centre for cultivation of the fruit, the French word became orange.

After the fall of the Roman Empire, the Arabs continued to cultivate oranges and lemons. The Jews also specialized in producing citrus fruit, and today many areas of citrus production were once places where Jews lived. Citron was used as a Jewish symbol on coins and gravestones and in synagogues. When the Jews were expelled from Spain and England, they went to live in northern and eastern Europe, returning to southern Italy, Spain and Sicily each year to buy a variety of citron – known as etrog in the Bible – to help them celebrate the Feast of Tabernacles or Sukkot. At the same time, Jewish merchants brought goods from the north and east, helping to establish trade routes in medieval Europe.

Right: Oranges are packed into crates for export in Andalucía, Spain 1888. Early on, merchants recognized the commercial value of citrus fruit.

Soldiers returned from the Crusades in Palestine via Italian ports, bringing oranges with them. One 11th-century pilgrim to the Holy Land found a fruit called "Adam's apple", a variety of pomelo. "Saracen" brides wore white orange blossoms in their hair as a symbol of innocence and fecundity – an orange tree can bear 3000–4000 oranges in a year. Centuries later, many brides in the Western world still feature orange blossoms in their headdress.

History and trade

In the 15th century, European explorers expanded their knowledge of the world, travelling to the Far East and to America. Christopher Columbus took all kinds of citrus seeds – bitter and sweet oranges, lemon, lime and citron – to Haiti on his second voyage in 1493. Fruit became an exciting commodity with its strong bright colours. In Italy, the Medici coat-of-arms showed five golden oranges. Sweet-smelling

pomanders, made from bitter oranges studded with cloves and herbs, were used by Cardinal Wolsey and others in Tudor England. The rich flavoured their food with bitter orange juice and aromatic citrus rind. In France, lemon juice made the lips red and the complexion pale.

By the 17th century, when "pretty, witty Nell Gwynne" sold sweet Portuguese oranges as an exotic snack in Drury Lane Theatre in London, orange marmalades and candied citrus fruits were incredibly popular. Unlike today, when the Seville orange season in Europe lasts a bare four weeks, it then extended from All Hallows Day (1 November) through to April. At that time, marmalade was a stiff candied paste that could be cut into squares as a sweetmeat.

Up until the 19th century most oranges were bitter, though the first sweet oranges were probably brought back to Europe by Vasco da Gama after

his Cape of Good Hope voyage in 1498. A growing interest in science and a desire for sweeter, tastier fruit led to the rapid development of many hybrids and cross-breeds. Grapefruits and tangerines were crossed to produce varieties of tangelo, including minneolas and Ugli fruit. Sweet oranges and Mexican limes were crossed with the kumquat to produce orangequats and limequats.

Artists and botanical painters such as Jan Pauwel Gillemans the Elder recorded these strange new fruits in still-lifes while Giuseppe Arcimboldo produced extraordinary fruit portraits such as Winter, which shows an old bearded man sprouting leaves and lemons. Architects designed orangeries, extravagant houses in which these rare fruits were grown and the fashionable could walk. Henri IV of France may have erected the first orangery at the Tuileries to shelter the trees from frost, but it was his grandson Louis XIV, the Sun King, who built at Versailles the most magnificent orangery in Europe.

There his chief gardener, la Quintinie produced asparagus in January, strawberries for nine months a year and sweet-scented orange blossom.

A variety of uses

As citrus fruit ceased to be a rare commodity and became more widely accepted, horticulturalists and cooks sought ways to preserve the acid scent of citrus fruit. Distillation produced neroli, an essential oil used in perfume making (named after Anne Maria de la Tremoille, Princess of Nerole), and orange flower water. Bergamot oil was used to perfume the barley sugar made in the French town of Nancy, and also Earl Grey tea, named after a British prime minister in the early 1800s.

People long ago discovered that if you can eat a food, you can also turn it into alcohol. Dutch settlers in the Caribbean island of Curaçao began the tradition of flavouring white rum with the bitter peel of green oranges. This technique was eventually adopted by the French who are today famous for

Above: A view of the orangerie in Lord Burlington's garden, Chiswick, England, 18th century.

the orange-based liqueurs Cointreau and Grand Marnier. Elsewhere, lemons were used in Limoncello in Italy and Limonnaya vodka in Russia, and Mandarine Napoléon is said to have been the Emperor's favourite tipple.

An expanding market

During this period of discovery and growth, there was a constant exchange of varieties of new fruit between Europe and the New World. Oranges from Paraguay and the West Indies were exported to Europe. Dutch settlers planted orange and lemon trees in South Africa. In 1828, the French count Odette Phillippe introduced the grapefruit into Florida, and the state started on its journey to becoming the world's largest producer of grapefruit. In the southern hemisphere, oranges, limes and lemons reached Australia by the end of the 18th century.

At this time doctors realized that citrus juice could prevent scurvy, and British sailors were nicknamed "limeys" by the Americans. After a certain number of days of sea, British sailors were issued with lime juice, liberally mixed with rum, to prevent scurvy, a killing disease. A whole area of London became known as Limehouse, after the great warehouses of limes stored there.

Imports of citrus continued to grow in number of variety and frequency: loose-skinned mandarins, for instance, were introduced to Europe and America in the 19th century. Children found mandarins in the toes of their Christmas stockings, since this fruit came into season around Christmas in Europe, and street-sellers cried, "Who will buy my sweet oranges?"

The modern era has seen a whole new range of fruit juices and fruit products in the shops. The development of sweet oranges from the original bitter oranges means that fruit juice has become an increasingly popular drink. Florida is famous for its oranges and grapefruits and most of the fruit grown there is turned into juice: its people are among the highest consumers of juice

Below: Every part of the Seville orange is highly valued, including the leaves, blossoms and fruit. Drawing from Kew Gardens Library, 19th century.

in the world. Fruit-growing is a major industry in the USA and Brazil, and production of oranges and lemons is a vital part of some countries' GNP. Citric acid is used as a flavouring in a huge variety of commercially produced foods and drinks. Scientists strive to synthesize the flavour for the food industry, but nothing can compare with the real thing.

Cooking with citrus

Virtually every cuisine is touched by the refreshing zesty tang of citrus. Oranges still claim the title of the world's favourite citrus fruit, while lemons and limes provide the undertones in hundreds of dishes. Every country has its own way of preparing citrus fruit. In Morocco, cooks store their harvest of lemons by preserving them with a generous amount of salt and water; in Italy, lemons flavour anything from ice cream to pasta sauces. Greek cuisine is liberally laced with lemons, from egg-and-lemon *avgolemono* to *limonato*, a rich pot-roast of beef flavoured with lemons. Sephardic Jews have many recipes for orange cakes and preserves. Seville orange marmalade is a British breakfast classic.

As well as the juice from the fruit, everything else can be used – flowers, leaves and rinds. The blossoms that form on trees of the bitter or Seville orange are turned into intensively perfumed orange flower or orange blossom water, particularly in the Middle East.

The age-old techniques of preserving the rinds by candying and caramelizing are perfect for decorating cakes and desserts, and a sliver of lemon, orange or lime peel tied up with the herbs that make a bouquet garni, gives it that something extra special.

Limes, although a relatively recent introduction to the West, have been used extensively in Asian cuisines for many centuries, their subtle fragrance enhancing curries, noodle and rice dishes, pickles and chutneys. In Peru, lime juice is used in the classic dish *ceviche*, where it "cooks" raw white fish without heat.

Above: Loading citrus at San Antonio, Paraguay, 1891.

Just juice?

Citrus fruit not only improves the flavour of food, it also nourishes. Nutritional values vary, so it is worth getting to know all the members of this diverse family of fruit. Choosing the best fruit can be difficult. An orange or lemon that feels heavy in the hand may indicate that it bears the maximum amount of juice. However, the Ugli fruit has a large central core, which makes it feel light for its size. Look out for organic fruit and try to use unwaxed fruit in recipes involving the zest.

Apart from vitamin C, present in all types, oranges contain vitamin A and many minerals. Lemons are an excellent source of bioflavonoids, which are a good antioxidant, cleansing the blood, and the juice is a well-known antiseptic, especially good for sore throats. Pink grapefruit contains an amazing five times the amount of vitamin A present in its white relative.

After reading all about this most fascinating family of fruit, turn to the wonderful collection of recipes. They are full of flavour and colour, and prove just how versatile citrus fruit can be. All that flavour is but a squeeze away.

THE CITRUS KITCHEN

Citrus fruits have many uses, from traditional
pomanders to scented pot-pourri, but it is in
the kitchen that they really come into their
own. The following pages explore the
wonderful range of citrus fruits available,
from the original bitter oranges to exotic
hybrids such as Ugli fruit. Information
is provided on their taste, appearance and uses,
as well as tips on buying, storage and
nutritional benefits. There are basic recipes
for marmalades, marinades and citrus curds,
plus an array of sauces and butters for both
savoury and sweet dishes.

ORANGES

Arguably the world's favourite citrus fruit, if not *the* favourite of all fruit, oranges are not always orange. They can be green, yellow or dappled with red. There are hundreds of varieties, ranging from the size of a tennis ball to almost football-size proportions. Some have honey-sweet flesh, while others are so bitter as to be quite inedible.

All citrus peel contains essential oils, and peel from the orange is used in perfume-making and cosmetics, as well as in cooking. Depending on the variety, oranges grow well in tropical, semi-tropical and sub-tropical regions. They ripen on the tree, and do not continue to ripen after picking, so have excellent keeping qualities.

History

The bitter orange probably originated around China and India, and the fruit has been grown in southern China for thousands of years. There is no record of the Romans having cultivated oranges, and it wasn't until around the middle of the 15th century that their cultivation reached the Mediterranean, having first travelled across the Middle East with Arab traders who brought the fruit across from China.

The name orange comes from the ancient Indian word *narayam*. Arabs called the fruit *narandj* and in Italy the word lost its initial vowel and became *arancia*. It is thought that, during medieval times in France, the fruit acquired the name by which it is most widely known today – taking the name of the town of Orange, where there was a large trade in the fruit. Like other commodities introduced by the Arabs into Europe, such as silks, sugar and spices, oranges were a rarity and were synonymous with wealth (the Medici family in Italy chose five oranges as their coat of arms). However, these early cultivars were far too bitter – and too precious – to eat raw, so they were made into preserves, and prized for their perfumed flowers.

The Portuguese, in particular, played a large part in cultivating the bitter orange, patiently developing new varieties. We have them to thank for most of the sweet oranges we eat today, which have their origin in trees that Portuguese farmers imported from China in the middle of the 17th century. These early varieties, which we would probably still consider to be quite bitter, became a novelty theatre snack and one that only the rich could afford.

Oranges do not flourish in cold climates, but this did not deter early 19th-century British gardeners, who were very taken with the exotic fruit. They eagerly adopted the Italian practice of cultivating the fruit in large glasshouses, which could be heated in the winter, and the orangery – the forerunner of the greenhouse – became a much sought-after status symbol.

Christopher Columbus is credited with introducing the orange to America. There is evidence that they were first cultivated in Florida in the 16th century, and introduced to California by Spanish missionaries about two hundred years later. The orange-growing industry was solidly established towards the end of the 19th century and the United States now grows more oranges than any other type of fruit; about one-sixth of the world's supply. Today, oranges are produced on a global scale: China, Spain, Greece, Italy, Morocco, the USA, Turkey, Israel, Australia and South Africa are the main producers.

> **Orange flower water**
> Also known as orange blossom water, this is distilled from the waxy white, star-shaped blossoms that appear before the citrus tree bears fruit. It will enhance the taste of any citrus fruit, especially oranges, and is wonderful in ice creams and fruit salads, jellies (flavoured gelatine) and sorbets (sherbets). Some Middle Eastern salads are dressed with a sprinkling of orange flower water, which lends them a fresh fragrant air.

*Above:
Valencia are
the world's most
popular variety
of orange.*

Varieties

Oranges fall into two principal groups: sweet oranges, which can be eaten raw, and bitter oranges, which cannot.

Sweet oranges, *Citrus sinensis*

Blond or common oranges These are pale-skinned winter varieties like Jaffa or Shamouti (the easiest oranges to peel). A variety called Pineapple is grown in Florida, mainly for its juice as it can be rather pippy, and Natal comes from Brazil. Valencia is the world's favourite eating orange and is grown in all the orange-producing countries: it was sent in the 1860s from the Azores islands, near Portugal, to Thomas Rivers of Hertfordshire, Great Britain, who cultivated it for the orangeries in grand houses. It was originally called Rivers Late, but was renamed Valencia Late in 1887, not because it had any real Spanish connections, but because an expert from Spain thought it was similar to an orange grown in Valencia. The fruits are medium to large, with reasonably thin rind, which is finely marked. Valencias are easy to peel, and have juicy flesh.

Blood or pigmented oranges If it's colour you are after, these are the oranges to use, especially for sorbets (sherbets) and similar iced desserts. With names such as Sanguina, Sanguigna and Sanguine, derived from *sanguis*, the Latin word for blood, they have red-tinged skin and

Above: Seedless navel oranges have very sweet juicy flesh.

golden or ruby red flesh. The red pigment develops naturally when the trees grow where the temperature at night is low; cold storage can also affect a similar change in the fruit's colour.

Bittersweet blood oranges originated in either Malta or Sicily, and the fruit is a key ingredient in the sauce Maltaise, an orange-flavoured mayonnaise, which takes its name from the island's juicy but sour variety of blood orange. Moro is a variety grown mainly in Italy, particularly on the island of Sicily.

Navel oranges These take their name from the small orange that grows inside the apex of the main fruit, a bit like a belly button. The navel, which is the earliest orange to mature, is seedless, sweet and juicy and great for eating in the hand. The most popular navel varieties are the Washington or Bahia navel, Cara Cara, and Lane Late from Australia, or its renamed Spanish version, Navelate. The thick skin is good for making candied peel.

Sugar or acidless oranges These varieties are not cultivated on a vast scale and have a very low acid content and a bland, rather insipid flavour. They are seldom exported, but are more usually grown for local consumption. In the countries where they grow – mainly the Mediterranean region and some parts of South America – they go by a range of different names, such as Lima (Brazil), Dolce (Italy) and Sucreña (Spain).

Above: Blood oranges

Left: Sweet oranges, Citrus sinensis

have enough freezer space, you can store them and make marmalade when you feel like it. The rind is good dried.

Seville oranges are also grown in California and Arizona, purely for their decorative shade on streets, and Japan and China also produce small numbers of their own bitter orange.

Nutrition

Packed with vitamin C, which is highest at the start of the season in winter, oranges are also a source of vitamin A and folic acid and the minerals calcium, potassium and phosphorus. The white pith contains pectin, which, as well as acting as a setting agent for marmalade, helps to lower blood cholesterol levels, and also bioflavonoids, which keep your gums and blood healthy.

Buying and storing

Oranges crop at different times of the year, depending on the variety and, as they are grown worldwide, climate dictates when that will be. You'll always be able to buy oranges all year round, but winter is the optimum time. Cup a fruit in your hand and if it feels heavy, the chances are that it will be full of juice. The skin should be taut and blemish-free. Although annoying, pips (seeds) are not a sign of inferior quality; their presence

Left: Bitter Seville oranges

Bitter oranges, *Citrus aurantium*

These were the first variety of oranges. They originated in India and China and gradually spread through Asia to Europe and North Africa, arriving eventually in the Iberian peninsula, from where they were said to be introduced to the New World by Christopher Columbus.

Seville oranges – known as Bigarade in France or Temple in the USA – taste bitter owing to a compound called neohesperidin. You can't eat them raw, but they are ideal for use in marmalade. In industry, they feature in liqueurs and some soft drinks, and the flowers

from special varieties called *bouquetiers* are used to make oil of neroli, which is used in perfumery. In Europe, Sevilles make a fleeting appearance for a couple of weeks in January, but they freeze well, as does their juice, so if you're not up to making marmalade then and you

Above: Seville oranges are considered by many to be the best type for making orange marmalade.

just depends on the variety. And, as a bowl of bright oranges is a welcome sight during any monochrome winter, it's good to know that they'll keep for two weeks in the refrigerator. The juice and pared or grated rind can be frozen.

Serving ideas

The simplest way to enjoy an orange is to cut it into quarters and use your teeth to extract the flesh. A less messy method is to separate the segments and serve them just as they are or moistened with freshly squeezed orange juice. The fruit makes an excellent flavouring for cakes, particularly rich fruit cakes and biscuits (cookies). Segments and slices are decorative as well as delicious, and look good in home-made fruit jellies, or as a caramelized topping for an orange flan. Oranges make very good sorbets (sherbets), ice creams and savoury or sweet sauces, especially when teamed with brandy or an orange liqueur as in the sauce for crêpes Suzette.

Oranges are equally at home in a savoury setting. Orange rind is used to flavour stews in both the French and Chinese traditions, while segments are famously used in the inimitable *canard à l'orange*. Juice and rind are excellent

partners in marinades, stuffings or sauces for meat, poultry and fish, and make a refreshing salad dressing, while segments are classically combined with beetroot (beet) and chicory (Belgian endive). The juice and rind perk up mild, creamy cheeses and complement sweet red onions and glazed carrots.

Commercial uses

Oranges are highly versatile so it is no surprise that they are used in many products, ranging from freshly squeezed orange juice to traditional marmalades.

Marmalades

These days, commercial marmalades may contain every type of citrus fruit, with ginger, vanilla and other spices joining spirits, such as brandy and whisky, to create exciting new flavours. Given the choice, however, many people will still plump for a traditional recipe, and thick-cut Seville orange is one of the best.

Liqueurs and cordials

Curaçao Dutch settlers on the Caribbean island of Curaçao first made this white rum-based liqueur. It is flavoured with bitter green oranges (not a bitter variety, just unripened). Although it is usually known by the name of its island home, versions of this liqueur are also made in many other countries, under a variety of names, and brandy is often used as a base instead of rum. Triple Sec is another name for Curaçao, although *sec*, a French word meaning dry, is a bit of a misnomer, as Triple Sec is sweet.

Curaçao is always flavoured with oranges, but comes in a variety of colours for novelty value – red, yellow, blue and vivid green – although the clear type is always Triple Sec.

Cointreau Cointreau is a Curaçao with a brandy base. Launched in 1849 by the brothers Edouard and Adolphe Cointreau, it was originally known as Triple Sec White Curaçao. However, at that time other branded Curaçaos were being sold as Triple Sec, so it seemed good business sense

to make theirs eponymous. It is very sweet and made with a blend of the Caribbean bitter green oranges and sweeter varieties from France.

Grand Marnier This branded Curaçao was devised in 1880 by Louis-Alexandre Marnier, who blended unripened oranges with the finest cognac, which was then aged in barrels. This aging gives it a superior taste to that of other Curaçaos. Grand Marnier has a highly refined, mellow flavour and the sweetness is tempered by the Cognac.

Aurum The name of this brandy-based Italian liqueur hints at gold, which it may once have contained. Today, however, the glorious golden colour is the result of a mixture of infused orange peel and whole oranges, enhanced by the addition of saffron.

Below: Grand Marnier is made from bitter green oranges and fine Cognac. Louis-Alexander Marnier first hit upon the idea for the drink after tasting bitter oranges in Haiti in 1880.

LEMONS

Where would we be without the lemon? We would have nothing to squeeze over our fish; our avocados and artichokes would turn brown; and we would be denied lemon curd and lemon meringue pie. With their wonderful, fresh, tart flavour, lemons are not only an excellent single flavouring in their own right, but also enhance the flavour of a vast range of other ingredients.

Lemons thrive in all climates, but most are grown in sub-tropical regions, as the humidity in hotter countries encourages pests and diseases. Unlike other citrus fruits, which usually flower once a year, lemon trees blossom several times during the season and you'll find fruit of various ages on the tree at the same time. Lemons do not ripen once they have been picked and will last for up to two weeks.

History

The familiar Italian or Mediterranean lemon is actually a cross between a citron, the Indian lime, and another (as yet unidentified) member of the citrus family. It is believed to have originated in the Punjab region of India and Pakistan, and may also have been cultivated in the Middle East. Unusually,

Below: Smooth-skinned lemons are best for juicing.

there is no Latin word for lemon, although there is some evidence that the Romans used the lemon as a condiment, in medicine and for decoration. They may also have grown the fruit themselves.

It was the Arabs who introduced lemons to Europe in the 4th century AD. They were soon extensively cultivated in Spain, Sicily and across the Mediterranean in North Africa. Lemons were also introduced into China – the Chinese name for lemon is *li ming*. The name lemon is derived from Persian via both Arabic and French.

Lemons were scarce in Northern Europe during the Middle Ages and were a luxury even for the wealthy.

Christopher Columbus took seeds to the New World in 1493, where lemons were hitherto unknown. The Portuguese introduced the fruit to Brazil, and the Brazilians, in turn, took it to Australia, where the first trees

Above: These Argentinian Eureka lemons are waxed, enhancing their golden colour.

were planted in 1788. Scurvy was rife on these early colonist ships, but it wasn't until the end of the 18th century that it was finally realized that the disease, caused by a deficiency of vitamin C, could be cured by eating citrus fruit. If only the sailors had known that the solution to their swollen gums and suppurating skin lay in the cargo they were carrying.

Varieties

Distinguishing between varieties of lemons can be extremely tricky. There is less difference between the types than is the case with oranges or mandarins, and the problem is further exacerbated by the fact that the shape of a lemon and the thickness of its skin varies, depending on the time of year. Their skin and pith can be thick or thin, the skin itself can be smooth or bumpy, and the juice mouth-puckering to almost sweet.

Eureka Although it was originally cultivated in Europe, and is still commonly grown in Spain, this variety is today the favourite of countries such as Australia, South Africa, Argentina and Israel. Fairly

Right: These fruit are Jambhiri lemons, though varietal names are rarely given in stores.

thin-skinned and very juicy, it is also a popular variety in California, where it was introduced from Sicily in 1858.

Femminello Commune This variety comprises around three-quarters of the Italian lemon crop, but is also grown in Argentina and Turkey. In Italy, it crops four times a year and each season's crop has a different name: Primofiori (September–November), Limoni (December–May), Bianchetti (April–June), and Verdilli (June–August). Femminello Commune lemons have medium skin and pith, but a lower than average juice content.

Lisbon As the name suggests, this was originally a Portuguese lemon variety, but it was developed in Australia, where it continues to be grown successfully. Lisbon lemons are also grown in California and South America. The juicy fruits are on the large side, with fairly thin, slightly rough rind. They crop during the winter and into early spring.

Fino or Primofiori A Spanish variety, this smooth-skinned lemon is relatively small, and can be rounded or oval in shape. In the northern hemisphere, it crops between October and February.

Verna This fruit accounts for about 60 per cent of the Spanish summer crop and has a rough, rather thick rind.

Above: Pale-skinned, unwaxed Italian Primofiori lemons.

Nutrition

As well as the vital vitamin C, lemons are an excellent source of bioflavonoids, which have important antioxidant properties that help maintain the immune system and protect against disease, including some forms of cancer. They also contain small amounts of the minerals potassium, calcium and phosphorus. A famous antiseptic, lemon juice soothes sore throats, especially when combined with a spoonful of honey in a warm drink – with or without a tot of whisky. It is also believed that lemons can ease rheumatism.

Lemon lore
• When rubbed on the hands, lemon juice will rid them of lingering fishy smells and other cooking odours.
• A glass of water spiked with lemon juice can aid digestion and help cleanse the system.
• If in need of something acidic to prevent browning (such as cut apples), lemon juice is perfect.

Left: Growers know lemons by the shape of their stalk and pointed end, which vary – albeit subtly – between varieties.

It is the skin of the lemon that holds the really powerful flavouring ingredient, however. If you rub a lump of sugar over the surface of a lemon it will soak up the aromatic oil. Use the sugar in a dessert sauce or cocktail, and it will add a subtle citrus flavour. Grated or pared lemon rind tastes wonderful in cakes, desserts and even savoury dishes, such as beef, lamb, pork or

Iced lemon tea

Although black tea tastes great hot with a slice of lemon, it is also very good chilled, especially on a hot, humid afternoon.

1 Mix the juice of 2 lemons with 1.75 litres/3 pints/7½ cups cold water in a large jug or pitcher. Add 3–4 Earl Grey or Lapsang Souchong tea bags and 6–8 fresh mint leaves.

2 Add about 90ml/6 tbsp sugar to the juice, to sweeten, stirring well. Remember that chilling will blunt the sweetness somewhat.

3 Cover tightly and chill for at least 8 hours to allow the flavours to develop. Strain into glasses and decorate with fresh lemon slices and mint leaves.

Buying and storing

Growers talk of nipples (the stalk end) and necks (where the lemon elongates) but, apart from minor differences in these two areas, the only feature that distinguishes one lemon from another at the market is whether the skin is rough or smooth. Lemons are seldom, if ever, labelled as to variety. The most you can hope for is a clue to the country of origin so, until you take the fruit home and cut it open, you cannot be sure whether what you have chosen is juicy or not, or if it will have thin skin and pith, or thick skin with sometimes as much as 1cm/½in of pith.

Sprightly, taut skin is what you are looking for with a good, clear, bright yellow colour. Lemons gradually become paler and less juicy as they ripen.

Where possible, always buy unwaxed lemons, sometimes also described as untreated, or organic lemons. The wax (diphenyl, an ethylene gas) works rather like shoe polish in that it makes the fruit shine and helps preserve it. It is considered to be harmless to health, but if you are intending to use the lemon rind, either by grating or paring it, thoroughly scrub a waxed lemon before using. This will also remove any pesticide residue.

When you buy a bag of lemons off the supermarket shelf use them as soon after purchase as possible. If stored in the refrigerator, they will be fine for up to two weeks; at room temperature they will keep for slightly less. However, the longer you leave them, the more their nutritional value will fade.

Serving ideas

All dishes, both sweet and savoury, benefit from the distinctive tang of this well-loved citrus fruit. It is seldom served solo, except when preserved or transformed into lemonade, but rather it is used primarily to enhance or flavour other foods.

Lemon juice will tenderize meat in a marinade, give fresh cream a soured taste, and prevent fruit and vegetables – especially apples, celeriac, artichokes, avocados and potatoes – from oxidizing and browning. It also makes a great marinade for both fish and shellfish, but do not marinate for more than an hour or the juice will start to "cook" or denature the protein. The juice can feature as the principal flavouring in such dishes as lemon mousse, sorbet (sherbet) or cheesecake or as a complementary flavour, for example, in a lemon mayonnaise or cake frosting.

chicken casseroles. When paring or grating lemons, take care not to include any of the pith, which is unpleasantly bitter. Where the pith is useful is in helping jam to set, since it contains a lot of pectin, as do the pips (seeds).

Preserved lemons feature in both sweet and savoury recipes. Sliced or quartered lemons, preserved in salt and stored in olive oil are widely used in North African cooking, especially in chicken and fish dishes. Candied lemon slices or half slices may be used to decorate creamy desserts and tarts.

Slices or wedges of lemon are classic garnishes for hot and cold fish and shellfish dishes. They are also natural partners for chicken and veal and the favourite decoration for cocktails. Finely grated lemon rind may be sprinkled over both sweet and savoury dishes and, combined with finely chopped flat leaf parsley and garlic cloves, it forms an Italian garnish called *gremolata*.

Commercial uses

By far, the most felicitious uses of lemon have been in drinks, spirits and liqueurs, but pre-squeezed lemon juice and lemon curd are also available for use in cooking. For light refreshment,

choose from lemon tea, lemon cordial or traditional, old-fashioned lemonade, and use lemon liqueurs to enliven cocktails or serve with coffee after dinner.

Lemon drinks

Limoncello This Italian lemon liqueur is made from a base alcohol steeped with lemon rind and sugar. Serve added to a fruit salad or drizzle over ice cream.

Limonnaya Fruit flavourings are quite common for vodka. Limonnaya is a leading lemon-flavoured brand.

Liquore al limone or Cedro This sticky, sweet liqueur is made from the peel of the lemons that grow in profusion around the Amalfi coast in south-west Italy. Almost every delicatessen in the region sells a home-made version of this opaque yellow drink, whose sweetness is toned down by the tangy citrus fruit. It should be served ice-cold straight from the refrigerator or freezer and makes a refreshing aperitif or digestif.

Lemon barley water

A traditional English cordial, this is made

from ground barley, water, lemon rind and juice, sweetened with sugar or honey. It is not so popular as it once was, but remains a good choice at picnics or after playing sport.

Lemon cordial In Britain, the name is given to a wide range of concentrated lemon drinks that are mixed with water. Some are full of sugar or artificial sweeteners, but better quality cordials are useful for making long, cold drinks for lazy summer afternoons. American cordials are alcoholic.

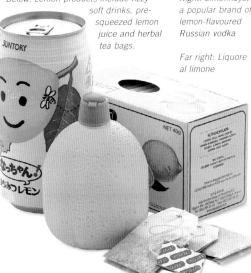

Below: Lemon products include fizzy soft drinks, pre-squeezed lemon juice and herbal tea bags.

Right: Limonnaya, a popular brand of lemon-flavoured Russian vodka

Far right: Liquore al limone

LIMES

Of the true members of the citrus family, limes are the smallest of the fruits. Their thin, bright green skin has an exquisite perfume, and the juice has a clean, sharp taste. Limes grow in tropical regions and need heat and high humidity if they are to thrive, although they do well in the dry heat of Egypt, where the crop outdoes that of the lemon. In cooking, lime plays a central role in the cuisines of Thailand and all of South-east Asia, as well as in the Caribbean, Mexico and south America.

History

Although India is often cited as the original home of the lime, historical data is scanty and each variety needs to be looked at independently. Limes seem to have been missing from both the Greek and the Roman cuisines and, when they were mentioned in early Arabic texts, a single word – *limah* – was used for both lemons and limes. One possible reason for this is that when limes are left to ripen fully on the tree, their skins turn a sunny yellow, giving them the appearance of lemons.

Limes grow well in the Caribbean, and it was from there that British sailors stocked up with the fruit as protection against scurvy. This led to the British being known as "limeys", and the area of London's docklands where the cargo was stored was named Limehouse.

Varieties

The glossy green fruit we collectively know as limes are so different from one another that they are actually classified as separate species. Most limes are picked before they are fully mature and still green.

Acid or sour limes

West Indian, Mexican or Key lime, *Citrus aurantifolia* Extreme heat is essential if this type of lime is to flourish, and it is not often found for sale in Europe. Originally from Malaysia, it is now grown in Mexico, the Caribbean (where it is used to make lime cordial), Brazil, Peru, India, Iran and Egypt. Traditionally used for Key lime pie, this variety now accounts for only a tiny proportion of the crop in Florida. Small and thin-skinned, with a powerfully scented rind and yellow flesh, it is full of pips (seeds) and very juicy.

Tahitian or Persian lime, *Citrus latifolia*
This is the lime you are most likely to buy in Europe, imported mainly from Mexico, Florida and Brazil. It has a complicated history: it is thought to have originated in Asia and made its way to the Americas via Persia, the Mediterranean, Australia and Tahiti, reaching California in the latter half of the 19th century. It is no longer grown in either Tahiti or Iran. In America it is known as the Bearrs lime. Thin-skinned,

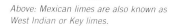

Above: Mexican limes are also known as West Indian or Key limes.

juicy and not so highly perfumed as the Key lime, it has yellowish-green flesh with no pips.

Makrut or Kaffir lime, *Citrus hystrix*
Grown on a small scale in Asia from Sri Lanka to the Philippines, this lime has extremely knobbly skin. The flesh inside is bitter, with lots of seeds and virtually no juice. The rind, however, is valued for its pungent fragrance. It is often grated and used in soups and salads.

Kaffir lime leaves are increasingly available, and are great in soups and noodle dishes. Their real name, Makrut, is seen by some to be more politically correct: Kaffir is an Arabic word for infidel, and in certain countries, notably South Africa, it is an offensive – and illegal – term of address.

Kalamansi or Musk lime, *Citrus mitis var. microcarpa* The flesh of this round, thin-skinned citrus fruit is bright yellow and full of flavour. Its alternative name – musk lime – refers to the flavour of the juice, which is less tart than that of most other limes and tastes musky. The kalamansi is native to the Philippines, but it is used throughout South-east Asia. It is the perfect partner for highly spiced chilli dishes. A popular drink is made from the sweetened juice.

Sweet or acidless limes

Australian wild limes *Microcitrus australasica* Fingerlimes, as these limes are known because of their shape, are wild fruit, native to Queensland and

Left: Tahitian lime blossom

northern New South Wales. They are cylindrical, 10cm/4in long and may be green, red, yellow, purple or black. They are mildly acidic and are seldom seen outside Australia. Other species of wild lime in that country include *Microcitrus australis*, a round fruit with thick skin that is good for candying.

Indian or Palestine lime, *Citrus limettioides* This lime is sweeter than other varieties and has a fairly bland flavour. It grows in India, Central and South America, and the Middle East. It is pale yellow when immature, ripening to orange. The flesh is very juicy, with few pips (seeds). You are unlikely to find it outside its growing areas.

Nutrition

Like lemons, limes are a rich source of vitamin C, and also contain potassium, calcium and phosphorus.

Buying and storing

Look for smooth, unblemished skins and fruit that feels a good weight for its size. Limes don't last as long as lemons and once a telltale browning appears around the ends, they should be thrown away. They look very pretty piled up in a bowl, but check the ones on the bottom as they will be susceptible to mould. It is better to keep them in the refrigerator, where they will last for up to one week.

Look for fresh and dried makrut or kaffir lime leaves at Asian and Indian stores and supermarkets.

Serving ideas

The most celebrated use for limes is in cocktails and drinks, such as margaritas and daiquiris. In cooking, Key lime pie from Florida, which is similar to a lemon meringue pie, but with a lime-flavoured filling, is perhaps the most famous dish. The meringue is sometimes omitted in favour of a cream topping. Grated lime

Left: Makrut limes are not eaten raw or cooked, but the finely grated rind and the shredded leaves are widely used for flavouring in much Asian cooking.

Above: Indian limes are sweeter and milder-tasting than other varieties.

rind and freshly squeezed juice flavour many iced desserts, and marmalade benefits from their pungent flavour.

In the Middle East, limes are dried and added to stews. In India, they are made into pickles and chutneys. Makrut or kaffir lime leaves are used in much the same way as bay leaves. A couple, torn or left whole, stirred into a Thai dish completes its flavour. In the classic South American dish of ceviche, chunks of raw white fish are marinated in lime juice. This changes or denatures the fish protein, so that it "cooks", turns opaque and tastes delicious.

A few pared strips of lime rind will perfume caster (superfine) sugar, and a little juice sprinkled over tropical fruit makes a fresh-tasting dessert.

Limes can be used as a substitute for lemons, but they have a sharper tang, so you will need fewer of them.

Commercial uses

The best-known lime product is cordial, but limes are also used in many pickles, chutneys and marmalades.

Lime cordial This lime concentrate makes a refreshing non-alcoholic drink with sparkling mineral water, though it is also essential in some classic cocktails.

MANDARINS

Strictly speaking, there is no such fruit as a mandarin. It is simply the umbrella name for a large group of citrus fruits, which includes the satsuma, tangelo, clementine and minneola. To further complicate the issue, the names are sometimes switched around so that the group is also designated as tangerine as well as mandarin. Furthermore, new hybrids are being developed.

All members of this extended family are smaller than the orange, have sweet and fragrant flesh, with a flavour that is distinctively different from that of the orange. They are also all characterized by their loose, sometimes puffy skins, which make them easy to peel. Some varieties are seedless, which makes them especially popular with children. There can be surprising differences between the various types: the satsuma, for instance, thrives in areas of the world that have cold winters, such as South America, New Zealand and its native Japan, while the clementine, which originated in Algeria, grows best in a Mediterranean climate.

Above: Ripe Citrus reticulata or common mandarin

History

The fruit is thought to have originated in China or India. Certainly, the Chinese have grown mandarins for many thousands of years – the earliest reference dates back to the 12th century BC. The name mandarin arrived some four hundred years later, a corruption of a Malay word derived from the Sanskrit *mantrin*, meaning counsellor, probably as a reference to the saffron-coloured robes worn by these Chinese court officials. By the beginning of the 10th century AD, Japan was also a prolific grower, but it wasn't until 1805 that the fruit was imported to England by Sir Abraham Hume, and from there sent on to Malta and Italy. A further seventy years passed before the mandarin reached the United States, where large crops are now produced in the western and southern states. Once popularly known as "easy peelers" in Europe, mandarins are now correctly known by their varietal names.

Varieties

Part of the huge family of citrus fruits, there are many varieties.
Common mandarin, *Citrus reticulata*
Fruits in this group are the least easy to peel, as the skin clings more tightly to the segments, and

Left: Clementines

Mediterranean mandarin, *Citrus deliciosa* This variety was introduced to the sunny climes of the Mediterranean in 1805 via a journey that included England, Malta and Italy. This fruit is today primarily grown for use in the perfume and cosmetics industry, and to flavour soft drinks.

King mandarin, *Citrus nobilis* There are two varieties of this species. The first is the yellow king, which is large and round, closely resembling an orange in appearance, although the skin is rather more knobbly. This came originally from Vietnam and Cambodia, and was sent to California in 1880, although it is now grown almost exclusively in South-east Asia. The second variety is the kunenbo from Japan, which is smaller, with a smoother skin.

Mandarin hybrids

Calamondin, *Citrus mitis* This hybrid originated in the Philippines, and is thought to be a cross between a sour, loose-skinned mandarin and a kumquat. It is closely related to the kalamansi or musk lime. Calamondins are not eaten whole (as they are too acidic), instead the juice is used to flavour food, such as soups and stews.

the clementine is a typical example. Once thought to be a cross between the Mediterranean mandarin and an inedible orange, the clementine is now believed to be a Chinese mandarin. It was named after a French missionary, Father Rodier, who found the fruit growing in his Algerian garden in 1902. It is now grown in Spain, Italy, South Africa and South America.

Satsuma or Unshiu mikan, *Citrus unshiu* This popular variety, with its sweet but tangy flavour, comes from an area that is now called Kagoshima in western Japan, but was formerly known as Satsuma. The fruit was given its name in 1878 by the wife of General Van Valkenberg, the United States Minister to Japan. It is now grown mostly in China and Korea, with smaller crops in Japan and Spain. It is also grown in Turkey, New Zealand, South America and California and Louisiana in the USA.

Satsumas are seedless and ideally suited to canning. Almost the entire Japanese crop is purchased every year for canning, and the fresh fruit is rarely available. It is generally marketed under the generic name of mandarin.

Above: Satsumas have a refreshing flavour and are relatively easy to peel.

Right: Calamondin

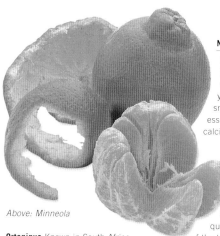

Above: Minneola

Ortanique Known in South Africa
as a tambor, this is actually a tangor,
which is a cross between a mandarin
and an orange. The skin is tough and
not very easy to peel, but it is worth
persevering with, for the flesh is juicy
and sweet.
Minneola This bright orange fruit is the
result of crossing a Duncan grapefruit
with a Dancy tangerine, a hybrid that
is known as a tangelo. The grapefruit
lends the fruit tartness and
the tangerine sweetness.
It is seedless, with juicy,
sweet flesh.

*Below: Dried
mandarin peel*

Nutrition

In common with oranges,
lemons and limes, all
mandarins and their hybrids
yield vitamin C, as well as
smaller amounts of the
essential minerals potassium,
calcium and phosphorus.

Buying and storing

Mandarins look like little
flattened oranges. Some
varieties have quite
loose, puffy skins, but
this isn't an indication of
quality; rather a characteristic
of the type. Again, it's the weight in
your hand that signifies a juicy fruit.
If buying pre-packed fruit, check that
there isn't a mouldy one lurking in the
bottom, as this will quickly taint all
the others. Keep mandarins in the
refrigerator for up to one week, but
bring them to room temperature first
if eating fresh, so that the full flavour
can reassert itself.

Serving ideas

With aromatic skins and juicy segments
that virtually separate themselves,
mandarins are ideal for eating in the
hand. They taste best fresh, as cooking
diminishes their delicate, sweet flavour.
Use them in the same ways you would
oranges. The rind is often soft, but can
be grated. It can also be cut into strips
and dried in a low oven, then used as
part of a bouquet garni or to flavour
a rich casserole, stew or soup.
Mandarin segments taste
delicious as part of a fruit
platter, in a mixed fruit salad,
caramelized or dipped in
melted chocolate. The shells
make pretty containers for ice
cream or sorbets (sherbets).
Mixed with Chinese five-
spice powder, or star
anise, ginger and
soy sauce, the
freshly squeezed
juice makes a
wonderful marinade
for chicken, duck
or pork.

Commercial uses

Apart from the canning industry, the
main commercial products are liqueurs.
Van der Hum This is South Africa's
version of Curaçao, made by steeping
the local mandarins or *naartjies* as they
are known, in brandy. Nutmeg is often
added as a flavouring, as are other
spices or aromatic herbs.
Mandarine Napoléon This is also a type
of Curaçao, made with the skins of
mandarins, which are then steeped in
Cognac. It was believed to have been
Napoleon Bonaparte's favourite tipple,
hence the name.

Tangerine

The name tangerine is sometimes
used to describe the mandarin
family but it has no real meaning:
the term is thought to have come
from the United States where the
seeds from an old variety called
Moragne tangerine were cultivated
by Colonel F.L. Dancy. The
Dancy tangerine was the result
and tangerine has now become
the accepted American name for
a mandarin. Another theory as to
the origin of its name is that the
fruit was called tangerine after the
town of Tangier, when mandarins
were imported from Morocco.

*Below: These mandarins, grown in
Italy, have sweet flesh, but often
contain a large number
of pips (seeds).*

POMELO AND UGLI FRUIT

Large and ungainly looking, these fruit are worth keeping an eye out for as they have a refreshing, delicious flavour.

Pomelo or Shaddock, *Citrus grandis*

Originally from Malaysia and Indonesia, pomelo seeds were taken from that part of the world to Barbados by English explorers and settlers in the 17th century. The pomelo was first introduced by a sea captain called Shaddock, hence its alternative name.

This fruit is the largest member of the citrus family, often with 16 segments as opposed to the 12 in its descendant, the grapefruit. There are three types – Thai, Indonesian and Chinese, each with several sub-species. Pomelos are considerably larger than grapefruit, and have thick yellow dimpled skin, pinky-yellow to deep red flesh and a sharp, refreshing flavour, which is improved with a sprinkling of sugar. They are used mostly in Asian and Thai cooking.

Look out for a new hybrid, the result of crossing a pomelo with a grapefruit. It is often labelled pummelo and has a smooth skin. If you come across one, the best way to prepare it is to cut it into segments as with an orange.

Ugli fruit

This citrus fruit owes its parentage to the grapefruit, mandarin and Seville (Temple) orange. Discovered growing wild in Jamaica at the beginning of the 20th century, it was called Ugli simply because of its appearance, the name patented with the "i" instead of the "y". Slightly larger than a grapefruit, it has orange skin mottled with green, with a large core surrounded by sweet, juicy orange flesh. The large core makes it seem light for its size, so the normal rule of choosing citrus that seem heavy in the hand does not apply. To eat, cut it in half, loosen the segments and spoon them out.

Below: Ugli fruit have a deliciously sweet flavour in spite of their less than sophisticated appearance.

Left: Pummelos

GRAPEFRUIT

It may not be so easy to peel as an orange or mandarin, but the grapefruit still has much to offer, and the ruby varieties are almost as sweet as their orange-fleshed cousins. All grapefruit have a refreshing, acidic flavour.

History

Both oranges and pomelos grew in Barbados in the 17th century, and it is thought that the grapefruit originated here, the result of a natural cross between the two.

The grapefruit was later introduced into Florida by Odette Phillipe, a French count, and production began in earnest at the end of the 19th century. Florida is still the major grower, followed by California, Mexico, Cuba, Argentina, South Africa, Israel and Cyprus. The name grapefruit is believed to reflect the way the fruit grows on the tree – in clusters, rather than as individual fruit – and has nothing to do with its flavour.

Varieties

There are two types: the white and the pigmented grapefruit, which is pink or ruby. White grapefruit, in fact, have bright yellow skins and flesh. There is also a sweet, emerald green variety, appropriately called Sweetie.

Right: The flesh of pink grapefruit can range from rosy pink to deep pink. As a general rule, the pinker the colour, the sweeter the grapefruit.

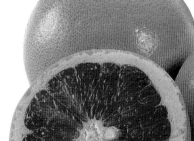

White grapefruit, *Citrus paradisi*
Marsh First grown as the Marsh Seedless by E. H. Tison in 1886, this grapefruit is now commonly known simply as the Marsh. Slightly smaller than the Duncan – about 11cm/4½in in diameter – it has a thicker rind. Nowadays, it is the most widely grown variety worldwide.

Duncan The first Duncan tree was grown in 1830 in Florida, and all other commercially cultivated varieties of grapefruit come from this one. It has firm, juicy flesh with a rich sweet flavour, and it is the most popular variety for canning.

Above: White Marsh grapefruit have pale yellow flesh.

Pigmented grapefruit These grapefruit get their colour from the pigment lycopene. They have varietal names such as Henderson and Ray Ruby, but are seldom labelled as such in the supermarket. You are more likely to find them marketed collectively under names such as Ruby Sweet and Sunrise. All pigmented grapefruits are sweet and juicy. In today's health-conscious world, they are proving more popular than their paler parents, as they need no extra sugar.

Nutrition

Grapefruit are a good source of vitamins A and C, with the usual citrus minerals of calcium, phosphorus and potassium. Pink grapefruit contains an astonishing five times the amount of vitamin A as white grapefruit. Although there's no way of establishing this when you buy the fruit, it is interesting to note that grapefruit that crop in autumn have the highest levels of vitamin C. The peel is a source of bioflavonoids and this, together with the vitamin C content, will help to keep gums strong, arteries healthy and the immune system functioning well.

Buying and storing

Look for plump, firm fruit. The first rule when buying any of the varieties of grapefruit is to choose specimens that weigh heavy in the hand. The skin can be thick or thin, depending on the variety, but if it is puffy, there won't be much juice. Avoid fruit with blemishes on the skin.

Right: Duncan grapefruit grows up to 17cm/7in in diameter, and is the most popular variety for canning.

Grapefruit will keep for about one week if stored in the refrigerator.

Serving ideas

The days when the height of sophistication meant sprinkling a cut grapefruit with brown sugar, grilling (broiling) it and then placing half a glacé (candied) cherry precisely in the middle are long gone but, minus the cherry, this is still a delicious way to serve this type of citrus, as is brushing with melted butter and grilling. At breakfast, the juice awakens the taste buds, while the fibre keeps the digestive system in good working order. The juice can also be used in a marinade, and it tastes great in a vinaigrette dressing.

As a first course, grapefruit goes particularly well with seafood – try a mixture of prawns (shrimp), avocado and grapefruit – and provides a flavour contrast to the richness of smoked fish. You can use segments from pink and red varieties in fruit salads and sorbets (sherbets). The candied peel can be coated in melted chocolate and left to set, then served as an after-dinner treat. The fruit also makes an excellent marmalade.

Commercial uses

Half the world crop is made into juice, with the rest being eaten fresh or canned.

Left: As its name suggests, Sweetie needs no sugar.

OTHER EXOTIC CITRUS FRUIT

Modern transportation and the curiosity of contemporary cooks means that even the lesser known types of citrus are becoming familiar. We may not find them all in our local store, but could certainly encounter them when we travel in their countries of origin.

Kumquat

It wasn't until Robert Fortune, an English plant expert, brought kumquat plants to the Royal Botanical Gardens, that the English got their first taste of this fascinating fruit, which must be grown under glass if it is to survive the British winter. Kumquats, which originated in central China, were originally classified as citrus, then later assigned to their own genus, Fortunella, named to commemorate Mr Fortune. They are not grown commercially in the UK, but are cultivated in Israel, Morocco, Florida, Brazil and Australia, with smaller crops in Corsica and in France.

There are three varieties of these miniature orange lookalikes – Oval, Round and Large Round. All are about the size of a large olive, and can be eaten whole. The soft peel is sweeter than the flesh but even so, they are an acquired taste eaten raw and are best bottled with sugar and alcohol or simmered in sugar syrup.

Kumquats can be sliced and used in sweet and savoury salads, and are often served with duck, red meat, cheese or ice cream. They go very well with bitter salad leaves such as

Below:
Limequats

chicory (Belgian endive) and frisée, and are excellent chopped and mixed with the stuffing for turkey. They make great marmalade and jam, and taste delectable when dipped in chocolate. Their thick skin means that they travel and keep well. Store in the refrigerator for up to one week.

Kumquat hybrids

New citrus hybrids are constantly appearing, sometimes naturally, other times through experimentation.
Orangequat This is a cross between the sweet orange and kumquat, and can be eaten fresh or used in cooking.

Limequat A cross between the Mexican lime and the kumquat, the main varieties of limequats are Eustis and Lakeland. If you come across them while they are still green, you can use them in cooking in the same way as limes.

Sudachi

A true citrus fruit, the sudachi has a firm, thick, green skin, light yellow flesh and fairly large pips (seeds). The juice and finely grated rind are used in Japanese cooking, especially with fish and in combination with matsutake (pine mushrooms), but the fruit is rarely seen in other countries. It has a similar flavour to limes, which may be used in its place in cooking.

Below: Sudachi

Below: Kumquats can be eaten whole – skin and all – although you will need to discard the pips (seeds).

Left: Bergamot is used for confectionery and pâtisserie, as well as perfumery.

One weird and wonderful variety is the Buddha's Hand, or Fingered Citron, which has about a dozen orange-yellow, finger-like protuberances, This fruit is inedible, but the scented skin makes them popular as room fresheners. The Chinese like to hang them in wardrobes to perfume their clothes.

Bergamot, *Citrus bergamia*

Not to be confused with the herb of the same name, the bergamot orange looks a bit like a large lime. The sour-tasting fruit is not grown for its eating qualities – although the peel makes excellent marmalade – but for the essential oil in the extremely aromatic rind. This is used in perfumery and confectionery, and, most famously, as a flavouring for Earl Grey tea. Tobacco is sometimes perfumed with bergamot oil, as is the barley sugar made in the French town of Nancy.

Known in the Mediterranean for centuries, the bergamot orange is today cultivated commercially in Calabria in Italy, with smaller crops coming from Turkey and the Ivory Coast in West Africa.

Citron, *Citrus medica*

This ancient ancestor of the lemon is believed to come from the foothills of the Himalayas, though it may also have come from China. Records show it was transported to the Middle East by the Medians in the 7th century BC. Media, from which the botanical name derives, is now part of Iran. This was where the Greeks came to know and value the citron. The Romans also appreciated the fruit, and used to soak the rind in fish sauce. After the Roman Empire fell, the citron became an important part of Arab cuisine.

Below: Candied green citron peel, with candied orange and grapefruit peel.

It is a large fruit, up to 30cm/12in long. It yields very little juice, but this is not important, as it is the aromatic thick, knobbly, greenish skin that is of most interest to the cook.

The citron is used in religious ceremonies, particularly in India, where Kuvera, the god of wealth, is depicted holding a citron; and a variety called etrog is essential in the celebration of the Jewish festival of Sukkot.

Citrons are cultivated in China, Japan, Greece, Corsica, Italy, Morocco and Israel, but only on a small scale. When it is grown commercially, the main reason is to utilize the peel, which, when candied, develops a lovely translucency. On the island of Corsica, citrons are used to make a liqueur called *Cédratine*, a rich, smooth drink usually drunk straight.

Above: The etrog, a variety of citron, is used in the Jewish festival of Sukkot, a celebration of the harvest. The fruit is considered unfit if it is dried up, too small, spotted or if the protuberance at the tip has been broken off.

EQUIPMENT

Although you can squeeze an orange with your bare hands, the job is made much easier with equipment designed especially for the job, whether this be a simple reamer or a sophisticated juicer. There are several other inexpensive gadgets that will prove handy in the citrus kitchen.

Vegetable peeler

Use a vegetable peeler to pare away thin strips of citrus rind, leaving the white pith behind. There are two types to choose from – the fixed blade peeler, which demands little dexterity in the hands of the user, but doesn't cut quite such a fine strip, and the swivel-blade peeler, which is sharper and more flexible and therefore more precise.

Cannelle knife (zester)

This handy tool has a tooth-like blade, which will shave citrus rind into ribbons or into fine julienne strips, leaving all the bitter white pith behind.

Citrus zester

Scrape the five-hole blade of the citrus zester over oranges, lemons or limes and the peel will come off in fine curly ribbons. A useful combination tool, which is both a citrus zester and a cannelle knife, is also available.

Citrus reamer

This curvy wooden device is simple but effective, letting you squeeze the juice straight into a bowl or pan. You simply insert the pointed end into a halved lemon or other

Above: Cannelle knife (left) and combination citrus zester and cannelle knife (right)

Below: Citrus reamer

Left: Fixed- and swivel-blade vegetable peelers

citrus fruit, and twist. Its only drawback is that you can't catch the pips (seeds), but if you hold the halved fruit in one hand with slightly opened fingers, and carefully twist the reamer with the other, you should be able to catch them. Alternatively, squeeze the juice into a jug (pitcher), then strain it into the bowl or pan.

Below: Lemon squeezer

Lemon squeezer

Most of us have one of these tucked away in the kitchen. The basic design has barely changed in generations, but they now come in a variety of shapes, sizes and materials – glass, plastic or chrome. The business end of the utensil is a dome on to which you push a halved fruit, then twist to extract the juice. All the pips are trapped in the rim and the juice either flows into a simple channel surrounding the dome, or into

a bowl beneath. Some models have interchangeable heads, which allows them to be used for anything from a small lime to a large grapefruit.

Citrus press

If you want to squeeze the maximum amount of juice from the minimum quantity of fruit, this is well worth the investment. The simplest version is a hand-operated gadget with a geared lever mechanism. As you pull the lever forward, the juice is squeezed into the integral container. A wide range of electric juicers is also available.

Below: A hand-operated citrus press

Box grater

Choose a grater with as many different grating surfaces as possible, preferably with a handle for a better grip. Make sure it stands firmly on the work surface or in a bowl, if you prefer to grate directly into that. Some models include a flat blade for thinly slicing lemons and limes, too.

Microplane grater

A real revolution when it comes to grating. The blade is actually a chemically sharpened grating surface that will take the outer rind off a lemon in next to no time, and with very little effort. It comes with an extremely comfortable soft grip handle, and it is very easy to brush off every last bit of grated rind from the back when it comes to cleaning.

Grapefruit knife

This is a small knife with a slim, serrated blade, which is curved to follow the natural shape of

Left: Grapefruit knife with curved blade

Right: A microplane grater makes speedy work of grating citrus rind.

Left: Box grater

the halved fruit. It makes short work of segmenting any type of citrus fruit.

Preserving pan

If you want to make marmalade, you will need a preserving pan. They come with a thick, heavy base to prevent burning and a sturdy handle, so that you can get a good grip as you lift the pan off the stove. The best preserving pan will also be wide and fairly shallow, which makes for rapid, highly effective boiling. Choose a pan that is made from stainless steel or pristine (that is, not cracked) enamel: avoid aluminium, which will taint the fruit. Preserving pans also come with a non-stick lining.

Right: Sugar thermometer

Below: Preserving pan with a square of muslin (cheesecloth) for straining marmalades.

Tips for grating citrus rind

• Grate citrus fruit on to a sheet of foil or baking parchment. You can then tip it into a bowl or pan.
• Use a small pastry brush or even a new toothbrush to remove the grated rind from the grater.
• Make sure that you only grate the coloured rind and not the bitter-tasting white pith.

Sugar thermometer

Expert marmalade makers will know just when it is ready to be potted, but for most of us, a sugar thermometer is the best and most accurate way to check the temperature, and also to determine just when the setting point has been reached.

BASIC TECHNIQUES

Preparing citrus for use in cooking, to eat fresh or for decoration, is not hard but it does help to master a few techniques. The cheering colours of citrus make it an ideal fruit for use in decoration, and even simple touches enliven dishes.

The following techniques are shown with the fruit most likely to demand that particular skill, but they can be used sucessfully with most citrus fruit.

Peeling and segmenting oranges

1 Using a serrated knife, cut a small slice off both the top and bottom of the orange or other fruit to expose the flesh and make it easier to remove the peel.

2 Holding the orange in one hand, cut off the peel in one continuous strip, starting at the top and cutting around the orange in a circular motion, using a gentle sawing action and making sure that you remove every scrap of white pith. Alternatively, stand the orange on a plate and cut off the peel in strips, working from top to bottom.

3 Holding the fruit over a bowl to catch all the juices, remove each segment in turn by cutting down either side of the membrane and easing it away.

4 When you have removed all the segments, squeeze the membrane over the bowl to extract the remaining juice.

Zesting and grating a lemon

If you intend to use the rind or peel of any fruit in cooking, choose an unwaxed or organic fruit or scrub thoroughly waxed fruit first.

1 To zest a lemon, hold the fruit very firmly in one hand. Scrape a lemon zester down the length of the fruit.

2 If you need the zest to be even finer, brush it into a neat pile on a chopping board, hold a large chef's knife at right angles to the board and rock it back and forth.

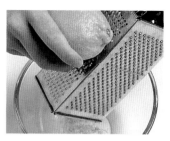

3 To grate a lemon, hold it against the fine side of the grater and work it up and down, taking off only the zest and not the pith. Work over a small bowl or a piece of foil to catch the rind.

Paring and cutting julienne strips

Julienne is the term used for fine strips or sticks. Choose fruit with firm, but not too thick rind, such as lemon and lime.

1 Wash and dry the fruit, then, using a swivel-blade vegetable peeler, remove long, wide strips of rind. Do not include the bitter white pith.

2 Square off the ends of the strips, then cut them lengthways. Use immediately or set aside, covered with cold water.

Segmenting grapefruit

Fresh grapefruit is delicious first thing in the morning. Serve it in its shell, with the segments loosened for easy eating.

1 Cut the fruit in half and remove the pips (seeds). Use a grapefruit knife with a curved blade to cut around between the skin and the flesh.

2 Loosen the segments by cutting between the membrane that surrounds each segment. Start in the centre, work out towards the skin, then cut around and back to the middle again.

3 Lastly, cut out the central core of the fruit and remove as much of the white membrane as you can before serving.

Drying mandarin rind

When dried, the peel of mandarins and other similar thin-skinned citrus fruit gives a wonderful flavour to meat stews and casseroles, and it can also be used in soups, vegetable dishes, sauces, salad dressings, desserts and cakes.

1 Wash unwaxed fruit thoroughly, then peel. Cut the peel into large pieces and place each piece on a board, skin-side down. Use a small knife to scrape away every trace of white pith.

2 Cut the peel into thin strips, about 2.5cm/1in long, and spread these out on a tray. Cover loosely and leave to dry in an airy room for about one week, until they are completely dry and have darkened in colour. Alternatively, dry in an oven preheated to 110°C/225°F/ Gas ¼ for 10–12 hours, then leave until completely cold.

3 Tip the peel into a clean, screwtop jar, replace the lid and keep in a cool, dry place. Use the rind whole, crumble between your fingers or powder in a coffee grinder. One or two strips, or 5ml/1 tsp ground peel, will be enough to flavour most dishes.

Making a citrus bouquet garni

In Provence in the South of France, it is traditional to add a strip of citrus rind to the herbs in a bouquet garni, especially when it is to be used to flavour a beef stew or casserole. It would also go well in rich game and duck dishes.

1 Pare a broad strip of rind from an orange or mandarin. A clementine or satsuma could be used instead, but avoid very thin-skinned fruit. Remove any white pith from the rind.

2 Tie the rind in a neat bundle with a sprig each of fresh thyme and rosemary and a few stalks of fresh parsley. Add a bay leaf if you like. Leave the end of the string long enough to loop around the handle of a pan or casserole. This prevents them from dispersing through the stew or casserole and also makes for easy retrieval before serving.

VARIATION
If a bouquet garni is to be used in fish or shellfish recipes, use lemon or grapefruit rind instead of orange or mandarin, and add a sprig of fresh tarragon and dill. If you like, tie the bouquet with a thin strip of celery.

Making caramelized citrus rind

The bold yellows and greens of lemons and limes combine to make a pretty decoration on cakes and desserts, such as Key lime pie or lemon and lime cheesecake. The caramelized rind is sweet, with an underlying citrus tang.

1 Using a swivel-bladed vegetable peeler, remove the rind from washed, unwaxed lemons and limes in long, even strips. Using a small, sharp knife, slice into fine julienne strips.

2 Place the strips in a small pan of water, bring to the boil, then lower the heat and simmer for about 5 minutes. Drain, refresh under cold water and then drain again. Pat dry with kitchen paper. Line a grill (broiler) pan with foil and preheat the grill.

3 Spread out the rind flat on a sheet of baking parchment and dredge with icing (confectioners') sugar. Toss to coat, then tip on to the foil-lined grill pan. Grill (broil) for 2–3 minutes, or until the sugar just begins to melt, then leave to cool and harden. Pile on top of a cooled cake or dessert, dusting with more icing sugar, if you like.

Making citrus corkscrews

Hang these over the edge of ice cream dishes or use to decorate a cocktail flavoured with citrus juice.

1 Using a cannelle knife (zester), pare long strips of rind from a lemon, lime or orange. The strips should be as long as it is possible to make them.

2 Pick up a cocktail stick (toothpick) and wind and twist the strip of citrus rind tightly around it. Slide the cocktail stick out, and you will be left with a little citrus corkscrew. Make more in the same way.

Making citrus loops

1 Cut a lemon in half lengthways, then cut each half into four equal segments. Holding one segment in your hand, use a sharp knife to ease away the flesh from the skin in a single piece, leaving about 1cm/½in still attached at the top.

2 Carefully cut away any bitter, white pith still remaining on the now bare piece of lemon peel, then fold it under the flesh segment to form a loop. Make three more lemon loops from the remaining segments.

Making citrus curls

These have a delicacy and elegance that makes them the ideal decoration for a citrus mousse.

1 Using a cannelle knife (zester), carefully pare the rind, avoiding the white pith.

2 Dust the curls with caster (superfine) sugar until coated.

Making citrus leaves

Two of these, placed side by side, make a dramatic garnish for a salmon terrine.

Cut a V-shaped wedge from the side of the lemon. Cut the lemon lengthways in slices, following the curve created by removing the wedge.

Making citrus shells

Oranges, lemons and limes look lovely filled with ice cream, sorbet (sherbet) or mousse. Grapefruit shells are a little large for desserts, but are wonderful for individual salads, such as grapefruit, prawn (shrimp) and watercress.

1 Cut the top off the fruit and set it aside to use as a lid. Loosen the flesh by running the blade of a small, sharp knife between the flesh and the skin. Scoop out the flesh with a teaspoon, keeping the shell intact, and set it aside for another dessert. Rinse the shell and leave it upside down to drain. Make more shells in the same way.

2 Pipe or spoon the filling into the fruit shells and replace the lids, setting them at an angle if you like. If the filling is ice cream or sorbet, wrap the filled fruit in clear film (plastic wrap) and freeze. If the filling is a mousse, cover loosely, chill and serve within the hour.

COOK'S TIP
To make shells more decorative, use a cannelle knife (zester) to make lengthways grooves in the skin of the fruit before cutting off the top and hollowing out the fruit.

Making a citrus ice bowl

This looks glorious filled with little balls of citrus sorbet (sherbet) or ice cream. Paler colours look more effective than bold ones.

1 You will need two freezerproof glass or plastic bowls that will fit one inside the other, leaving a gap between them of about 2.5cm/1in all around. Add some crushed ice to the larger bowl to hold up the inner bowl, then tape them together with parcel tape. It is essential to make sure that the gap between them is the same all the way around.

2 Put the pair of bowls on to a large plate to catch any drips. Carefully fill the gap between the bowls with water. It should come almost to the top, and the smaller bowl should float slightly.

3 Slide thin slices of lime, orange and lemon, with, perhaps, a few sliced kumquats, into the water between the bowls. Use a skewer to push them into position. Check the bowl from all angles until you have achieved an attractive and well-balanced effect. Carefully lift the bowls into the freezer and freeze overnight, until required.

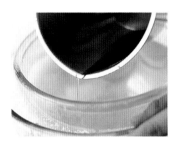

4 To unmould the ice bowl, peel off the tape. Put the bowls in another larger bowl half-filled with hot water, then pour a little hot water into the smaller bowl. Leave it there for about 30 seconds or so, then lift both bowls out of the water. Pour the water out of the smaller bowl and loosen the inner bowl with a thin, round-bladed knife.

5 Lift out the inner bowl, turn out the ice bowl and put it on a large plate. You can sprinkle a few extra slices of citrus fruit or curled rind around the edge if you like, or add a few flowers, such as nasturtiums or calendula marigolds. Fill with scoops of ice cream or sorbet and serve.

COOK'S TIPS
• For a crystal-clear ice bowl, use water that has been boiled and then left to cool completely or use still mineral water; for a more frosted appearance, use water straight from the tap (faucet).
• If your ice bowl is to be part of a buffet, make the ice bowl in advance, unmould it, fill with ice cream or sorbet (sherbet), then put back into the freezer until required. Leave any final decorations to the last minute.

PRESERVING CITRUS

The tradition of preserving citrus goes back to the time when the fruit was a rare luxury. Today we are lucky to have a plentiful supply of fruit all year round, but it is still worth making preserves, if only to experience the wonderful depth of flavour that develops when orange peel is candied, kumquats are bottled in brandy syrup or Seville (Temple) oranges metamorphose into marmalade. The best time for preserving citrus is during the winter months when the fruit is at its juiciest.

Quick candied lemon slices

Translucent candied lemon slices look gorgeous on a fresh lemon tart. Use this method when you are going to serve the slices soon after candying.

1 Cut two large, thin-skinned, unwaxed lemons into thin slices, put them in a pan and cover with plenty of water. Simmer for 15–20 minutes, or until the skin is tender, then drain.

2 Put 200g/7oz/scant 1 cup caster (superfine) sugar in a large, shallow pan and stir in about 105ml/7 tbsp water. Heat until the sugar has all dissolved, stirring constantly, then bring to the boil. Boil for 2 minutes, add the lemon slices and cook for 10–15 minutes, until they look shiny and candied.

3 Lift the candied lemon slices out of the syrup using tongs or a slotted spoon and arrange them on top of a tart or cake. Return the syrup to the heat and boil, without stirring, until reduced to a thick glaze. Brush this over the lemon slices and leave to cool completely before serving.

Candying orange peel

When you squeeze oranges for juice, the peel is wasted. Transforming it into candied peel will provide you with a flavoursome ingredient for adding to fruit cakes, scones and desserts. When the candied peel is cool, store it in a clean jar and it will keep for months.

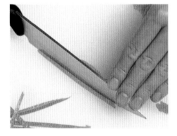

1 Choose unwaxed oranges with thick skins. Wash and dry them. Remove the rind in long thin strips. Using a sharp knife, cut the peel into julienne strips.

2 For each orange you use, put 250ml/8fl oz/1 cup water and 115g/4oz/½ cup granulated sugar into a pan. Stir well over a medium heat until the sugar has dissolved. Bring to the boil, add the strips of orange rind, half-cover the pan and simmer until the syrup has reduced by three-quarters. Remove the pan from the heat and leave to cool completely.

3 Preheat the oven to 110°C/225°F/Gas ¼. Sift icing (confectioners') sugar in a thick, even layer over a baking tray. Drop in the candied peel and roll the pieces in the sugar. Dry in the oven for 1–2 hours, checking often. When the strips are crisp, they are done.

Preserved lemons

These are surprisingly mild and sweet, despite the salt used to preserve them. Although they will be ready after a month, they'll keep for at least another six. They are used all over the Middle East and in North Africa, particularly Morocco, where they form an essential part of the flavouring for a traditional *tagine*. Add strips of preserved lemon to any lamb or chicken stew and you'll notice the difference. The following makes about 1.3kg/3lb.

1 Put 14 unwaxed lemons of average size in a large bowl and pour over cold water to cover. Cut 12 of the lemons into quarters, but keep them attached at one end.

2 Ease slightly apart the sections on one of the lemons, then spoon 5ml/1 tsp of sea salt into the centre. Close the lemon again. Repeat with the remaining fruit.

3 Pack the salted lemons in sterilized jars, sprinkling with salt, and pressing them down. Squeeze the juice of the remaining 2 lemons over the top, then top up with olive oil. Cover and seal, then store in a cool dark place.

Glacé citrus slices

These luxury sweetmeats are very popular, and if you make them yourself, they will cost just a fraction of the price in the stores.

MAKES 24–32 SLICES

INGREDIENTS
 450g/1lb citrus fruit, such as oranges, lemons, limes and clementines, along with apricots or cherries, according to the season
 1kg/2¼lb/4½ cups granulated sugar
 115g/4oz/1 cup powdered glucose

1 Wash and dry the fruit. Thinly slice the citrus fruit, remove the pits from apricots and prick the skins of cherries. Place enough in a preserving pan to cover the base, then cover with water. Simmer gently to avoid breaking the fruit. Using a slotted spoon, transfer to a shallow heatproof dish. Cook any remaining fruit in the same way.

2 Measure the liquid from the pan. You will need 300ml/½ pint/1¼ cups, so make it up with water if necessary. Tip it into the preserving pan and stir in 60ml/4 tbsp of the sugar. Add all the glucose. Heat gently until the sugar has dissolved. Bring to the boil and pour over the fruit in the dish, making sure they are submerged. Leave overnight.

3 Next day, drain the syrup into the pan and add a further 60ml/4 tbsp sugar. Dissolve the sugar and bring to the boil. Pour over the fruit and leave overnight. Repeat this process on the next five days, so that the syrup becomes more and more concentrated.

4 On the next day – day 8 – repeat the process of draining the concentrated syrup into the pan, but this time add 90ml/6 tbsp sugar. Bring to the boil, stirring, then add the fruit to the pan and cook them gently for about 3 minutes. Return the fruit and syrup to the dish and leave for two days.

5 On day 10, repeat the process carried out on day 8. The syrup will now look like honey. Having returned the fruit to the dish, leave it for at least ten days, or up to three weeks.

6 Preheat the oven to 110ºC/225ºF/Gas ¼. Place a wire rack over a baking tray. Using a fork or tongs, transfer the fruit to the rack in a single layer. Dry in the oven for 1–2 hours, until they no longer feel sticky.

7 To coat the slices in sugar, briefly dip each slice in boiling water, then roll in granulated sugar. To coat in syrup, place the remaining sugar in a pan, add 175ml/6fl oz/¾ cup water and heat gently until dissolved. Boil for 1 minute. Dip each citrus slice into boiling water, then into the syrup. Place on the wire rack and leave in a warm place to dry.

Spiced poached kumquats

These are ideal served after Christmas or Thanksgiving, with the rich pickings left over from the previous day's feast. Cold turkey, ham – even sausages – will all be enhanced by this preserve.

MAKES ABOUT 900G/2LB

INGREDIENTS
 500g/1¼lb kumquats
 350ml/12fl oz/1½ cups white wine vinegar
 500g/1¼lb/2½ cups granulated sugar
 1 cinnamon stick
 15 cloves
 6 allspice berries

1 Cut the kumquats in quarters and remove the pips (seeds). Place the kumquats in a large heavy pan and pour in just enough water to cover. Bring to the boil, then lower the heat and simmer until the fruit is tender.

2 With a slotted spoon, remove the kumquats from the pan and set them aside. Add the vinegar, sugar, cinnamon stick, cloves and allspice berries to the cooking liquid and bring to the boil, stirring only occasionally. Return the kumquats to the pan, lower the heat and simmer for 30 minutes.

3 Carefully lift the kumquats out of the syrup and place them in jars that have been sterilized with boiling water and warmed in the oven. Boil the syrup until thick and syrupy. Pour over the kumquats, cover and leave in a cool place for at least two weeks before using.

MARMALADES

Breakfast just wouldn't be the same without marmalade. The name comes from the Portuguese *marmelada*, which was a sweet, stiff paste made from quinces. In Tudor times, peach, apple, pear, lemon and orange pastes were all called marmalades. Resembling fruit cheeses, they were usually cut into pieces and presented in fancy boxes as a sweetmeat. By the 18th century, a clear, looser version existed, which was a precursor to today's preserves. Then and now, Seville (Temple) oranges, grapefruit, lemons and limes are the most popular fruits to use.

Seville orange marmalade

This classic recipe is made with the best oranges for the job: Sevilles.

MAKES ABOUT 4KG/9½LB

INGREDIENTS
1kg/2¼lb Seville oranges
1 unwaxed lemon
2.2 litres/4 pints/9 cups water
2kg/4½lb/9 cups preserving sugar

1 Wash the oranges and lemon and cut them into quarters. Remove the flesh, pips (seeds) and pulp and tie them in a square of muslin (cheesecloth). Shred the peel finely or coarsely, depending on how you like your marmalade.

2 Place the peel in a preserving pan and add the water and the muslin bag. Bring to the boil, then lower the heat and simmer for 1½–2 hours. About 15 minutes before the peel is ready, preheat the oven to 110°C/225°F/ Gas ¼. Put the sugar in a heatproof bowl and place it in the oven to warm.

3 Remove the muslin bag and hold it over the pan between two plates. Press to extract as much liquid as possible. Stir in the sugar until it has dissolved, then boil rapidly until setting point is reached. Pour into warm, sterilized jars and seal. Label when cold.

Clementine and coriander marmalade

This marmalade has a sweet and spicy flavour that goes well with toast, but also with cold meats or hot sausages.

MAKES ABOUT 2.75KG/6LB

INGREDIENTS
1.6kg/3½lb clementines, washed
6 unwaxed lemons, washed
30ml/2 tbsp coriander seeds, roasted and coarsely crushed
3 litres/5 pints/12 cups water
1.6kg/3½lb preserving sugar

1 Cut the fruit in half, then squeeze and pour the juice into a preserving pan.

2 Scrape the pith from the citrus shells and tie it up, with the pips (seeds) and half the coriander, in a square of muslin (cheesecloth). Tie the bag to the handle of the pan so it dangles in the juice.

3 Slice the peel into shreds and add them to the pan with the water. Bring to the boil, then simmer for 1½ hours. Preheat the oven to 110°C/225°F/ Gas ¼. Put the sugar in a heatproof bowl and place it in the oven to warm.

4 Remove the muslin bag. Hold it over the pan and squeeze it between two plates to extract all the liquid. Stir in the sugar and the remaining coriander, then boil rapidly until setting point is reached. Skim off any scum, then leave for about 30 minutes. Pour into sterilized jars and cover with waxed discs. Leave to cool before sealing and labelling the jars.

> **Tips for a successful marmalade**
> The best way to test for setting point is with a sugar thermometer. When it registers about 105°C/ 220°F, the marmalade is ready.
>
>
>
> To sterilize jars, preheat the oven to the highest setting. Wash the jars in hot, soapy water, then rinse. Stand them in the sink and pour over boiling water. Place them on a baking tray in the oven for 10 minutes.

Three fruit marmalade

You could use sweet oranges, such as Valencia or Navelina, in place of the bitter Seville oranges, but the flavour of the marmalade would not be so intense and tangy. Most marmalades require all the pith to be included on the peel, but in this case, err on the cautious side and don't have it too thick.

MAKES ABOUT 2.25KG/5LB

INGREDIENTS
2 unwaxed or well-scrubbed Seville oranges
2 unwaxed lemons
1 grapefruit
1.75 litres/3 pints/7½ cups water
1.5kg/3lb/6¾ cups preserving sugar

1 Wash the fruit and cut them in half. Squeeze all the fruit and pour the juice into a preserving pan. Tie the pips (seeds) and pulp securely in a square of muslin (cheesecloth). Tie the bag to the handle of the pan so that it dangles in the citrus juice.

Marmalade or jam?
The main difference between marmalade and jam is that the former invariably contains citrus fruit. Oranges, lemons and limes are used to make fruit curds or cheeses, but we seldom find them in jam, except in order to boost pectin levels. One exception, however, is a light orange jam, from Portugal, which makes a delicious spread.

2 Cut the citrus skins into thin wedges; scrape off and discard the membranes and pith. Cut the peel in slivers and add them to the pan with the water. Bring to simmering point and cook gently for 2 hours, or until all the peel is tender and the water has reduced by half.

3 About 15 minutes before the peel is ready, preheat the oven to 110°C/225°F/ Gas ¼. Put the sugar in a heatproof bowl and place in the oven to warm.

4 Remove the muslin bag. Holding it over the pan, squeeze it between two plates to extract all the liquid. Stir in the sugar until dissolved.

5 Bring to the boil and boil rapidly until setting point is reached. Pour a small amount on to a chilled saucer. Chill for 2 minutes, then push the marmalade with your finger; if wrinkles form on the surface, it is ready.

6 Skim off any scum from the surface, then leave the marmalade to stand for 30 minutes. Stir, then pour into warm, sterilized jars and cover with waxed discs. Leave to cool before adding the lids and labelling the jars.

Other citrus marmalades
Toast was invented for delicious treats like these.
Lime marmalade Wash 450g/1lb limes, then slice them thinly, removing the pips (seeds) and putting them in a small muslin (cheesecloth) bag. Put the lime slices and bag of pips in a large pan and pour in 1.5 litres/ 2½ pints/6 cups water. Leave overnight to soften the lime rind, which can be tough. Next day, bring the water to the boil, simmer for 1¼–1½ hours until the lime rind is tender. Remove the muslin bag, squeeze out all the liquid between two plates and stir 1.2kg/2½lb/5 cups preserving sugar into the pan. Continue as for Three Fruit Marmalade.

Kumquat marmalade Halve 1.3kg/ 3lb kumquats and scoop out the pips (seeds). Peel and segment one orange and one lemon, then chop the segments coarsely, removing any tough membrane and pips. Put the citrus flesh in a pan with the kumquat halves and tie everything else in a muslin (cheesecloth) bag. Add 750ml/ 1¼ pints/3 cups water. Bring to the boil, then simmer for about 30 minutes, until the kumquats are tender. Remove the muslin bag and squeeze out all the liquid between two plates. Carefully stir 675g/1½lb/3 cups preserving sugar into the pan. Continue as for Three Fruit Marmalade.

CITRUS CURDS

Strictly speaking, citrus curds are not preserves as they contain butter and eggs, but they still make great spreads.

Lemon curd

Creamy, buttery and tangy, lemon curd is well worth making yourself. The home-made version tastes nothing like the bright yellow bought stuff, which owes its set more to copious amounts of cornflour (cornstarch) than eggs. Use lemon curd to fill a sponge cake, flavour a trifle or stir it through vanilla ice cream for a quick sweet sensation. Best of all, spoon it generously on to a thick slice of fresh white bread, spread with a little unsalted (sweet) butter.

MAKES ABOUT 450G/1LB

INGREDIENTS
    3 unwaxed lemons
    115g/4oz/½ cup caster
        (superfine) sugar
    15ml/1 tbsp cornflour (cornstarch),
        mixed to a paste with
        15ml/1 tbsp water
    2 egg yolks
    50g/2oz/¼ cup unsalted
        (sweet) butter

1 Grate the lemons and squeeze the juice. Add to a pan with the sugar and stir over a low heat to dissolve the sugar. Stir in the cornflour paste.

2 Remove from the heat and whisk in the egg yolks. Return to a low heat, whisk for about 2 minutes; remove from the heat. Gradually whisk in the butter. Pour into a sterilized jar, cover and seal at once. Leave to cool, then store in the refrigerator and use within three weeks.

Lemon and lime curd

The tart lime rind and juice gives this spread an added dimension. It makes a lovely filling for a roulade.

MAKES ABOUT 800G/1¾LB

INGREDIENTS
    3 large unwaxed lemons
    3 unwaxed limes
    175g/6oz/¾ lb unsalted
        (sweet) butter
    225g/8oz/1 cup caster
        (superfine) sugar
    4 large (US extra large) eggs, beaten

1 Wash the lemons and limes and finely grate the rinds.

2 Squeeze the juice from the lemons and limes, then strain it into a bowl.

3 Melt the butter in a heatproof bowl set over a pan of barely simmering water or in the top of a double boiler. Beat in the citrus rind and juice, the sugar and eggs. Cook, beating constantly, until the mixture is smooth and thickened. Do not let it boil. Pour the curd into warm, sterilized jars and seal. When cold, store in the refrigerator for three weeks.

Passion fruit and lemon curd

This tastes wonderful when stirred into thick yogurt or spooned over ice cream.

MAKES ABOUT 450G/1LB

INGREDIENTS
    2 passion fruit
    1 lemon
    175g/6oz/¾ cup unsalted
        (sweet) butter
    115g/4oz/½ cup caster
        (superfine) sugar
    2 egg yolks

1 Cut the passion fruit in half and strain all the pulp and seeds into a bowl. Cut the lemon in half and squeeze the juice. Strain it into the bowl.

2 Melt the butter in the top of a double boiler or in a heatproof bowl set over a pan of barely simmering water. Beat in the passion fruit pulp, lemon juice, sugar and egg yolks. Cook, beating constantly, until the mixture thickens. Do not let it boil. Pour into a warm sterilized jar and seal. When cold, store in the refrigerator for three weeks.

Tips for successful citrus curds
• The important thing to remember when making citrus curd is to stir it constantly and avoid letting it boil. If you are not confident about making it in a heavy pan, use a double boiler.
• Stabilize the mixture by adding 10ml/2 tsp cornflour (cornstarch) mixed to a paste with some water. Add to the mixture before the eggs.

CITRUS IN ALCOHOL

Fruit can be preserved very successfully in alcohol, as 18th-century sailors discovered when they macerated their booty of tropical fruits in rum. The liquor takes on the flavour of the fruit, while the fruit absorbs the alcohol.

Orange brandy

This traditional English recipe produces a delicious drink with a flavour similar to that of orange liqueur. It is ready to drink within about three weeks of being bottled, but tastes even better if left for longer. The following makes about 750ml/1¼ pints/3 cups.

1 Thinly pare the rind from one lemon and two oranges, taking care to remove only the bright outer layer. Cut the rind in julienne strips and put it in a large earthenware bowl.

2 Add 225g/8oz/1 cup preserving sugar and a pinch of saffron, then pour in a 70cl bottle of brandy. Stir well.

3 Cover and set aside for three days. Stir four times a day. Strain, bottle and seal. Store in a cool, dark place for at least three weeks before opening.

Alternative spirits

Brandy and rum are popular and the most commonly used spirits for preserving citrus fruits, but liqueurs can also be used. Orange or mandarin liqueurs, such as Cointreau, Grand Marnier, Van der Hum and Mandarine Napoléon are obvious choices, but Kirsch and cherry brandy also work well.

Satsumas in brandy

Serve these juicy satsumas straight from the jar or gently heated. They make a delicious dessert accompanied by ice cream or cream, with a little of the brandy poured over. The satsumas are preserved in brandy here, but you could happily substitute it with an orange- or mandarin-flavoured liqueur. The following makes about 1.3kg/3lb.

1 Peel the satsumas, making sure you remove every last trace of the bitter, white pith.

2 Weigh them, place them in a large bowl and cover with the same weight of caster sugar. Cover the bowl and leave for 1 hour. Approximately 1kg/2¼lb each of peeled fruit and sugar will need a 70cl bottle of brandy.

3 Spoon the sugared fruit into cold, sterilized preserving jars and then pour in just enough brandy to cover the satsumas.

4 Seal the jars and store in a cool, dark place. Leave for at least two months before using, although the fruit will keep for up to six months.

Kumquats in Cointreau

These bright orange kumquats look truly spectacular and taste very good, too. Serve spooned over ice cream or mixed into fresh fruit salads.

MAKES ABOUT 675G/1½LB

INGREDIENTS
 450g/1lb kumquats, or a mixture of
  kumquats and limequats
 175g/6oz/¾ cup granulated sugar
 300ml/½ pint/1¼ cups water
 150ml/¼ pint/⅔ cup Cointreau
 15ml/1 tbsp orange flower water

1 Using a cocktail stick (toothpick), prick each fruit in several places.

2 Put the sugar in a heavy pan and pour in the water. Heat gently, stirring occasionally, until the sugar has dissolved. Bring to the boil.

3 Add the citrus fruit, lower the heat and simmer gently for 25 minutes, until it is tender, but still intact.

4 Using a slotted spoon, transfer the fruit to warm sterilized jars.

5 Boil the syrup until it reaches 107°C/ 225°F. If you do not have a sugar thermometer, test by pressing a small amount between two teaspoons. When they are pulled apart, a thread should form. Pour the syrup into a jug (pitcher).

6 Let the syrup cool slightly, then stir in the Cointreau and orange flower water. Pour over the fruit in the jars until covered. Seal immediately. Store in a cool place and use within six months.

CHUTNEYS AND RELISHES

There's something very satisfying about making your own chutneys, and the sight of jars with hand-written labels is always impressive. This type of preserve is easier to make than a marmalade, as you don't have to worry about setting points or skimming. Fresh chutneys and relishes are even easier.

Spicy chutney

Grated orange rind gives this dried fruit chutney real piquancy. Although it is intended as festive fare, it keeps well, and you'll still be enjoying it when summer comes around.

MAKES ABOUT 1.6KG/3½LB

INGREDIENTS
grated rind of 1 orange
450g/1lb cooking apples
500g/1¼lb/3 cups luxury mixed
 dried fruit
30ml/2 tbsp mixed (apple pie) spice
150ml/¼ pint/⅔ cup cider vinegar
350g/12oz/2 cups soft light
 brown sugar

1 Put the grated orange rind in a large, heavy pan. Cut the apples into quarters, remove the cores and skin, then chop coarsely. Add to the pan, with the dried fruit, mixed spice, vinegar and brown sugar. Heat gently, stirring constantly until all the sugar has dissolved.

2 Bring to the boil, then lower the heat and simmer for about 45 minutes, stirring frequently, until the mixture is thick. Stir more frequently towards the end of cooking, as it thickens. Ladle into warm sterilized jars, cover and seal. Keep for one month before using.

Fresh lemon and coriander chutney

This is a fresh chutney. It is not cooked, and it is made a few hours before being served, so that the flavours can blend.

MAKES ABOUT 475ML/16FL OZ/2 CUPS

INGREDIENTS
115g/4oz/4 cups fresh coriander
 (cilantro) leaves
1 fresh green chilli
2 garlic cloves, coarsely chopped
5ml/1 tsp salt
2.5ml/½ tsp granulated sugar
25ml/1½ tbsp lemon juice
45ml/3 tbsp ground peanuts
120ml/4fl oz/½ cup water

1 Put the coriander leaves on a board. Pile them in rough heaps, then chop them coarsely.

2 Cut the chilli in half lengthways. Scrape out the seeds and core, then chop the flesh coarsely.

3 Put all the ingredients in a blender or food processor and process together until smooth. Spoon the chutney into a bowl or jar, then cover and chill for 2–3 hours before serving.

Spiced cranberry and orange relish

This relish is a great one to serve with roast turkey, goose or duck. Eat within one week of making.

MAKES ABOUT 450G/1LB

INGREDIENTS
225g/8oz cranberries, chopped
1 onion, finely chopped
150ml/¼ pint/⅔ cup port
115g/4oz/½ cup caster
 (superfine) sugar
finely grated rind and juice of
 1 orange
2.5ml/½ tsp English (hot)
 mustard powder
1.5ml/¼ tsp ground ginger
1.5ml/¼ tsp ground cinnamon
5ml/1 tsp cornflour (cornstarch)
50g/2oz/⅓ cup raisins

1 Put the cranberries in a pan. Add the onion, port and sugar. Cook gently for about 10 minutes, stirring frequently, until the cranberries are tender.

2 Mix together the orange juice, mustard powder, ginger, cinnamon and cornflour in a bowl. Add the mixture to the pan.

3 Add the raisins and orange rind. Cook over a high heat, stirring constantly, until the mixture thickens, then lower the heat and simmer for 2 minutes. Cool, then spoon into a bowl or jar, cover and chill until ready to serve.

COOK'S TIP
When making chutneys and relishes, use a heavy pan that is large enough to leave room to stir the mixture well to prevent it from catching on the base.

Red onion, garlic and lemon relish

A powerful combination of sweet red onions, spices, hot chillies and citrus. Serve with kebabs or grilled fish.

MAKES ABOUT 450G/1LB

INGREDIENTS
45ml/3 tbsp olive oil
3 large red onions, sliced
2 heads of garlic, separated into cloves and peeled
10ml/2 tsp coriander seeds, crushed
10ml/2 tsp light muscovado (brown) sugar, plus a little extra
pinch of saffron threads
45ml/3 tbsp warm water
5cm/2in piece cinnamon stick
2–3 whole dried red chillies
2 fresh bay leaves
30–45ml/2–3 tbsp sherry vinegar
juice of ½ small orange
30ml/2 tbsp chopped fresh or preserved lemon
salt and ground black pepper

1 Heat the oil in a heavy pan. Stir in the onions, cover and cook over a very low heat for 10–15 minutes, stirring occasionally, until soft.

2 Add the garlic cloves and coriander seeds. Cover and cook for 5–8 minutes, until the garlic is soft.

3 Add a pinch of salt, plenty of pepper and the sugar. Cook, uncovered, for 5 minutes. Soak the saffron threads in the warm water for 5 minutes, then add to the onions, with the soaking water. Add the cinnamon stick, dried chillies and bay leaves. Stir in 30ml/2 tbsp of the sherry vinegar and the orange juice.

4 Cook over a low heat, uncovered, until the onions are soft. Stir in the lemon and cook for 5 minutes more. Taste and adjust the salt, sugar and/or vinegar, if necessary. The relish is best if left to stand for 24 hours.

Tropical lime relish

This colourful Indonesian side dish is served with almost every meal, but goes especially well with fish.

MAKES ABOUT 450G/1LB

INGREDIENTS
1cm/½in cube shrimp paste
1 small or ½ large fresh pineapple
½ cucumber, halved lengthways
50g/2oz dried shrimp
1 large fresh chilli, seeded and coarsely chopped
juice of 1 large lime or lemon
light brown sugar, to taste (optional)

1 To prepare the shrimp paste, wrap the cube in foil and dry-fry over a low heat for 5 minutes, turning occasionally.

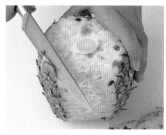

2 Cut off both ends of the pineapple. Stand it upright, then slice off the skin from top to bottom.

3 Cut the pineapple flesh into slices and remove any remaining eyes. Chop each slice into small chunks and set aside.

4 Trim the cucumber and slice it thinly. Spread out the slices in a colander, sprinkle with salt and set aside.

5 Place the dried shrimp in a food processor and chop finely, then add the chilli. Unwrap the shrimp paste and add to the food processor, pour in the lime or lemon juice and process to a paste.

6 Rinse the cucumber, drain and dry on kitchen paper. Mix with the pineapple and chill. Just before serving, spoon in the spice mixture with sugar to taste, if you like. Mix well.

SALSAS AND DIPS

Great for all sorts of meals, salsas and dips are always a delight, and they do double duty as side dishes and sauces.

Fiery citrus salsa

This versatile salsa can be served with kebabs or sausages.

MAKES ABOUT 475ML/16FL OZ/2 CUPS

INGREDIENTS
  1 orange
  1 eating apple, peeled
  2 fresh red chillies, seeded
  1 garlic clove
  8 fresh mint leaves
  juice of 1 lemon
  salt and ground black pepper

1 Slice the ends off the orange so that it will stand upright. Slice off the peel. Holding the orange over a bowl, cut it into segments. Squeeze what remains of the orange over the bowl. Slice the apple into wedges and remove the core.

2 Put the chillies in a food processor or blender with the orange segments and juice, apple, garlic and mint. Process until smooth, then pour in the lemon juice. Season and serve.

Salsa verde

Serve this classic sauce over mashed potatoes or drizzled over grilled fish.

MAKES ABOUT 300ML/½ PINT/1¼ CUPS

INGREDIENTS
  2–4 fresh green chillies, seeded
  8 spring onions (scallions)
  2 garlic cloves, halved
  50g/2oz salted capers
  fresh tarragon sprig
  bunch of fresh parsley
  grated rind and juice of 1 lime
  juice of 1 lemon
  90ml/6 tbsp olive oil
  15ml/1 tbsp green Tabasco sauce
  ground black pepper

1 Put the chillies, spring onions and garlic in a food processor and pulse briefly until they are coarsely chopped.

2 Rub the salt off the capers. Add the capers and herbs to the food processor and pulse until very finely chopped.

3 Spoon the salsa into a bowl. Lightly stir in the lime rind and juice, lemon juice and oil. Add Tabasco and pepper. Cover and chill for up to 8 hours.

Habanero salsa

This is a fiery salsa. Habañero chillies, also called scotch bonnets, are very hot, whereas costeno amarillo chillies have a sharp citrus flavour, which harmonizes with the grapefruit or orange and lime.

MAKES ABOUT 250ML/8FL OZ/1 CUP

INGREDIENTS
  2 dried roasted habañero chillies
  2 dried costeno amarillo chillies
  2 spring onions (scallions),
    finely chopped
  juice of ½ large grapefruit or
    1 Seville (Temple) orange
  grated rind and juice of 1 lime
  small bunch of fresh
    coriander (cilantro)
  salt

1 Soak all the chillies in hot water for about 10 minutes, until softened. Drain, reserving the soaking water.

2 Remove the stalks from the chillies, then slit them and scrape out the seeds with a small, sharp knife. Put the chillies in a food processor, add a little of the reserved soaking liquid and then process to a fine paste. Spoon the chilli purée into a bowl.

3 Put the spring onions in another bowl and add the grapefruit or orange juice, then the lime rind and juice. Coarsely chop the coriander and add to the spring onions.

4 Add the coriander mixture to the chilli paste and mix thoroughly, then season to taste with salt. Cover and chill for at least one day before using.

Orange and chive salsa

Sweet oranges and fresh chives are teamed with rich tomato to make a tasty salsa, which is not at all spicy. This is a great one to serve with chicken tikka.

MAKES ABOUT 350ML/12FL OZ/1½ CUPS

INGREDIENTS
  2 large oranges
  1 beefsteak tomato
  bunch of fresh chives
  1 garlic clove, thinly sliced
  30ml/2 tbsp olive oil
  sea salt

1 Slice the bottom off one orange so that it will stand upright. Slice off the peel. Cut the orange into segments. Squeeze the membrane for any juice. Repeat with the second orange. Chop the segments, and add them to the bowl.

2 Halve the tomato and use a teaspoon to scoop the seeds into the bowl. Finely dice the flesh and add it to the bowl.

3 Use a pair of kitchen scissors to snip the chives into the bowl. Add the garlic slices. Pour on the olive oil, season with sea salt and stir. Serve within 2 hours.

Lime guacamole

An essential part of a Tex-Mex spread, enjoy this creamy avocado dip with corn chips or serve it as a cold sauce with chicken, fish or a juicy steak.

MAKES ABOUT 475ML/16FL OZ/2 CUPS

INGREDIENTS
  2 large ripe avocados
  1 small red onion, finely chopped
  1 fresh red or green chilli, seeded
    and very finely chopped
  1 garlic clove, crushed with salt
  finely shredded rind of ½ lime
  juice of 1½ limes
  pinch of caster (superfine) sugar
  225g/8oz tomatoes, seeded
    and chopped
  30ml/2 tbsp coarsely chopped fresh
    coriander (cilantro)
  15ml/1 tbsp olive oil
  salt and ground black pepper

1 Halve, stone (pit) and peel the avocados. Set one half aside. Chop the remaining halves and put them in a bowl. Mash coarsely with a fork.

2 Add the onion, chilli, garlic, lime rind and about two-thirds of the lime juice. Stir in the sugar, tomatoes and chopped coriander. Season with salt and pepper and add more lime juice to taste. Stir in the olive oil.

3 Dice the remaining avocado and stir it into the guacamole, then leave to stand for 15 minutes before serving.

COOK'S TIP
As well as adding a citrus zing, the lime juice helps prevent discoloration.

Pickled lemon and chilli dip

The piquancy of pickled lemons and the sweet bite of the chillies makes this a delicious dip for tortilla chips.

MAKES ABOUT 350ML/12FL OZ/1½ CUPS

INGREDIENTS
  200g/7oz soft (white farmer's) cheese
  30ml/2 tbsp double (heavy) or
    sour cream
  1 drained pickled lemon
  8 drained bottled Peppadew chillies
    (pickled cherry chillies)
  paprika, for dusting
  cucumber, carrot and celery sticks or
    tortilla chips, to serve

1 Put the soft cheese in a bowl and beat it until soft. Beat in the cream or sour cream.

2 Rinse the pickled lemon if it is still salty, then carefully scrape away the pulp, leaving the rind. Chop this finely. Chop the Peppadews to a similar size.

3 Stir the lemon and chillies into the cheese mixture, dust the surface lightly with paprika and serve with crudités or tortilla chips.

MARINADES AND STUFFINGS

Citrus juice makes an excellent basis for a marinade, since the acid is a valuable tenderizer. This is very useful when it comes to meat and poultry, but if you are marinating fish, keep the marinating time short or the fish may break up.

Citrus is also a very good ingredient in stuffings. Choose between the warm, sweet flavour of orange or mandarin, or the tartness of a lemon or lime.

Lemon and rosemary marinade

This is lovely with lamb for roasting. If used with chicken pieces, lift them out of the marinade before cooking, or the chicken could become tough.

MAKES ABOUT 350ML/12FL OZ/1½ CUPS

INGREDIENTS
  1 lemon, sliced
  6 fresh rosemary sprigs
  15ml/1 tbsp cornflour (cornstarch)
  150ml/¼ pint/⅔ cup lemon juice
  150ml/¼ pint/⅔ cup dry white wine
  60ml/4 tbsp olive oil
  salt and ground black pepper

1 Place your chosen meat in a large shallow pan or dish that will not react with the acid in the marinade. Sprinkle the lemon slices and rosemary on top.

2 Put the cornflour in a bowl and stir in enough of the lemon juice to make a paste. Stir in the remaining juice, with the wine, oil and a little salt and pepper. Pour over the meat, cover and leave for 4–6 hours, turning occasionally. Roast meat – but not poultry – in the marinade. If grilling the meat over a barbecue, use the marinade for basting.

Orange and green peppercorn marinade

A perfect marinade for fish. If a whole fish is used, you can afford to marinate it for up to 4 hours; marinate steaks or fillets for no more than 1 hour.

MAKES ABOUT 750ML/1¼ PINTS/3 CUPS

INGREDIENTS
  1 red onion, sliced
  2 small oranges, peeled and sliced
  90ml/6 tbsp mild olive oil
  30ml/1 tbsp cider vinegar
  30ml/2 tbsp drained green
    peppercorns in brine
  30ml/2 tbsp chopped fresh parsley
  salt and sugar

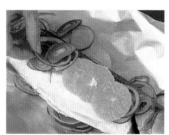

1 Slash a whole fish three or four times on either side. Line an ovenproof dish with foil. Lay half the onion and orange slices on the foil, place the whole fish or portions on top and cover with the remaining onion and orange slices.

2 Mix the remaining ingredients in a jug (pitcher) and pour them over the fish. Cover and set aside for up to 4 hours, depending on whether you are using portions or a whole fish. Bake the fish in the oven.

Lemon rub

This makes a marvellous dry marinade for chicken. Rub it on to the skin about 1 hour before roasting or grilling on the barbecue. You need to allow time to dry the lemon rind, so make this a few days before you intend to use it.

MAKES ABOUT 50G/2OZ

INGREDIENTS
  2 lemons
  30ml/2 tbsp chopped fresh
    lemon thyme
  15ml/1 tbsp chopped fresh
    lemon verbena
  15ml/1 tbsp chopped lemon grass

1 Peel the lemon in fine strips and then air-dry the rind and herbs on a rack in a warm place for up to two days.

2 When thoroughly dry, powder the lemon rind, using a pestle and mortar. Add the dried herbs and crush to blend together and make a powder.

COOK'S TIP
You can dry the lemon peel in an airing cupboard, if you have one, though a warm kitchen will do just as well.

Parsley, lemon and thyme stuffing

This is a very good stuffing to use with poultry. Slide it under the breast of a chicken before roasting it, or use it to stuff a poussin.

MAKES ABOUT 175G/6OZ

INGREDIENTS
  30g/1oz/2 tbsp butter
  1 small onion, finely chopped
  1 celery stick, finely chopped
  115g/4oz/2 cups fresh
    white breadcrumbs
  15ml/1 tbsp chopped fresh parsley
  10ml/2 tsp chopped fresh thyme
  grated rind of ½ lemon
  beaten egg, to bind
  salt and ground black pepper

1 Melt half the butter in a frying pan and cook the onion and celery over a low heat for about 5 minutes, or until the onion is tender. Remove from the heat and leave to cool.

2 Mix the breadcrumbs, parsley, thyme, and lemon rind in a small bowl. Add the onion mixture, the remaining butter, and enough of the egg to bind. Season with salt and pepper, and mix well.

Apricot and mandarin stuffing

An aromatic, golden mixture that makes the perfect stuffing for pork. Try it as a filling for pork fillet or tenderloin. Use the handle of a wooden spoon to make a hole right through the centre of the fillet, insert the stuffing and roast.

MAKES ABOUT 175G/6OZ

INGREDIENTS
  15g/½oz/1 tbsp butter
  1 small onion or leek, finely chopped
  115g/4oz/2 cups fresh white or
    wholemeal (whole-wheat)
    breadcrumbs
  50g/2oz/¼ cup ready-to-eat
    dried apricots
  6 mandarin segments, chopped
  grated rind of ½ orange
  beaten egg, to bind

1 Melt the butter in a frying pan and cook the onion or leek over a low heat for about 5 minutes, or until tender. Leave to cool.

2 Mix the breadcrumbs, dried apricots, mandarin segments and orange rind in a bowl. Add the onion with enough egg to bind. Season and mix well.

Prune, orange and nut stuffing

This makes enough to stuff a 4.5kg/ 10lb turkey, so amounts are generous. Reduce the quantities if you want to use it for a duck or chicken.

MAKES ABOUT 500G/1¼LB

INGREDIENTS
  115g/4oz/1 cup pitted prunes
  60ml/4 tbsp sherry
  25g/1oz/2 tbsp butter
  1 onion, finely chopped
  225g/8oz/4 cups fresh
    white breadcrumbs
  finely grated rind of 1 orange
  2 eggs, beaten
  30ml/2 tbsp chopped fresh parsley
  15ml/1 tbsp mixed dried herbs
  large pinch of ground allspice
  large pinch of freshly grated nutmeg
  115g/4oz/1 cup chopped walnuts
  2 celery sticks, finely chopped
  salt and ground black pepper

1 Put the prunes and sherry in a small pan. Cover and simmer gently until the prunes are tender. Remove from the heat and set aside to cool.

2 Melt the butter in a heavy frying pan and cook the onion over a low heat for about 5 minutes, or until it is softened. Remove the pan from the heat and leave to cool.

3 The prunes should have absorbed most, if not all, of the sherry. Cut each prune into four pieces. Place in a large bowl and add the onions. Stir in all the remaining ingredients, seasoning with salt and pepper. Use immediately, or cover and chill until needed.

CITRUS BUTTERS

Adding flavour to your food is easy when you top a steak, a succulent piece of white fish, chicken, or lamb chops with a pat of tangy citrus butter. If your sandwiches need updating, soften the citrus butter and use it to spread over the bread. Sweet butters are wonderful melted over waffles and pancakes too.

Maître d'hôtel butter

This is the classic parsley and lemon butter, frequently used for fish, but also great on steak or chops.

MAKES ABOUT 115G/4OZ/½ CUP

INGREDIENTS
    115g/4oz/½ cup unsalted (sweet)
      butter, at room temperature
    30ml/2 tbsp finely chopped
      fresh parsley
    2.5ml/½ tsp lemon juice
    cayenne pepper
    salt and ground black pepper

1 Put the butter into a mixing bowl and soften it by beating it with a spoon. Beat in the parsley, lemon juice and cayenne pepper. Season with salt and pepper.

2 Spread the butter 1cm/¼in thick on a piece of baking parchment, greaseproof (waxed) paper or foil. Chill until firm, then stamp out small rounds or other shapes using pastry (cookie) cutters.

3 If you want to make a butter roll, which can later be cut into slices, spoon the butter on to the foil or paper, then shape it, using the foil or paper as a guide. Do this as quickly as you can, as the heat from your hands will melt the butter. Wrap and chill.

Fennel and lime butter

Scallops taste sublime when teamed with this delectable butter. It also tastes wonderful on swordfish steaks. Only the feathery tops of the fennel are used, but don't waste the bulb – cut it into wedges and cook to serve with the fish.

MAKES ABOUT 225G/8OZ/1 CUP

INGREDIENTS
    1 fennel bulb, with plenty of
      feathery leaves
    2 egg yolks
    grated rind and juice of 1 lime
    175g/6oz/¾ cup butter
    salt and ground black pepper

1 Trim the feathery leaves from the fennel bulb and chop them finely.

2 Place the egg yolks in a bowl and whisk in the grated lime rind and juice. Continue to whisk until the mixture is pale and smooth.

3 Melt the butter in a pan. Gradually whisk it into the egg yolk mixture, until the sauce is thick and smooth. Add the chopped fennel leaves, salt and pepper to taste and stir well to mix.

Maître d'hôtel butter variations

These ideas are a good way of using up extra citrus. Use 115g/4oz/½ cup unsalted (sweet) butter.

Lemon and lime butter Add 15ml/1 tbsp finely grated lemon or lime rind and 15ml/1 tbsp juice. Omit the cayenne pepper.

Citrus butter Increase the lemon juice to 5ml/1 tsp or use 10ml/2 tsp orange juice or 5ml/1 tsp lime juice. Add the grated rind of 1 lemon, orange or lime. Omit the parsley and cayenne pepper.

Coriander-lime butter Omit the lemon juice, parsley and the cayenne pepper. Chop 25g/1oz/1 cup fresh coriander (cilantro). Mix into the butter with the grated rind and juice of 1 lime.

Sweet orange butter Instead of using lemon juice, add 10ml/2 tsp orange juice and the finely grated rind of 1 orange. Omit the parsley, cayenne pepper and seasoning. Sweeten it with 30ml/2 tbsp icing (confectioners') sugar.

CITRUS DRESSINGS

Although lemon is the juice most closely associated with dressings, other citrus juices can be used to delicious effect. Orange juice, for instance, works very well in a dressing that contains soy sauce, and grapefruit juice has an affinity for balsamic vinegar and virgin olive oil. Gremolata, a dry mixture of lemon rind, garlic and parsley, makes a tasty garnish sprinkled over stews.

Lemon vinaigrette

The original salad dressing for green leaves, this is often also called French dressing (except in France, that is). It is basically a mixture of oil and lemon juice, with extra ingredients that vary, depending on what kind of salad it is to be used for. Vinegar can be the acid element, but the ratio of oil to acid must be adjusted because vinegar has a stronger flavour than lemon. You can make it hours before you need it – just give it a quick whisk to bring it back up to scratch – but don't let green leaves sit in it for too long or they'll wilt. Some cooks mix vinaigrette by the jam-jar-full and keep it in the refrigerator, but it tastes infinitely better freshly made.

MAKES ABOUT 150ML/¼ PINT/⅔ CUP

INGREDIENTS
 1 garlic clove
 5ml/1 tsp Dijon mustard
 45–60ml/3–4 tbsp lemon juice
 150ml/¼ pint/⅔ cup good quality
  olive oil
 salt and ground black pepper

1 Put the garlic on a board, sprinkle it with a little salt and crush with the flat side of the blade of a cook's knife.

2 Scrape the crushed garlic into a small bowl and beat in the mustard, then the lemon juice.

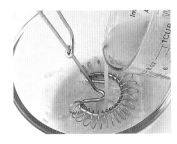

3 Using a whisk (the horseshoe-shaped type works best), gradually whisk in the oil until the dressing thickens and emulsifies. Season to taste.

Grapefruit vinaigrette

Tangy and full of flavour, grapefruit juice makes an excellent salad dressing. Try it with romaine leaves or watercress.

MAKES ABOUT 150ML/¼ PINT/⅔ CUP

INGREDIENTS
 45ml/3 tbsp grapefruit juice
 10ml/2 tbsp balsamic vinegar
 5ml/1 tsp Provençal or red
  pepper mustard
 120ml/4fl oz/½ cup mild, fruity
  olive oil or a mixture of sunflower
  oil and extra virgin olive oil
 salt, ground black pepper and sugar

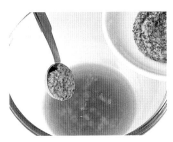

Mix the grapefruit juice and balsamic vinegar in a bowl. Whisk in the mustard and a pinch each of salt, pepper and sugar. Slowly whisk in the oil. Taste and adjust the seasoning if necessary.

Grapefruit and yogurt dressing

This oil-free dressing makes a healthy change from vinaigrette.

MAKES ABOUT 250ML/8FL OZ/1 CUP

INGREDIENTS
 30ml/2 tbsp pink grapefruit juice
 15ml/1 tbsp sherry vinegar
 1 garlic clove, crushed
 5ml/1 tsp wholegrain mustard
 150ml/¼ pint/⅔ cup natural (plain)
  low-fat yogurt
 15ml/1 tbsp chopped fresh herbs

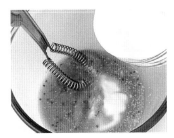

Mix the grapefruit juice and vinegar in a bowl. Add the garlic, mustard, then whisk in the yogurt and herbs.

Gremolata

The traditional finishing flourish for the Milanese dish of osso buco. This makes enough for one stew, four lamb kebabs, four pork chops, or four portions of chunky white fish.

Grate 1 lemon. Crush 2 garlic cloves to a paste or chop very finely with salt. Chop a small bunch of parsley then mix with the lemon rind and garlic. Sprinkle over the food just before serving.

SAVOURY SAUCES

The most popular lemon-based sauce is mayonnaise, but because it does not have a strong citrus flavour, few people connect it with the fruit. Other sauces featuring citrus include orange butter sauce, Cumberland sauce and the famous Sauce bigarade.

Never-fail mayonnaise

The capital of the Balearic island of Minorca is almost certain to have lent its name to this famous sauce, when the French duc de Richelieu took the city of Mahon in 1756. Mayonnaise has many different uses, in sandwiches and hamburgers, as a salad dressing and as a sauce with fish and chicken. This version is made with a food processor for ease. Have all the ingredients at room temperature before you start.

MAKES ABOUT 350ML/12FL OZ/1½ CUPS

INGREDIENTS
  1 egg, plus 1 egg yolk
  5ml/1 tsp Dijon mustard
  juice of 1 large lemon
  175ml/6fl oz/¾ cup olive oil
  175ml/6fl oz/¾ cup rapeseed
    (canola), sunflower or corn oil
  salt and white pepper

1 Process the whole egg and yolk in a food processor for 20 seconds. Add the mustard, half the lemon juice, and a pinch of salt and pepper. Process for about 30 seconds until mixed.

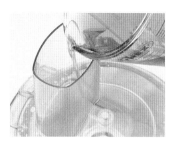

2 With the motor running, pour in the oils through the feeder tube in a thin stream. Process until the mayonnaise is thick. Taste and add more lemon juice and seasoning if necessary.

Basil and lemon mayonnaise

This is delicious served with baked new potatoes or used as a dip for French fries. It also make a great partner for lightly poached salmon.

MAKES ABOUT 350ML/12FL OZ/1½ CUPS

INGREDIENTS
  2 large (US extra large) egg yolks
  15ml/1 tbsp lemon juice
  150ml/¼ pint/⅔ cup mild olive oil
  150ml/¼ pint/⅔ cup sunflower oil
  a handful of fresh green basil leaves
  a handful of fresh opal basil leaves
  4 garlic cloves, crushed
  salt and ground black pepper

1 Place the egg yolks and lemon juice in a food processor or blender and process them briefly to mix. With the motor running, add the oils, slowly at first, then in a steady stream. Continue processing until the mixture forms a thick, creamy mayonnaise.

2 Tear both types of basil into pieces and stir them into the mayonnaise with the crushed garlic. Add salt and pepper to taste. Spoon into a serving bowl, cover and chill until ready to serve.

Tartare sauce

This is the real thing – tartare sauce made from scratch – but if you are short of time, you could always stir the flavourings into a good quality bought mayonnaise. It is perfect with fish.

MAKES 200ML/7FL OZ/SCANT 1 CUP

INGREDIENTS
  2 hard-boiled eggs
  1 egg yolk
  10ml/2 tsp lemon juice
  175ml/6fl oz/¾ cup olive oil
  5ml/1 tsp each chopped capers,
    gherkin, fresh chives and parsley
  salt and ground black pepper

1 Halve the hard-boiled eggs, scoop the yolks into a sieve placed over a bowl and push them through with the aid of a spoon. Stir in the raw egg yolk until smooth. Stir in the lemon juice.

2 Whisk in the oil, a little at a time. When the mixture starts to thicken, add the oil more quickly, so that it forms an emulsion. Finely chop one egg white (save the other for another dish) and stir it into the sauce with the capers, gherkin and herbs. Season to taste.

Avgolemono sauce

This frothy, light lemon mixture is the sauce version of a classic Greek recipe that is more often served as a soup. It tastes great with oily fish, such as sardines, with chicken or with a medley of roasted Mediterranean vegetables. Adjust the stock accordingly.

MAKES ABOUT 250ML/8FL OZ/1 CUP

INGREDIENTS
  10ml/2 tsp arrowroot
  grated rind and juice of
    1 large lemon
  120ml/4fl oz/½ cup vegetable,
    chicken or fish stock
  3 egg yolks

1 Put the arrowroot and lemon rind in a heavy pan. Strain the lemon juice, then add to the pan and mix thoroughly. Stir in the stock, then bring the mixture to the boil over a low heat, whisking constantly until smooth and thickened.

2 Remove the pan from the heat and add the egg yolks, whisking constantly. Return the pan to the heat and cook, still whisking constantly, for 1 minute. Serve immediately.

Hollandaise sauce

This classic sauce has a reputation for being quite difficult to make, as it will separate if it gets too hot. This version is much easier. Serve it with asparagus, artichokes, poached eggs (to make eggs Benedict), peas, broccoli, poached salmon and fish mousses.

MAKES ABOUT 300ML/½ PINT/1¼ CUPS

INGREDIENTS
  3 egg yolks
  15–30m/1–2 tbsp lemon juice
  175g/6oz/¾ cup unsalted (sweet)
    butter, diced
  salt and ground black pepper

1 Add the egg yolks and 15ml/1 tbsp of the lemon juice to a heavy pan. Season and whisk well to combine.

2 Add the butter and set the pan over a medium heat. Whisk constantly so that as the butter melts, it is blended into the egg yolks.

3 Continue whisking over a medium heat until the sauce is thick. Taste and add more lemon juice, salt and pepper if needed.

Simple sauce variations

Mayonnaise and hollandaise can be easily varied, with great results.
Aioli Add 4 garlic cloves with the eggs when making mayonnaise. Great as a dip for potato chunks, and superb with mussels.

Remoulade To 300ml/½ pint/ 1¼ cups mayonnaise, add 15ml/ 1 tbsp each of chopped fresh chives, tarragon and parsley, Dijon mustard and chopped, drained gherkins, and 5ml/1 tsp each of anchovy essence and chopped capers. Serve with braised celeriac.

Mousseline Add 150ml/¼ pint/ ⅔ cup of whipped cream to a cooled hollandaise sauce, and whisk well. Serve as a dip with artichoke hearts.
Sauce Maltaise Grate the rind from 1 blood orange, taking care to avoid the pith, and squeeze the juice from 2 blood oranges. Whisk the juice into warm hollandaise, then stir in the grated rind. Serve with cooked green vegetables.

Orange butter sauce

A simple sauce, this is wonderful tossed with wild mushrooms that have been fried in butter. Sprinkle over chopped fresh parsley and serve with toast.

MAKES ABOUT 350ML/12FL OZ/1½ CUPS

INGREDIENTS
    juice of 4 large oranges
    pinch of cayenne pepper
    175g/6oz/¾ cup unsalted (sweet)
      butter, diced
    salt

1 Pour the orange juice into a small, heavy pan and bring to the boil. Boil until the liquid has reduced to about 30ml/2 tbsp. Add salt and cayenne pepper to taste.

2 Over a low heat, gradually whisk in the butter, piece by piece, to produce a creamy and smooth sauce. It is best if each piece of butter is fully incorporated before adding the next cube. Serve the sauce immediately.

COOK'S TIP
Use unsalted butter as its sweeter flavour is more suited to this sauce.

Cumberland sauce

This British classic is served with a hot piece of gammon or ham, cold game or tongue, and is good brushed over lamb for the last few minutes of cooking.

MAKES ABOUT 475ML/16FL OZ/2 CUPS

INGREDIENTS
    1 unwaxed lemon
    1 unwaxed orange
    2 sugar cubes
    150ml/¼ pint/⅔ cup port
    4 allspice berries
    4 cloves
    5ml/1 tsp mustard seeds
    225g/8oz redcurrant jelly
    10ml/2 tsp arrowroot
    30ml/2 tbsp orange liqueur
    pinch of ground ginger

1 Pare the lemon, avoiding the pith. Snip or cut the peel into thin strips.

2 Put the lemon rind in a pan, cover with water and bring to the boil. Cook for 5 minutes, drain and set aside.

3 Wash the orange, then rub it all over with the sugar cubes, until they are saturated with the citrus oil.

4 Pour the port into a small pan and add the sugar cubes and whole spices. Bring to the boil, then leave to cool. Strain the port into a pan, add the jelly and stir over a low heat until dissolved.

5 Mix the arrowroot with the orange liqueur and stir it into the sauce. Bring the sauce to the boil and cook gently for 1–2 minutes until thickened.

6 Remove from the heat and add the lemon rind and ground ginger. Cool to room temperature before serving.

COOK'S TIP
To develop a rich flavour, store this sauce in the refrigerator for a few days then bring to room temperature before serving.

Orange and caper sauce

Fish gets the luxury treatment with this sweet-and-sour sauce. It is classically served with poached skate, but tastes just as good with an oily fish such as mackerel. Adding the fish bones and trimmings will give the sauce depth.

MAKES ABOUT 475ML/16FL OZ/2 CUPS

INGREDIENTS
  25g/1oz/2 tbsp butter
  1 onion, chopped
  fish bones and trimmings
  5ml/1 tsp black peppercorns
  300ml/½ pint/1¼ cups dry
    white wine
  2 small oranges
  15ml/1 tbsp drained capers
  60ml/4 tbsp crème fraîche
  salt and ground black pepper

1 Melt the butter in a pan and sauté the onion over a medium heat until it is lightly browned. Add the fish trimmings and peppercorns, then pour in the wine. Cover and simmer for 30 minutes.

2 Using a sharp knife, peel the oranges. Working over a bowl, ease the segments away from the membranes.

3 Strain the stock into a clean pan. Add the capers and orange segments, with any juice. Heat through. Reduce the heat to the lowest setting and stir in the crème fraîche. Season and serve hot.

Sauce bigarade

The classic orange sauce to serve with duck and rich game.

MAKES ABOUT 550ML/18FL OZ/2½ CUPS

INGREDIENTS
  roasting pan juices or 25g/1oz/
    2 tbsp butter
  40g/1½oz/3 tbsp plain
    (all-purpose) flour
  300ml/½ pint/1¼ cups hot stock
  150ml/¼ pint/⅔ cup red wine
  2 unwaxed Seville (Temple) oranges
    or 2 sweet oranges plus 10ml/2 tsp
    lemon juice
  15ml/1 tbsp orange liqueur
  30ml/2 tbsp redcurrant jelly
  salt and ground black pepper

1 Pour off any excess fat from the roasting pan, leaving the juices, or melt the butter in a small pan. Add the flour and cook, stirring constantly, for about 4 minutes, or until lightly browned.

2 Remove from the heat and gradually blend in the stock and wine. Bring to the boil, stirring constantly. Lower the heat and simmer gently for 5 minutes.

3 Meanwhile, using a zester, pare the rind thinly from one orange. Squeeze the juice from both oranges.

4 Blanch the rind by putting it in a pan, pouring over boiling water to cover and cooking for 5 minutes. Drain the rind then return it to the pan. Add the sauce to the pan.

5 Add the orange juice and lemon juice to the pan, if using, with orange liqueur and redcurrant jelly, stirring to dissolve the jelly. Season to taste and serve.

SWEET SAUCES

One of the many reasons that makes citrus so special is its affinity for both sweet and savoury dishes. In sweet sauces, citrus really stars.

Lemon custard

This creamy sauce is perfect spooned over a steamed lemon sponge pudding, or poured over the sponges in a trifle. It is also delicious with sliced bananas.

MAKES ABOUT 600ML/1 PINT/2½ CUPS

INGREDIENTS
    15ml/1 tbsp cornflour (cornstarch)
    15ml/1 tbsp custard powder (see Cook's tip)
    15ml/1 tbsp caster (superfine) sugar
    finely grated rind of 2 lemons
    600ml/1 pint/⅔ cup milk
    15g/½oz/1 tbsp butter

1 Mix the cornflour and custard powder in a large bowl. Stir in the sugar and lemon rind.

2 Stir in 15–30ml/1–2 tbsp of the milk and mix to a paste. Heat the remaining milk in a pan. As soon as bubbles start to appear on the surface, around the edge, remove the pan from the heat.

3 Gradually stir the hot milk into the paste, until the mixture is very smooth. Return it to the pan and heat gently, stirring until thick. Whisk in the butter to finish.

COOK'S TIP
If you cannot find custard powder use cornflour (cornstarch) instead. The colour will not be so bright, but the flavour will not be compromised.

Orange honey sauce

This is a quick and easy sauce to make. Try it over hot pancakes or waffles for a delicious dessert.

MAKES ABOUT 300ML/½ PINT/1¼ CUPS

INGREDIENTS
    175ml/6fl oz/¾ cup clear honey
    50g/2oz/¼ cup butter
    50g/2oz/⅓ cup muscovado (molasses) sugar
    grated rind and juice of 2 large oranges

Mix all the ingredients in a heavy pan. Place over a low heat and stir constantly until the sugar has dissolved and the sauce is warm.

Sabayon

Serve this sauce hot over a steamed pudding or chill as described and serve just as it is with dessert cookies. Never let it stand, as it will collapse.

MAKES ABOUT 250ML/8FL OZ/1 CUP

INGREDIENTS
    1 egg
    2 egg yolks
    75g/3oz/⅔ cup caster (superfine) sugar
    150ml/¼ pint/⅔ cup sweet white wine
    grated rind and juice of 1 lemon

1 Whisk the egg, yolks and sugar until they are pale and thick.

2 Stand the bowl over a pan of hot water. Add the wine and lemon juice, a little at a time, whisking vigorously. Continue whisking until the mixture leaves a trail from the whisk. Whisk in the lemon rind. If serving hot, serve immediately.

3 To serve cold, place over a bowl of iced water and whisk until chilled. Pour into small glasses and serve at once.

Hot orange and red wine sauce

This tangy sauce has a vibrant colour. It looks and tastes great with fruit pies, and is also good with crêpes.

MAKES ABOUT 300ML/½ PINT/1¼ CUPS

INGREDIENTS
 4 oranges, such as Valencia
 250ml/8fl oz/1 cup fruity red wine
 25g/1oz/2 tbsp soft light brown sugar
 1 cinnamon stick
 2 cloves
 5ml/1 tsp cornflour (cornstarch)
 15ml/1 tbsp water or orange liqueur, such as Cointreau or Grand Marnier
 25g/1oz/2 tbsp butter, diced

1 Using a zester, thinly pare the rind from half an orange and place it in a small pan. Squeeze the juice from all the oranges and strain it into the pan. Add the wine, brown sugar, cinnamon stick and cloves. Heat until the sugar has completely dissolved, then simmer for 10 minutes until reduced.

2 Mix the cornflour with the water or liqueur in a small cup. Add to the red wine mixture and simmer for 1 minute, until slightly thickened.

3 Remove and discard the cloves and cinnamon stick and gradually whisk in the butter, one piece at a time until smooth and glossy. Make sure each piece is incorporated before adding more. Serve immediately.

Orange, lemon or lime crème pâtissière

This is also known as pastry cream, which gives a clue to its most common use. Spread it in a cold baked pastry case (pie shell) and top with kiwi fruit and mandarin segments, then add an orange glaze for a sophisticated treat. It is a good idea to make the custard the day before you need it, so that it can be thoroughly chilled.

MAKES ABOUT 300ML/½ PINT/1¼ CUPS

INGREDIENTS
 3 egg yolks
 50g/2oz/¼ cup caster (superfine) sugar
 1 orange, lemon or lime
 40g/1½oz/6 tbsp plain (all-purpose) flour
 250ml/8fl oz/1 cup milk
 1 vanilla pod (bean), split lengthways

1 In a heatproof bowl, whisk the egg yolks with the sugar until pale. Finely grate the orange, lemon or lime directly into the bowl or, if easier, grate onto a sheet of baking parchment and then add to the egg mixture. Sift over the flour and whisk it in.

2 Pour the milk into a small pan and add the vanilla pod. Bring to the boil, remove the vanilla pod and slowly pour the hot milk over the egg mixture, whisking constantly.

3 Pour the mixture into a heavy pan and return the vanilla pod. Bring to the boil, lower the heat and gently simmer for 2 minutes, stirring constantly with a wooden spoon, until thickened. Transfer the mixture to a bowl and cover closely with clear film (plastic wrap). Leave to cool, then chill until needed.

Citrus cream

The simplest sauce of all, this flavoured whipped cream is very good with a rich sweet pie and adds an extra boost to a plate of mixed summer berries.

MAKES 300ML/½ PINT/1¼ CUPS

INGREDIENTS
 300ml/½ pint/1¼ cups double (heavy) cream
 5ml/1 tsp icing (confectioners') sugar
 grated rind of 1 lemon, 1 orange or 1 lime

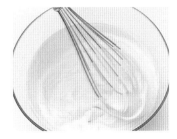

Whip the cream to soft peaks with a small balloon whisk or electric mixer. Add the icing sugar and grated citrus rind and beat until the cream holds its shape. Transfer to a serving dish and serve immediately.

CITRUS DRINKS

Orange, lemon and lime go well in many drinks, but grapefruit can also be used for colour and flavour.

THIRST QUENCHERS

These home-made drinks are cooling, but without the cloying sweetness or additives typical of commercial drinks.

Old-fashioned lemonade

The traditional drink for a long summer, this is best enjoyed in a hammock after a vigorous game of tennis.

SERVES TWO

INGREDIENTS
2 lemons
75g/3oz/6 tbsp caster
  (superfine) sugar
2 egg whites
300ml/½ pint/1¼ cups boiling water
75ml/5 tbsp sherry (optional)
ice cubes

1 Pare a few strips of rind from one of the lemons, and add to a pan. Cut both lemons in half and squeeze the juice.

2 Strain the juice to remove any pips, then add to the pan containing the rind.

3 Add the sugar and egg whites and whisk until frothy. Whisk in the water. Continue to whisk for 2 minutes more, until the sugar has dissolved. Pour in the sherry, if using, a little at a time, whisking after each addition.

4 To serve, put several ice cubes into tall glasses, pour over the lemonade, and decorate with mint, if you like.

Orange and raspberry smoothie

This combines the fragrant flavour of raspberries and the tang of citrus with creamy yogurt – a perfect way to start the day or a great pick-me-up when your energy begins to flag.

SERVES THREE

INGREDIENTS
250g/9oz/about 2 cups
  raspberries, chilled
200ml/7fl oz/scant 1 cup natural
  (plain) yogurt
300ml/½ pint/1¼ cups freshly
  squeezed orange juice, chilled

1 Put the chilled raspberries and yogurt in a food processor or blender and process for 1 minute to make a smooth and creamy purée. Reserve a few raspberries for decoration.

2 Add the orange juice to the raspberry and yogurt mixture and process for about 30 seconds, or until thoroughly combined and smooth.

3 To serve, pour into tall glasses and decorate with a few whole raspberries. Serve immediately with a swizzle stick for stirring, if you like.

Citrus shake

It would be hard to find a drink with more flavour and zest than this mix of three citrus and pineapple.

SERVES FOUR

INGREDIENTS
1 pineapple
3 grapefruit, using 1 each white,
  pink and ruby grapefruit
2 oranges, peeled and chopped
juice of 1 lemon

1 To prepare the pineapple, cut the bottom and the top off the fruit. Stand the pineapple upright and cut off the skin, removing all the spikes, but taking off as little of the flesh as possible. Cut the flesh into bitesize chunks.

2 Peel and segment the grapefruit, removing the membrane, if you wish. Put in a food processor or blender along with the pineapple, oranges and lemon juice. Process until combined.

3 Press the fruit juice through a sieve to remove any pith or membranes. Pour into tall glasses and serve the shakes chilled, with straws, if you wish.

HOT CITRUS DRINKS

Adding a slice or two of orange, lemon or lime to mulled wine or hot coffee is a great way to bring out their flavour and is wonderfully aromatic.

Mulled wine

The perfect way to welcome guests on a chilly winter evening.

SERVES FOUR

INGREDIENTS
70cl bottle red wine
75g/3oz/6 tbsp soft light brown sugar
2 cinnamon sticks
1 lemon, sliced
4 whole cloves
150ml/¼ pint/⅔ cup brandy or port
lemon slices, to serve

1 Put all the ingredients, except the brandy or port, into a large pan. Bring to the boil, then remove from the heat. Cover and leave to stand for 5 minutes, to allow the flavours to infuse (steep).

2 Strain the liquid into a heatproof bowl, to remove the spices and lemon slices. Add the brandy or port. Serve warm, decorated with a half slice of lemon.

Café brûlot

This mixture of coffee, brandy and orange liqueur, with pared citrus rinds, makes a spectacular drink when flamed at the table.

SERVES FOUR TO SIX

INGREDIENTS
1 orange
1 lemon
30ml/2 tbsp caster (superfine) sugar
6 cloves
1 cinnamon stick
175ml/6fl oz/¾ cup brandy
45–60ml/3–4 tbsp Curaçao or other orange liqueur
475ml/16fl oz/2 cups hot strong black coffee
4–6 cinnamon and orange rind twists

1 Pare the rind of the orange and the lemon in one strip and place in a pan.

2 Add the sugar, cloves, cinnamon, brandy and liqueur, and heat to dissolve the sugar. Have the hot coffee ready. Carefully ignite the brandy mixture, then add the coffee in a steady stream. Serve in heatproof glasses, decorated with a cinnamon stick and orange rind twist.

Café à l'orange

Sip this drink slowly and savour the contrast between the thick citrus cream topping and hot liqueur coffee beneath.

SERVES FOUR

INGREDIENTS
120ml/4fl oz/½ cup whipping or double (heavy) cream
30ml/2 tbsp icing (confectioners') sugar
5ml/1 tsp grated orange rind
600ml/1 pint/2½ cups hot strong black coffee
150ml/¼ pint/⅔ cup orange liqueur
4 orange wedges, to decorate

1 Whip the cream until stiff, then fold in the icing sugar and orange rind. Chill for 30 minutes, or until the flavoured cream is firm enough to support a wedge of orange.

2 Divide the hot black coffee equally among four tall glass mugs and stir about 30ml/2 tbsp liqueur into each. Top with a generous swirl of the chilled whipped cream, then place an orange wedge on the cream. Serve immediately, sipping the drink through the cream.

CITRUS COCKTAILS

Ever since their heyday in the 1920s and 1930s, cocktails have been very popular, and continue to be so today. Citrus is a favourite ingredient, whether juiced, sliced or rubbed around the rim of a glass to provide a tart tingle as a prelude to the drink itself.

Harvey wallbanger

Galliano has a wonderful affinity for orange juice, as this extremely popular cocktail demonstrates.

SERVES ONE

INGREDIENTS
    30ml/2 tbsp vodka
    15ml/1 tbsp Galliano liqueur
    150ml/¼ pint/⅔ cup orange juice
    crushed ice
    1 small orange, to decorate

1 Pour the spirits and juice into a tall glass or cocktail shaker full of crushed ice. Mix or shake the cocktail for about 30 seconds to chill it.

Bartender's tips
Freshly squeezed orange juice or bottled fresh orange juice is one of the most important elements in drinks based on single spirit shots, particularly with the white spirits such as gin, vodka and white rum. In cocktails, freshly squeezed lemon juice is great for cutting through the sweetness of many liqueurs. Fresh lime juice is even sourer, and is used in drinks that demand a powerful tang.

2 Use a canelle knife (zester) to take strips of rind off the orange. Cut the orange into thin, even slices.

3 Cut the orange slices in half and sit them between cracked ice in a highball glass. Strain the cocktail into the glass, decorate with the rind and serve.

Morning glory fizz

Despite the name, it's not necessary to drink this first thing in the morning.

SERVES ONE

INGREDIENTS
    15ml/1 tbsp brandy
    5ml/1 tsp orange Curaçao
    5ml/1 tsp lemon juice
    1 dash anisette
    2 dashes Angostura bitters
    soda water (club soda), to taste
    twist of lemon rind, to decorate

Pour the brandy, Curaçao, lemon juice and anisette into a cocktail shaker filled with crushed ice and shake for about 20 seconds. Strain into a small, chilled cocktail glass. Add bitters to taste and top up the glass with soda water. Decorate with the lemon twist.

Tequila sunset

Try this recipe for a different take on a tequila sunrise. For that drink, bright red grenadine sinks to the bottom and then blends upwards into the orange juice. Here, the orange, tequila and crème de cassis represent a glowing sunset sky above a honeyed horizon.

SERVES ONE

INGREDIENTS
    30ml/2 tbsp tequila
    120ml/4fl oz/½ cup lemon
    juice, chilled
    40ml/1½ tbsp orange juice, chilled
    30ml/2 tbsp clear honey
    15ml/1 tbsp crème de cassis

1 Pour the tequila and then the lemon and orange juices straight into a tall, well-chilled cocktail glass.

2 Mix the ingredients by twisting a swizzle stick between the palms of your hands. Drizzle the honey into the glass so that it falls in a layer at the bottom.

3 Add the crème de cassis – but don't stir – to add a glowing layer above the honey in the glass.

Gin and lemon fizz

The citrus sorbet here is enhanced by pretty ice cubes, filled with curls of pared lemon rind, berries or flowers.

SERVES TWO

INGREDIENTS
  berries and currants
  pieces of thinly pared lemon and
  orange rind
  tiny edible flowers, such as rose
  4 scoops lemon sorbet (sherbet)
  30ml/2 tbsp gin
  120ml/4fl oz/½ cup tonic water

1 To make the ice cubes, place a mixture of fruit, pared rind and flowers in separate sections of an ice cube tray.

2 Carefully fill with water and freeze for several hours until solid. Divide the sorbet between two glasses. Pour over the gin and add a couple of the ice cubes to each glass. Top up with tonic water and serve.

VARIATION
Substitute orange sorbet for the lemon, sparkling mineral water for the tonic and add 30ml/2 tbsp Cointreau with the gin.

Iced citrus Margarita

This smooth, cooling tangy sorbet drink has all the punch of Mexico's renowned cocktail. Serve in tall, slim glasses.

SERVES TWO

INGREDIENTS
  30ml/2 tbsp lime juice
  30ml/2 tbsp caster (superfine) sugar,
  plus extra for frosting
  4 lime and 4 lemon slices
  60ml/4 tbsp tequila
  30ml/2 tbsp Cointreau
  6–8 small scoops of orange or lime
  sorbet (sherbet)
  150ml/¼ pint/⅔ fizzy lemonade

1 Frost the glasses, using lime juice and sugar. Carefully add two lime and two lemon slices to each glass, standing them on end.

2 Mix the tequila, Cointreau and lime juice in a bowl. Scoop the sorbet into the glasses, pour the tequila mixture over and top up with the lemonade.

VARIATION
Frost the rims of the glasses with salt instead of sugar, for a traditional taste.

Snowball

Lime, nutmeg and ice cream give this cocktail an irresistible smooth and very creamy taste.

SERVES FOUR

INGREDIENTS
  8 scoops vanilla ice cream
  120ml/4fl oz/½ cup advocaat
  60ml/4 tbsp lime juice
  freshly grated nutmeg
  300ml/½ pint/1¼ cups chilled
  fizzy lemonade

1 Put half the vanilla ice cream in a food processor or blender and add the advocaat and the lime juice, with plenty of freshly grated nutmeg. Process the mixture briefly until well combined.

2 Scoop the remaining ice cream into four glasses. Pour over the advocaat mixture and top up the glasses with lemonade. Sprinkle with more nutmeg.

Quick citrus cocktails
Milano Mix equal measures of gin and Galliano liqueur with crushed ice and the juice of ¼ lemon in a cocktail shaker. Shake, then strain into a cocktail glass.
Gimlet Stir equal measures of Plymouth gin and lime cordial in a glass with a couple of ice cubes.
Gin rickey Half-fill a tall glass with ice. Add 45ml/3 tbsp gin, the juice of ¼ lime or ¼ lemon and a generous dash of grenadine. Stir vigorously, then top with fresh soda water (club soda).

COOKING
WITH
CITRUS

*Citrus fruits are among the most versatile
and useful of ingredients, providing flavour,
aroma, colour and liveliness to a vast range
of dishes. In savoury recipes, lemon and lime
are classic flavouring agents for all sorts of
soups, tagines and fish dishes; orange and
kumquats combine perfectly with duck; and
grapefruit makes a superb addition to salads.*

*In sweet dishes, citrus fruits add a
wonderfully refreshing touch, and are found
in dishes from sorbets and cheesecakes to
compôtes and puddings. Cakes and breads also
benefit from their inimitable flavour.*

SOUPS AND APPETIZERS

Summery soups and tangy appetizers are the perfect way to get the taste buds tingling at the start of a meal. Refreshing citrus flavours — whether the sharpness of limes, the piquancy of preserved lemons or the sweetness of oranges — cleanse the palate and stimulate the appetite. Recipes range from creamy and fragrant soups to fiery spiced shellfish and subtly flavoured vegetable medleys, all with the special lift and zest that comes from citrus fruit.

AVGOLEMONO

THIS IS THE MOST POPULAR OF GREEK SOUPS. THE NAME MEANS EGG AND LEMON, THE TWO MOST IMPORTANT INGREDIENTS, WHICH PRODUCE A LIGHT, NOURISHING SOUP. ORZO IS GREEK, RICE-SHAPED PASTA, BUT YOU CAN USE ANY SMALL SOUP PASTA.

SERVES FOUR TO SIX

INGREDIENTS
1.75 litres/3 pints/7½ cups
   chicken stock
115g/4oz/½ cup orzo pasta
3 eggs
juice of 1 large lemon
salt and ground black pepper
lemon slices, to garnish

COOK'S TIP
This egg and lemon combination is also widely used in Greece as a sauce for pasta or with meatballs.

1 Pour the stock into a large pan, and bring it to a rolling boil. Add the pasta and cook for 5 minutes.

2 Beat the eggs until frothy, then add the lemon juice and 15ml/1 tbsp of cold water. Slowly stir in a ladleful of the hot chicken stock, then add one or two more. Return this mixture to the pan, remove from the heat and stir well.

3 Season to taste with salt and pepper and serve immediately, garnished with lemon slices. (Do not let the soup boil once the eggs have been added or it will curdle.)

CARROT AND ORANGE SOUP

THIS TRADITIONAL, BRIGHT AND SUMMERY SOUP IS ALWAYS POPULAR FOR ITS WONDERFULLY CREAMY CONSISTENCY AND VIBRANTLY FRESH CITRUS FLAVOUR. USE A GOOD, HOME-MADE CHICKEN OR VEGETABLE STOCK IF YOU CAN FOR THE BEST RESULTS.

SERVES FOUR

INGREDIENTS
50g/2oz/¼ cup butter
3 leeks, sliced
450g/1lb carrots, sliced
1.2 litres/2 pints/5 cups chicken or
  vegetable stock
rind and juice of 2 oranges
2.5ml/½ tsp freshly grated nutmeg
150ml/¼ pint/⅔ cup Greek
  (US strained plain) yogurt
salt and ground black pepper
fresh sprigs of coriander (cilantro),
  to garnish

1 Melt the butter in a large pan. Add the leeks and carrots and stir well, coating the vegetables with the butter. Cover and cook for about 10 minutes, until the vegetables are beginning to soften but not colour.

2 Pour in the stock and the orange rind and juice. Add the nutmeg and season to taste with salt and pepper. Bring to the boil, lower the heat, cover and simmer for about 40 minutes, or until the vegetables are tender.

3 Leave to cool slightly, then purée the soup in a food processor or blender until smooth.

4 Return the soup to the pan and add 30ml/2 tbsp of the yogurt, then taste the soup and adjust the seasoning, if necessary. Reheat gently.

5 Ladle the soup into warm individual bowls and put a swirl of yogurt in the centre of each. Sprinkle the fresh sprigs of coriander over each bowl to garnish, and serve immediately.

CHICKPEA, LEMON AND PARSLEY SOUP

LEMON ENHANCES THE FLAVOUR OF FRESH PARSLEY IN THIS TASTY NORTH AFRICAN INSPIRED SOUP, WHICH MAKES A SUBSTANTIAL LUNCH SERVED WITH MOROCCAN OR CRUSTY BREAD.

2 Place the onion and parsley in a food processor or blender and process until finely chopped.

3 Heat the mixed oils in a large frying pan and gently cook the onion mixture for about 4 minutes over a low heat, or until slightly softened.

4 Add the chickpeas, cook gently for about 2 minutes, then add the stock. Season well with salt and pepper. Bring the soup to the boil, then cover and simmer for 20 minutes, or until the chickpeas are very tender.

5 Leave the soup to cool a little and then part-purée in a food processor or blender, or mash the chickpeas fairly coarsely with a fork, so that the soup is thick, but still quite chunky.

SERVES SIX

INGREDIENTS
225g/8oz/1¼ cups chickpeas, soaked overnight
1 small onion, coarsely chopped
1 bunch fresh parsley (about 40g/1½oz/1½ cups)
30ml/2 tbsp olive oil and sunflower oil, mixed
1.2 litres/2 pints/5 cups chicken stock
juice of ½ lemon
salt and ground black pepper
lemon wedges and thinly pared and shredded lemon rind, to garnish
crusty bread, to serve

1 Drain the chickpeas and rinse well under cold running water. Cook them in rapidly boiling water for 10 minutes, then simmer for 1–1½ hours, or until tender. Drain and, using your fingertips, gently peel away the skins.

6 Return the soup to a clean pan, stir in the lemon juice, then taste and adjust the seasoning, if necessary. Heat it through gently, then serve, garnished with lemon wedges and shredded lemon rind, and accompanied by crusty bread.

THAI FISH BROTH

LIMES, LEMON GRASS, CHILLIES AND GALANGAL ARE AMONG THE FLAVOURINGS USED IN THIS FRAGRANT SOUP. IT LOOKS AND TASTES DELICIOUS, AND WOULD BE THE PERFECT CHOICE FOR A DINNER PARTY.

SERVES TWO TO THREE

INGREDIENTS

1 litre/1¾ pints/4 cups fish or light chicken stock
4 lemon grass stalks
3 limes
2 small fresh hot red chillies, seeded and thinly sliced
2cm/¾ in piece fresh galangal or ginger, peeled and thinly sliced
6 coriander (cilantro) stalks
2 kaffir lime leaves, coarsely chopped (optional) (see Cook's Tip)
350g/12oz monkfish fillet, membrane removed and cut into 2.5cm/1in pieces
15ml/1 tbsp rice vinegar
45ml/3 tbsp Thai fish sauce
30ml/2 tbsp chopped coriander (cilantro) leaves, to garnish

1 Pour the stock into a heavy pan and bring it to the boil over a medium heat. Meanwhile, slice the bulb end of each lemon grass stalk diagonally into pieces about 3mm/⅛in thick.

2 Peel off four wide strips of lime rind with a vegetable peeler, taking care to avoid the white pith underneath which would make the soup bitter. Squeeze the limes and reserve the juice.

3 Add the sliced lemon grass, strips of lime rind, chillies, galangal or ginger slices and coriander stalks to the stock, with the kaffir lime leaves, if using. Simmer for 1–2 minutes.

COOK'S TIP
If you use kaffir lime leaves, you will need the juice of only 2 limes.

4 Add the monkfish, rice vinegar and Thai fish sauce, with half the reserved lime juice. Simmer for about 3 minutes, or until the fish is just cooked. Lift out and discard the coriander stalks, taste the broth and add more lime juice, if necessary; the soup should taste quite sour. Sprinkle with the coriander leaves and serve very hot.

OLIVES ᵂᴵᵀᴴ MOROCCAN LEMON MARINADES

PRESERVED AND FRESH LEMONS PROVIDE THEIR OWN DISTINCT QUALITIES TO THESE APPETIZERS FROM NORTH AFRICA. START PREPARATIONS A WEEK IN ADVANCE TO ALLOW THE FLAVOURS TO DEVELOP.

SERVES SIX TO EIGHT

INGREDIENTS

450g/1lb/2⅔ cups olives (unpitted)
For the piquant marinade
  45ml/3 tbsp chopped fresh
    coriander (cilantro)
  45ml/3 tbsp chopped fresh parsley
  1 garlic clove, finely chopped
  good pinch of cayenne pepper
  good pinch of ground cumin
  30–45ml/2–3 tbsp olive oil
  30–45ml/2–3 tbsp lemon juice
For the spicy marinade
  60ml/4 tbsp chopped fresh
    coriander (cilantro)
  60ml/4 tbsp chopped fresh parsley
  1 garlic clove, finely chopped
  5ml/1 tsp grated fresh root ginger
  1 red chilli, seeded and sliced
  ¼ preserved lemon, cut into strips

1 Using the flat side of a large knife blade, crack the olives, hard enough to break the flesh, but taking care not to crack the stone (pit). Place the olives in a bowl of cold water, cover and leave overnight in a cool place to remove the excess brine. Next day, drain them thoroughly and divide among two sterilized screwtop jars.

2 To make the piquant marinade, mix the coriander, parsley and garlic together in a bowl. Add the cayenne pepper and cumin and 30ml/2 tbsp of the olive oil and lemon juice. Add the olives from one jar, mix well and return to the jar. Add more olive oil and lemon juice to cover if necessary. Seal.

3 To make the spicy marinade, mix together the coriander, parsley, garlic, ginger, chilli and preserved lemon. Add the olives from the second jar, mix well and return to the jar. Seal.

4 Store the olives in the refrigerator for at least one week before using, shaking the jars occasionally.

GLOBE ARTICHOKES WITH BEANS AND AIOLI

MAKE THE MOST OF FRESH ARTICHOKES WHEN IN SEASON BY SERVING THEM WITH A SQUEEZE OF
LEMON AND THIS DELICIOUS GARLIC AND MAYONNAISE DRESSING FROM SPAIN.

SERVES THREE

INGREDIENTS
  225g/8oz green beans
  3 small globe artichokes
  15ml/1 tbsp olive oil
  pared rind of 1 lemon
  coarse salt, for sprinkling
  lemon wedges, to garnish
For the aioli
  6 large garlic cloves,
    thinly sliced
  10ml/2 tsp white wine vinegar
  250ml/8fl oz/1 cup olive oil
  salt and ground black pepper

1 First, make the aioli. Put the garlic and vinegar in a food processor or blender. With the motor running, slowly pour in the olive oil through the lid or feeder tube until the mixture is quite thick and smooth. (Alternatively, crush the garlic to a paste with the vinegar and gradually beat in the oil using a hand whisk.) Season with salt and pepper to taste.

2 To make the salad, cook the green beans in lightly salted boiling water for 1–2 minutes until slightly softened. Drain well.

3 Trim the artichoke stalks close to the base. Cook the artichokes in a large pan of salted water for about 30 minutes, or until you can easily pull away a leaf from the base. Drain well.

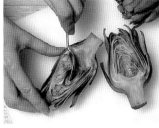

4 Using a large, sharp knife, cut the artichokes in half lengthways and carefully scrape out the hairy choke using a teaspoon.

5 Arrange the artichokes and beans on serving plates and drizzle with the olive oil. Sprinkle the lemon rind over them and season to taste with coarse salt and a little pepper. Spoon the aioli into the artichoke hearts and serve the salad warm, garnished with lemon wedges.

6 To eat the artichokes, squeeze a little lemon juice over them, then pull the leaves from the base one at a time and use to scoop a little of the aioli sauce. Gently scrape away the fleshy end of each leaf with your teeth and discard the remainder of the leaf. Eat the tender base or "heart" of the artichoke with a knife and fork.

RICOTTA FRITTERS WITH AVOCADO SALSA

THE FRESH-FLAVOURED SALSA SPIKED WITH A LITTLE RED ONION, CHILLI AND LIME IS EXCELLENT
WITH THESE MELT-IN-THE-MOUTH HERBED SPRING ONION FRITTERS.

MAKES ABOUT TWELVE

INGREDIENTS
   250g/9oz/generous 1 cup
     ricotta cheese
   1 large (US extra large) egg, beaten
   90ml/6 tbsp self-raising
     (self-rising) flour
   90ml/6 tbsp milk
   1 bunch spring onions (scallions),
     thinly sliced
   30ml/2 tbsp chopped fresh
     coriander (cilantro)
   sunflower oil, for shallow frying
   salt and ground black pepper
   fresh coriander (cilantro) sprigs and
     lime wedges, to garnish
   200ml/7fl oz/scant 1 cup crème
     fraîche, to serve
For the salsa
   225g/8oz tomatoes
   2 ripe, but not soft, avocados
   1 small red onion, diced
   grated rind and juice of 1 lime
   ½–1 fresh green or red chilli, seeded
     and finely chopped
   30–45ml/2–3 tbsp chopped mixed
     fresh mint and coriander (cilantro)
   pinch of caster (superfine) sugar
   5–10ml/1–2 tsp Thai fish sauce

1 First, make the salsa. Peel and seed
the tomatoes and roughly dice the flesh.
Peel, stone (pit) and dice the avocados.
Place in a small bowl with the onion,
lime rind and juice. Add chilli to taste,
the tomatoes, mint and coriander.
Season with salt, pepper, sugar and
Thai fish sauce. Mix well and set aside
for about 30 minutes.

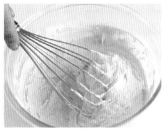

2 Beat the ricotta until smooth, then
beat in the egg and flour, followed by
the milk to make a smooth, thick batter.
Beat in the spring onions and coriander.
Season well with pepper and a little salt.

3 Heat a little oil in a non-stick frying
pan over a medium heat. Add spoonfuls
of the mixture to make fritters about
7.5cm/3in across, and fry for 5 minutes
each side, or until set and browned.
The mixture makes about 12 fritters.

4 Taste the salsa and adjust the
seasoning, adding more sugar to taste.
Serve the ricotta fritters immediately,
with the salsa and a spoonful of crème
fraîche. Garnish with coriander sprigs
and lime wedges.

VARIATION
The fritters are also excellent served with
thinly sliced smoked salmon.

CITRUS FISHCAKES WITH CUCUMBER RELISH

THESE WONDERFUL, SMALL FISHCAKES ARE A VERY FAMILIAR AND POPULAR APPETIZER IN THAILAND AND INCREASINGLY THROUGHOUT SOUTH-EAST ASIA. THEY ARE USUALLY SERVED WITH CHILLED BEER.

MAKES ABOUT TWELVE

INGREDIENTS
    3 kaffir lime leaves, plus extra
      to garnish
    300g/11oz cod fillet, cut into chunks
    30ml/2 tbsp red curry paste
    1 egg
    30ml/2 tbsp Thai fish sauce
    5ml/1 tsp sugar
    30ml/2 tbsp cornflour (cornstarch)
    15ml/1 tbsp chopped fresh
      coriander (cilantro)
    50g/2oz green beans, thinly sliced
    vegetable oil, for frying
For the cucumber relish
    60ml/4 tbsp rice or coconut vinegar
    50g/2oz/¼ cup sugar
    1 head pickled garlic
    15ml/1 tbsp chopped fresh
      root ginger
    1 cucumber, cut into thin batons
    4 shallots, thinly sliced

1 First, make the cucumber relish. Place the vinegar and sugar in a small pan with 60ml/4 tbsp water and bring to the boil, stirring constantly until the sugar has dissolved. Set aside to cool.

2 Separate the head of pickled garlic into individual cloves. Chop these finely and place in a bowl with the ginger. Add the cucumber and shallots, stir, then add to the vinegar mixture and mix well.

3 Thinly slice the kaffir lime leaves. Put the chunks of fish, curry paste and egg in a food processor and process to a smooth paste.

4 Transfer the mixture to a small bowl and stir in the Thai fish sauce, sugar, cornflour, sliced kaffir lime leaves, coriander and green beans. Mix well, then shape the mixture into 12 or more cakes, measuring about 5mm/¼in thick and 5cm/2in in diameter.

5 Heat the oil in a wok or deep frying pan. Fry the fishcakes, a few at a time, for about 4–5 minutes, or until cooked and evenly brown.

6 Lift out the fishcakes and drain them on kitchen paper. Keep each batch hot while frying successive batches. Garnish with the extra kaffir lime leaves and serve with the cucumber relish.

BUTTERFLIED MEDITERRANEAN PRAWNS

SKEWERED PRAWNS, MARINATED IN A FIERY HERB AND LIME DRESSING, THEN GRILLED UNTIL PINK AND TENDER, MAKE A DELICIOUS FIRST COURSE OR LIGHT LUNCH.

SERVES FOUR

INGREDIENTS
32 raw king prawns (jumbo shrimp)
2 garlic cloves, finely chopped
90ml/6 tbsp finely chopped
    fresh parsley
1 fresh rosemary sprig, leaves
    removed and finely chopped
pinch of dried chilli flakes
juice of 2 limes
30ml/2 tbsp olive oil
salt and ground black pepper
green salad, to serve

1 Wash the prawns in salted water and remove their heads and shells. Make a shallow cut down the centre of the curved back of each prawn. Pull out the black vein with the point of a knife or a cocktail stick (toothpick).

2 To butterfly the prawns, cut more deeply along the deveining cut, without completely cutting through them, then carefully fan out.

3 Blend the garlic, parsley, rosemary, chilli flakes, lime juice and olive oil in a large bowl. Stir in the prawns, season and leave to marinate for 1 hour.

4 Meanwhile, soak 32 wooden skewers in warm water for at least 30 minutes.

5 Preheat the grill (broiler) until very hot. Thread two prawns on to each pair of skewers and grill (broil) for about 2 minutes, or until each side has turned pink. Remove the prawns from the skewers and serve with green salad.

SEARED SCALLOPS WITH LEMON AND THYME

TENDER SCALLOPS NEED VERY LITTLE COOKING. THEY ARE DELICIOUS MARINATED WITH THYME AND GARLIC AND COOKED WITH LEMON AND BALSAMIC VINEGAR. THE CURVED TOP SHELLS MAKE ATTRACTIVE DISHES FOR SERVING — MAKE SURE THEY ARE WELL SCRUBBED FIRST.

SERVES FOUR

INGREDIENTS
50ml/2fl oz/¼ cup olive oil
2 garlic cloves, finely chopped
4 fresh thyme sprigs
1 bay leaf
15ml/1 tbsp chopped fresh parsley
16 fresh scallops, prepared and rinsed
1 shallot, finely chopped
15ml/1 tbsp balsamic vinegar
30ml/2 tbsp lemon juice
150ml/¼ pint/⅔ cup chicken or
    vegetable stock
salt and ground black pepper
24 baby spinach leaves, to garnish

1 Blend the olive oil, garlic, thyme, bay leaf and parsley in a shallow bowl. Add the scallops and leave to marinate in a cool place for 1 hour.

2 Heat a large, heavy frying pan until it smokes. Remove the scallops from the marinade and drain well. Add them to the pan and sear for about 30 seconds on each side until they turn opaque. This will seal in their juices, but do not overcook them or they will become tough. Transfer the scallops to a plate and keep warm.

3 Add the marinade to the pan, then add the shallot, balsamic vinegar, lemon juice and stock. Cook over a high heat for 5 minutes. Discard the bay leaf and season well.

4 Neatly arrange six spinach leaves around each scallop shell in the centre of each of four serving plates. Place four scallops on each shell and pour over the juices. Serve immediately.

COOK'S TIP
To prepare the scallops, use a sturdy, short-bladed knife to prise the shell apart. Scrape away the fringe next to the edible white and orange (coral) part, and remove the intestinal thread. Remove the edible part. Retain four shells for serving. If you prefer, buy shelled scallops and serve in small dishes.

PRAWN COCKTAIL

THERE IS NO NICER APPETIZER THAN A GOOD, FRESH PRAWN COCKTAIL, FLAVOURED WITH LEMON AND WORCESTERSHIRE SAUCE AND DRESSED IN A CREAMY MAYONNAISE.

SERVES SIX

INGREDIENTS
   60ml/4 tbsp double (heavy) cream,
      lightly whipped
   60ml/4 tbsp mayonnaise, preferably
      home-made
   60ml/4 tbsp tomato ketchup
   5–10ml/1–2 tsp Worcestershire sauce
   juice of 1 lemon
   ½ cos or romaine lettuce, or other
      very crisp lettuce
   450g/1lb cooked peeled
      prawns (shrimp)
   salt, ground black pepper
      and paprika
   6 large whole cooked prawns in the
      shell, to garnish (optional)
   thinly sliced and buttered brown
      bread and lemon wedges,
      to serve

1 Lightly whisk the cream, mayonnaise and tomato ketchup together in a bowl. Add Worcestershire sauce to taste, then whisk in enough of the lemon juice to make a tangy sauce.

COOK'S TIP
Partly peeled prawns, with the tail "fan" intact, make a pretty garnish.

2 Finely shred the lettuce and fill six individual glasses one-third full.

3 Stir the prawns into the sauce, then season with salt and pepper. Spoon the mixture over the lettuce. If you like, drape a whole prawn over the edge of each glass, and sprinkle the cocktails with black pepper and/or paprika.

SALMON MARINATED WITH THAI SPICES

PIQUANT THAI SPICES, ENHANCED BY KAFFIR LIME LEAVES AND LIMES, TRANSFORM A SCANDINAVIAN RECIPE TO MAKE AN EXOTIC DISH FOR ENTERTAINING.

SERVES FOUR TO SIX

INGREDIENTS

20ml/4 tsp coarse sea salt
20ml/4 tsp granulated sugar
2.5cm/1in piece fresh root ginger, peeled and grated
2 lemon grass stalks, coarse outer leaves removed, thinly sliced
4 kaffir lime leaves, shredded
grated rind of 1 lime
1 fresh red chilli, seeded and finely chopped
5ml/1 tsp black peppercorns, coarsely crushed
30ml/2 tbsp chopped fresh coriander (cilantro)
tail piece of 1 salmon, about 675g/1½lb, cleaned and prepared (see Cook's Tip)
coriander (cilantro) and kaffir lime wedges, to garnish

For the dressing
150ml/¼ pint/⅔ cup mayonnaise
juice of ½ lime
10ml/2 tsp chopped fresh coriander (cilantro)

1 Mix together the salt, sugar, ginger, lemon grass, kaffir lime leaves, lime rind, chilli, peppercorns and coriander.

2 Place one quarter of the spice mixture in a shallow dish. Place one salmon fillet, skin-side down, on top of the spices. Spread two-thirds of the remaining spice mixture over the flesh, then place the remaining fillet on top, flesh-side down. Sprinkle the rest of the spice mixture over the fish.

3 Cover the fish with foil, then place a board on top. Add some weights, such as clean cans of fruit. Chill the fish for 2–5 days, turning the fish daily in the spice mixture.

4 Make the dressing by mixing the mayonnaise, lime juice and chopped coriander in a bowl.

5 Scrape the spices off the fish. Slice the flesh as thinly as possible. Serve with the lime dressing, garnished with coriander and wedges of kaffir limes.

COOK'S TIP
Ask your fishmonger to scale the fish, split it lengthways and remove it from the backbone in two fillets.

SEARED SWORDFISH WITH CITRUS DRESSING

THE JAPANESE TRY OUT NEW DISHES FROM ALL OVER THE WORLD AND THEN ARRANGE THEM IN A TRADITIONAL WAY. THIS SALAD IS A GOOD EXAMPLE OF THAT PRACTICE. FRESH FISH IS SLICED THINLY AND SEARED, THEN SERVED WITH CRISP SALAD VEGETABLES WITH A LIME DRESSING.

2 To make the dressing, mix together all the ingredients in a small bowl. Stir well, then chill.

3 Heat the oil in a frying pan until smoking hot. Sear the fish for about 30 seconds on all sides. Immediately plunge it into cold water in a bowl to stop the cooking. Gently pat dry on kitchen paper and wipe off as much oil as possible.

4 Using a sharp knife, cut the swordfish steak in half lengthways before slicing it into 5mm/¼in thick pieces in the opposite direction, against the grain.

5 Arrange the fish slices in a ring on individual dinner plates. Mix together the vegetable strands, mustard and cress and sesame seeds. Fluff up with your hands, then shape them into four spheres. Gently place each sphere in the centre of the plate, on top of the swordfish. Pour the dressing around the plate's edge and serve immediately.

SERVES FOUR

INGREDIENTS
  75g/3oz mooli (daikon), peeled
  50g/2oz carrot, peeled
  1 cucumber
  10ml/2 tsp vegetable oil
  300g/11oz skinned fresh swordfish
    steak, cut against the grain
  2 cartons mustard and cress
  15ml/1 tbsp toasted sesame seeds
For the dressing
  105ml/7 tbsp shoyu
  105ml/7 tbsp water mixed with
    5ml/1 tsp dashi-no-moto
  30ml/2 tbsp toasted sesame oil
  juice of ½ lime
  rind of ½ lime, shredded into strips

1 Use a very sharp knife, mandolin or vegetable slicer with a julienne blade to make very thin (4cm/1½in long) strands of mooli, carrot and cucumber. Soak the mooli and carrot in iced water for about 5 minutes, then drain and chill.

COOK'S TIPS
• Dashi-no-moto are freeze-dried granules that are used to make a quick dashi stock. They are available from Japanese supermarkets and some other specialist stores.
• This dish is traditionally made with fillet cut with the grain. To prepare, cut it in half lengthways, then slice against the grain by holding a knife horizontally to the chopping board.

CEVICHE WITH RED ONION, AVOCADO AND SWEET POTATO

MARINATING FISH IN CITRUS JUICE HAS A SIMILAR EFFECT TO COOKING, MAKING THE FISH OPAQUE AND FIRM. KNOWN AS CEVICHE, THIS DISH IS A TRADITIONAL SOUTH AMERICAN ONE, AND HERE IT IS COMBINED WITH SWEET POTATOES, AVOCADOS AND PRAWNS TO MAKE A DELICIOUS SALAD.

SERVES SIX

INGREDIENTS
500–675g/1¼–1½ lb white fish
  fillets, skinned
1 red onion, thinly sliced
pinch of dried red chilli flakes
grated rind of 1 small lime and juice
  of 5 limes
450–500g/1–1¼ lb sweet
  potatoes, unpeeled
75ml/5 tbsp mild olive oil
15–25ml/1–1½ tbsp rice vinegar
2.5–5ml/½–1 tsp caster
  (superfine) sugar
2.5ml/½ tsp ground toasted
  cumin seeds
½–1 fresh red or green chilli, seeded
  and finely chopped
1 large or 2 small avocados, peeled,
  stoned (pitted) and sliced
225g/8oz cooked peeled
  prawns (shrimp)
45ml/3 tbsp chopped fresh
  coriander (cilantro)
30ml/2 tbsp roasted
  peanuts, chopped
salt and ground black pepper

1 Cut the fish into strips or chunks. Sprinkle half the onion over the base of a glass dish and lay the fish on top. Sprinkle on the dried red chilli flakes and pour in the lime juice. Cover and chill for 2–3 hours, spooning the lime juice over the fish once or twice. Drain, and discard the onion.

2 Steam or boil the sweet potatoes for 20–25 minutes, or until just tender. Peel and slice, or cut into wedges.

3 Place the oil in a bowl and whisk in the rice vinegar and sugar to taste, then add the cumin, season, and whisk in the fresh chilli and grated lime rind.

4 In a glass bowl, toss the fish, sweet potatoes, avocado slices, prawns and most of the coriander with the dressing.

5 Add the remaining half of the sliced red onion and toss to mix. Sprinkle over the remaining coriander and the peanuts and serve immediately.

CHINESE CHICKEN WINGS

LEMON IS FREQUENTLY USED FOR MARINADES IN CHINESE CUISINE. HERE IT COMBINES WITH GINGER, CHILLI AND GARLIC TO GIVE ROASTED CHICKEN WINGS AN EXOTIC FLAVOUR. THE WINGS MAKE A TASTY FIRST COURSE; AS THEY ARE BEST EATEN WITH THE FINGERS, MAKE SURE YOU PROVIDE FINGER BOWLS AND PLENTY OF PAPER NAPKINS.

SERVES FOUR

INGREDIENTS
   12 chicken wings
   3 garlic cloves, crushed
   4cm/1½in piece fresh root ginger,
      peeled and grated
   juice of 1 large lemon
   45ml/3 tbsp soy sauce
   45ml/3 tbsp clear honey
   2.5ml/½ tsp chilli powder
   150ml/¼ pint/⅔ cup chicken stock
   salt and ground black pepper
   lemon and lime wedges, to garnish

1 Remove the wing tips (pinions) and discard. Cut the wings into two pieces.

2 Put the chicken pieces into a shallow dish, cover and set aside.

3 Mix together the garlic, ginger, lemon and soy sauce in a small jug (pitcher). Blend in the honey, chilli powder, seasoning and chicken stock. Pour the mixture over the chicken wings and turn to coat completely. Cover and marinate in the refrigerator overnight.

4 Preheat the oven to 220°C/425°F/ Gas 7. Remove the chicken wings from the marinade and arrange them in a single layer in a large roasting pan. Roast for about 25 minutes, generously basting at least twice with the marinade during cooking.

5 Place the wings on a serving plate. Add the remaining marinade to the roasting pan and bring to the boil. Cook until it turns a syrupy consistency and spoon a little over the wings. Serve the chicken wings immediately, garnished with the lemon and lime wedges.

CARPACCIO WITH ROCKET

INVENTED IN VENICE, CARPACCIO IS NAMED IN HONOUR OF THE RENAISSANCE PAINTER. IN THIS FINE ITALIAN DISH RAW BEEF IS LIGHTLY DRESSED WITH LEMON JUICE AND OLIVE OIL AND IS TRADITIONALLY SERVED WITH FLAKES OF PARMESAN CHEESE. USE VERY FRESH MEAT OF THE BEST QUALITY AND ASK THE BUTCHER TO SLICE IT VERY THINLY.

SERVES FOUR

INGREDIENTS

1 garlic clove, peeled and cut in half
1½ lemons
50ml/2fl oz/¼ cup extra virgin
  olive oil
2 bunches rocket (arugula)
4 very thin slices of beef fillet
115g/4oz Parmesan cheese, shaved
salt and ground black pepper

1 Rub the cut side of the garlic over the inside of a bowl. Squeeze the lemons into the bowl, then whisk in the olive oil. Season with salt and pepper. Leave to stand for at least 15 minutes.

2 Carefully wash the rocket and tear off any thick stalks. Spin or pat dry with kitchen paper. Arrange the rocket around the edge of a serving platter or divide among four individual plates.

3 Place the sliced beef in the centre of the platter, and pour the sauce over it, spreading it evenly over the meat. Arrange the shaved Parmesan on top of the meat slices and serve immediately.

VARIATION
You can also serve meaty fish, such as tuna, in the same way. Place a tuna steak between sheets of clear film (plastic wrap) and pound with a rolling pin. Then roll it up tightly and wrap in clear film. Place in the freezer for about 4 hours until firm. Unwrap and, using a very sharp knife, cut the fish crossways into very thin slices. Serve with the rocket (arugula), sauce and Parmesan.

SIDE DISHES
AND SALADS

Although careful planning often goes into the main course,
accompaniments are frequently something of an afterthought, yet
complementary combinations of flavours and colours turn an ordinary
meal into a special occasion. Citrus sauces, glazes, dressings and
flavourings pep up even the most mundane vegetables, enhance
luxurious ingredients and give salads a refreshing lift. Besides such
classic combinations as carrots and oranges, the recipes feature some
more unusual and utterly delicious mixtures, from orange-glazed
potatoes to spicy cauliflower with a hint of lemon.

ASPARAGUS WITH EGG AND LEMON SAUCE

EGGS AND LEMONS ARE OFTEN FOUND IN DISHES FROM GREECE, TURKEY AND THE MIDDLE EAST. THIS SAUCE HAS A FRESH, TANGY TASTE AND BRINGS OUT THE BEST IN ASPARAGUS.

2 Blend the cornflour with the cooled, reserved cooking liquid and place in a small pan. Bring to the boil, stirring constantly, and cook over a low heat until the sauce thickens slightly. Stir in 10ml/2 tsp sugar, then remove the pan from the heat and leave to cool slightly.

3 Beat the egg yolks thoroughly with the lemon juice and then stir gradually into the cooled sauce. Cook over a very low heat, stirring constantly, until the sauce is fairly thick. Be careful not to overheat the sauce or it may curdle. As soon as the sauce has thickened, remove the pan from the heat and continue stirring for 1 minute. Taste and add salt or sugar as necessary. Leave the sauce to cool slightly.

4 Stir the cooled sauce, then pour a little over the asparagus. Cover and chill for at least 2 hours before serving with the rest of the sauce.

COOK'S TIP
Use tiny asparagus spears for an elegant first course or a special dinner party.

SERVES FOUR

INGREDIENTS
    675g/1½lb asparagus, tough ends removed, and tied in a bundle
    15ml/1 tbsp cornflour (cornstarch)
    about 10ml/2 tsp sugar
    2 egg yolks
    juice of 1½ lemons
    salt

VARIATIONS
This sauce goes very well with young vegetables. Try it with baby leeks, cooked whole or chopped, or serve it with other baby vegetables, such as carrots and courgettes (zucchini).

1 Cook the bundle of asparagus in salted boiling water for 7–10 minutes. Drain well and arrange the asparagus in a serving dish. Reserve 200ml/7fl oz/ scant 1 cup of the cooking liquid.

ORANGE CANDIED SWEET POTATOES

A TRUE TASTE OF AMERICA – NO THANKSGIVING OR CHRISTMAS TABLE IS COMPLETE UNLESS SWEET POTATOES ARE ON THE MENU. SERVE WITH EXTRA ORANGE SEGMENTS TO MAKE IT REALLY SPECIAL.

SERVES EIGHT

INGREDIENTS

900g/2lb sweet potatoes
250ml/8fl oz/1 cup freshly squeezed
   orange juice
50ml/2fl oz/¼ cup maple syrup
5ml/1 tsp fresh peeled and grated
   fresh root ginger
7.5ml/1½ tsp ground cinnamon
6.5ml/1¼ tsp ground cardamom
7.5ml/1½ tsp salt
ground black pepper
ground cinnamon, to garnish
orange segments, to serve

1 Preheat the oven to 180°C/350°F/ Gas 4. Peel and dice the potatoes and then boil in water for 5 minutes.

2 Meanwhile, put the remaining ingredients in a bowl and mix together. Spread out on a shallow roasting pan.

3 Drain the potatoes and spread them out over the pan. Cook for 1 hour, stirring the potatoes every 15 minutes, until they are tender and well coated. Garnish with ground cinnamon, and serve with the orange segments to accompany a main dish.

COOK'S TIP
Use Florida Pineapple oranges or Valencia oranges for their high juice yield.

HASSELBACK POTATOES

THIS IS AN UNUSUAL WAY TO COOK WITH POTATOES: EACH POTATO HALF IS SLICED ALMOST TO THE BASE AND THEN ROASTED WITH OIL AND BUTTER. THE CRISPY POTATOES ARE THEN COATED IN AN ORANGE GLAZE AND RETURNED TO THE OVEN UNTIL DEEP GOLDEN BROWN AND CRUNCHY.

SERVES FOUR

INGREDIENTS
4 large potatoes
25g/1oz/2 tbsp butter, melted
45ml/3 tbsp olive oil
For the glaze
juice of 1 orange
grated rind of ½ orange
15ml/1 tbsp demerara (raw) sugar
ground black pepper

COOK'S TIP
To make potato fans, cut through the potato halves at a slight angle, without cutting all the way through. Gently press on the top of the potato until it flattens out and fans slightly.

1 Preheat the oven to 190°C/375°F/ Gas 5. Cut each potato in half lengthways. Place the flat side down on the chopping board and then cut down as if making very thin slices, but leaving the bottom 1cm/½in intact.

2 Place the potatoes in a large roasting pan. Coat them with the melted butter and pour the olive oil over and around. Roast the potatoes for 50 minutes.

3 Meanwhile, make the glaze. Place the orange juice, orange rind and sugar in a pan and heat gently, stirring, until the sugar has dissolved. Simmer over a low heat for 3–4 minutes until thick, then remove the pan from the heat.

4 When the potatoes begin to brown, brush them all over with the orange glaze and return them to the oven for a further 15 minutes, or until golden brown. Tip on to a warmed serving plate and serve immediately.

PEAS <u>WITH</u> BABY ONIONS <u>AND</u> CREAM

A CREAMY SAUCE WITH A HINT OF LEMON IS THE PERFECT CHOICE FOR SWEET BABY ONIONS AND FRESH GARDEN PEAS. THIS MAKES A DELIGHTFUL, SUMMERY SIDE DISH THAT IS VERSATILE ENOUGH TO ACCOMPANY GRILLED MEAT, CHICKEN OR FISH.

2 Add the peas and stir-fry briefly. Add 120ml/4fl oz/½ cup water, bring to the boil and simmer for about 10 minutes until tender. There should be a thin layer of water on the base of the pan.

3 Blend the cream with the flour. Remove the pan from the heat and stir in the cream mixture and parsley. Season to taste with salt and pepper.

SERVES FOUR

INGREDIENTS

175g/6oz baby (pearl) onions
15g/½oz/1 tbsp butter
900g/2lb fresh peas or 350g/12oz/
  3 cups shelled or frozen peas
150ml/¼ pint/⅔ cup double
  (heavy) cream
15g/½oz/2 tbsp plain
  (all-purpose) flour
10ml/2 tsp chopped fresh parsley
15–30ml/1–2 tbsp lemon juice
salt and ground black pepper

1 Remove the skin from the onions and halve any large ones. Melt the butter in a frying pan and cook them for about 5 minutes until tender and just golden.

4 Cook over a low heat for 3 minutes, or until the sauce has thickened slightly. Add lemon juice to taste, stir through, and serve immediately.

SPICED TURNIP, SPINACH AND TOMATO STEW

PAPRIKA AND LEMON JUICE ADD A DELICATE PIQUANCY TO SWEET BABY TURNIPS, TENDER SPINACH AND RIPE TOMATOES IN THIS SIMPLE EASTERN MEDITERRANEAN VEGETABLE STEW. USE PLUM TOMATOES OR VINE-RIPENED TOMATOES FOR THE BEST AND MOST INTENSE FLAVOUR.

SERVES SIX

INGREDIENTS
450g/1lb plum or other
  well-flavoured tomatoes
60ml/4 tbsp olive oil
2 onions, sliced
450g/1lb baby turnips, peeled
5ml/1 tsp paprika
2.5ml/½ tsp caster
  (superfine) sugar
60ml/4 tbsp chopped fresh
  coriander (cilantro)
450g/1lb fresh young spinach,
  stalks removed
15–30ml/1–2 tbsp lemon juice
salt and ground black pepper

1 Make a small cross in the tops of the tomatoes, plunge them into a bowl of boiling water for 30 seconds, then refresh in a bowl of cold water. Peel off the skins and chop the tomatoes.

2 Heat the olive oil in a large, heavy frying pan or sauté pan and cook the onion slices for about 5 minutes, or until golden brown.

3 Add the baby turnips, tomatoes and paprika to the pan with 60ml/4 tbsp water and cook over a medium heat until the tomatoes are pulpy. Cover with a lid and continue cooking until the baby turnips have softened.

4 Stir in the sugar and coriander, then add the spinach and salt and pepper. Add lemon juice to taste and cook for a further 2–3 minutes, or until the spinach has wilted. Serve warm or cold.

LEMON-SPICED RED CABBAGE

PEARS AND RED CABBAGE MAKE DELICIOUS PARTNERS, AND HERE THEIR FLAVOURS ARE ENHANCED WITH RED WINE, LEMON AND CARAWAY. SERVE THIS EAST EUROPEAN VEGETABLE DISH AS AN ACCOMPANIMENT TO ROAST PORK OR GAME, SUCH AS WILD BOAR OR VENISON.

SERVES SIX TO EIGHT

INGREDIENTS

3 thick rindless bacon rashers (strips), diced
1 large onion, chopped
1 large red cabbage, evenly shredded
3 garlic cloves, crushed
15–25ml/1–1½ tbsp caraway seeds
120ml/4fl oz/½ cup water
2 firm, ripe pears, cored and evenly chopped
juice of 1 lemon
475ml/16fl oz/2 cups red wine
45ml/3 tbsp red wine vinegar
150g/5oz/⅔ cup clear honey
salt and ground black pepper
caraway seeds and chopped fresh chives, to garnish

1 Dry-fry the diced bacon in a pan over a gentle heat for 5–10 minutes, or until golden brown.

2 Add the onion and cook, stirring occasionally, for 5 minutes, or until pale golden brown.

3 Stir the cabbage, garlic, caraway seeds and the water into the pan. Cover and cook for 8–10 minutes.

4 Season to taste with salt and pepper, then add the chopped pears, lemon juice, red wine and wine vinegar. Cover and cook over a low heat for about 15 minutes. Stir in the honey.

5 If there is too much cooking liquid, remove the lid and continue to cook to allow it to reduce. The pears will have broken up in the pan, and the quantity will have reduced by one-third. Adjust the seasoning to taste, if necessary. Transfer to a warm serving dish and serve sprinkled with caraway seeds and chopped fresh chives.

CAULIFLOWER WITH TOMATOES AND CUMIN

WARM SPICES ARE SHARPENED WITH LEMON JUICE IN THIS UNUSUAL SIDE DISH OF CAULIFLOWER BRAISED WITH TOMATOES. IT IS EXCELLENT SERVED WITH BARBECUE-COOKED MEAT OR FISH.

SERVES FOUR

INGREDIENTS

4 tomatoes
30ml/2 tbsp sunflower or olive oil
1 onion, chopped
1 garlic clove, crushed
1 small cauliflower, broken
  into florets
5ml/1 tsp cumin seeds
a good pinch of ground ginger
15–30ml/1–2 tbsp lemon juice
30ml/2 tbsp chopped fresh
  coriander (cilantro) (optional)
salt and ground black pepper

1 Cut a small cross in the top of the tomatoes, plunge them into boiling water for 30 seconds, then refresh in cold water. Peel off the skins, cut the tomatoes into quarters and remove and discard the seeds.

2 Heat the oil in a flameproof casserole, add the onion and garlic and stir-fry for 2–3 minutes, or until the onion is softened. Add the cauliflower and stir-fry for a further 2–3 minutes, or until the cauliflower is flecked with brown. Add the cumin seeds and ginger, fry briskly for 1 minute, and then add the tomatoes, 175ml/6fl oz/¾ cup water and some salt and pepper.

3 Bring to the boil and then reduce the heat, cover with a plate or with foil and simmer for 6–7 minutes, or until the cauliflower is just tender.

4 Stir in a little lemon juice to sharpen the flavour, and taste and adjust the seasoning if necessary. Sprinkle over the chopped coriander, if using, and serve immediately.

ROASTED MEDITERRANEAN VEGETABLES

OVEN ROASTING BRINGS OUT THE ROBUST FLAVOURS OF COURGETTE, ONION, PEPPER AND TOMATO. TOSS THEM IN A PIQUANT LEMON AND HARISSA DRESSING FOR EXTRA TANG.

SERVES FOUR

INGREDIENTS

2–3 courgettes (zucchini)
1 Spanish onion
2 red (bell) peppers
16 cherry tomatoes
2 garlic cloves, chopped
pinch of cumin seeds
5ml/1 tsp fresh thyme or 4–5 torn
  basil leaves
60ml/4 tbsp olive oil
juice of ½ lemon
5–10ml/1–2 tsp harissa or
  Tabasco sauce
fresh thyme sprigs, to garnish

COOK'S TIP
Harissa is a fiery-hot sauce from Tunisia. It is usually sold in jars and can be found in Middle Eastern stores.

1 Preheat the oven to 220°C/425°F/ Gas 7. Trim the courgettes and cut into long strips. Cut the onion into thin wedges. Cut the peppers into chunks, discarding the seeds and core.

2 Place the vegetables in a roasting pan, add the tomatoes, chopped garlic, cumin seeds and thyme or basil.

3 Sprinkle with the olive oil and toss to coat. Roast for 25–30 minutes, or until the vegetables are very soft and slightly charred at the edges.

4 Blend the lemon juice with the harissa or Tabasco sauce and stir into the vegetables before serving, garnished with the thyme.

CARROT AND ORANGE SALAD

THIS IS A WONDERFUL, FRESH-TASTING SALAD WITH SUCH A FABULOUS COMBINATION OF CITRUS FRUIT AND VEGETABLES THAT IT IS DIFFICULT TO KNOW WHETHER IT IS A SALAD OR A DESSERT. IT MAKES A REFRESHING ACCOMPANIMENT TO GRILLED MEAT, CHICKEN OR FISH.

SERVES FOUR

INGREDIENTS
    450g/1lb carrots
    2 large Navelina oranges, such as
      Washington or Bahia
    15ml/1 tbsp extra virgin
      olive oil
    30ml/2 tbsp freshly squeezed
      lemon juice
    pinch of sugar (optional)
    30ml/2 tbsp chopped pistachio nuts
      or toasted pine nuts
    salt and ground black pepper

1 Peel the carrots and coarsely grate them into a large bowl.

2 Cut a thin slice of peel and pith from each end of the oranges. Place cut-side down on a plate and cut off the peel and pith in strips. Holding the oranges over a bowl, cut out each segment leaving the membrane behind. Squeeze the juice from the membrane.

3 Blend the oil, lemon juice and orange juice in a small bowl. Season with salt and pepper, and sugar, if you like.

4 Toss the oranges with the carrots and pour the dressing over. Sprinkle over the pistachios or pine nuts and serve.

AVOCADO AND PINK GRAPEFRUIT SALAD

A LUXURIOUS, REFRESHING AND ATTRACTIVE CITRUS AND AVOCADO SALAD THAT IS EXCELLENT SERVED AS A SIDE DISH OR FIRST COURSE. IT CAN BE PARTIALLY PREPARED IN ADVANCE, THEN ASSEMBLED JUST BEFORE SERVING, BUT DON'T LET THE AVOCADO DISCOLOUR.

2 Put the sugar and water in a small pan and heat gently until the sugar has dissolved. Add the shreds of orange rind, increase the heat and boil steadily for 5 minutes, or until the rind is tender. Using two forks, remove the orange rind from the syrup and spread it out on a wire rack to dry. Reserve the cooking syrup to add to the dressing.

3 Wash and dry the lettuce or other salad leaves and tear or chop them into bitesize pieces. Using a sharp knife, remove the pith from the oranges and the pith and peel from the grapefruit. Hold the citrus fruits over a bowl and cut out each segment leaving the membrane behind. Squeeze the remaining juice from the membrane into the bowl.

SERVES EIGHT

INGREDIENTS
mixed red and green lettuce or other
salad leaves
2 sweet pink grapefruit
1 large or 2 small avocados, peeled,
stoned (pitted) and cubed
For the dressing
90ml/6 tbsp light olive oil
30ml/2 tbsp red wine vinegar
1 garlic clove, crushed
5ml/1 tsp Dijon mustard
salt and ground black pepper
For the caramelized peel
4 oranges
50g/2oz/¼ cup caster
(superfine) sugar
60ml/4 tbsp cold water

1 To make the caramelized peel, using a vegetable peeler, carefully remove the rind from the oranges in thin strips and reserve the fruit. Scrape away the white pith from the underside of the rind with a small, sharp knife, and cut the rind into fine shreds.

4 Put all the dressing ingredients into a screw-top jar and shake well. Add the reserved syrup and adjust the seasoning to taste. Arrange the salad ingredients on plates with the cubed avocado. Spoon over the dressing and sprinkle with the caramelized peel. Serve.

FENNEL, ORANGE AND ROCKET SALAD

THIS LIGHT AND REFRESHING SALAD IS IDEAL TO SERVE WITH SPICY OR RICH FOODS. ZESTY ORANGE BLENDS PERFECTLY WITH THE DELICATE FLAVOUR OF FENNEL AND THE PEPPERY ROCKET.

SERVES FOUR

INGREDIENTS
2 oranges, such as Jaffa, Shamouti or blood oranges
1 fennel bulb
115g/4oz rocket (arugula) leaves
50g/2oz/⅓ cup black olives
For the dressing
30ml/2 tbsp extra virgin olive oil
15ml/1 tbsp balsamic vinegar
1 small garlic clove, crushed
salt and ground black pepper

1 With a vegetable peeler, cut strips of rind from the oranges, leaving the pith behind, and cut into thin julienne strips. Cook in boiling water for a few minutes. Drain and set aside. Peel the oranges, removing all the white pith. Slice them into thin rounds and discard any seeds.

2 Trim the fennel bulb, then cut in half lengthways and slice across the bulb as thinly as possible, preferably in a food processor fitted with a slicing disc or using a mandolin.

3 Combine the slices of orange and fennel in a serving bowl and toss with the rocket leaves.

4 To make the dressing, mix together the oil, vinegar, garlic and seasoning. Pour over the salad, toss together well and leave to stand for a few minutes. Sprinkle with the black olives and julienne strips of orange. Serve.

VARIATION
Substitute minneolas for the oranges.

AUBERGINE, LEMON AND CAPER SALAD

LEMON SUBTLY UNDERLINES THE FLAVOUR OF MELTINGLY SOFT AUBERGINE IN THIS CLASSIC SICILIAN DISH. IT IS DELICIOUS SERVED AS AN ACCOMPANIMENT TO A PLATTER OF COLD MEATS, WITH PASTA OR SIMPLY ON ITS OWN WITH SOME GOOD CRUSTY BREAD.

SERVES FOUR

INGREDIENTS
1 large aubergine (eggplant), weighing about 675g/1½lb
60ml/4 tbsp olive oil
grated rind and juice of 1 lemon
30ml/2 tbsp capers, rinsed
12 pitted green olives
30ml/2 tbsp chopped fresh flat leaf parsley
salt and ground black pepper

COOK'S TIP
This salad will taste even better when made the day before. It will keep well, covered in the refrigerator, for up to 4 days. Return the salad to room temperature before serving.

1 Cut the aubergine into 2.5cm/1in cubes. Heat the olive oil in a large, heavy frying pan. Add the aubergine cubes and cook over a medium heat for about 10 minutes, tossing frequently, until golden and softened. You may need to do this in two batches. Remove with a slotted spoon, drain on kitchen paper and sprinkle with a little salt.

2 Place the aubergine cubes in a large serving bowl, toss with the lemon rind and juice, capers, olives and chopped parsley and season well with salt and pepper. Serve at room temperature.

VARIATION
Add toasted pine nuts and shavings of Parmesan cheese for a main course dish.

PIQUANT ROASTED RED PEPPER SALAD

THIS IS THE MOROCCAN COUSIN OF GAZPACHO — INDEED, THE SPANIARDS LEARNED OF GAZPACHO FROM THE MOORS, WHO MADE IT WITH GARLIC, BREAD, OLIVE OIL AND LEMON JUICE. TOMATOES AND PEPPERS WERE ADDED LATER, AND THIS VERSION OF THE DISH MADE ITS WAY BACK TO NORTH AFRICA.

2 Cut the peppers into small pieces, discarding the seeds and core, and place in a serving dish.

3 Plunge the tomatoes into a pan of boiling water for about 30 seconds, then refresh in cold water. Peel off the skins, then quarter them, discarding the core and seeds. Chop coarsely and add to the peppers. Sprinkle the chopped garlic on top and chill for 1 hour.

4 Blend together the olive oil, lemon juice, paprika and cumin and pour over the salad. Season with salt and pepper.

5 Rinse the preserved lemon in cold water and remove the flesh and pith. Cut the peel into slivers and sprinkle over the salad. Garnish with coriander and flat leaf parsley.

SERVES FOUR

INGREDIENTS
3 green (bell) peppers, quartered
4 large tomatoes
2 garlic cloves, finely chopped
30ml/2 tbsp olive oil
30ml/2 tbsp lemon juice
good pinch of paprika
pinch of ground cumin
¼ preserved lemon
salt and ground black pepper
fresh coriander (cilantro) and flat leaf
   parsley, to garnish

1 Grill (broil) the peppers skin-side up until the skins are blackened, place in a plastic bag and tie the ends. Leave for about 10 minutes, or until the peppers are cool enough to handle, then peel off the skins.

COOK'S TIP
It is always better to use fresh, rather than bottled lemon juice; as an easy guide, 30ml/2 tbsp is the average yield from half a lemon.

LEMONY COUSCOUS SALAD

THIS IS A POPULAR SALAD OF OLIVES, ALMONDS AND COURGETTES MIXED WITH FLUFFY COUSCOUS AND DRESSED WITH HERBS, LEMON JUICE AND OLIVE OIL. IT HAS A DELICATE FLAVOUR AND MAKES AN EXCELLENT ACCOMPANIMENT TO GRILLED CHICKEN OR KEBABS.

SERVES FOUR

INGREDIENTS

275g/10oz/1⅔ cups couscous
550ml/18fl oz/2½ cups boiling
  vegetable stock
2 small courgettes (zucchini)
16–20 black olives
25g/1oz/¼ cup flaked (sliced)
  almonds, toasted
60ml/4 tbsp olive oil
15ml/1 tbsp lemon juice
15ml/1 tbsp chopped fresh
  coriander (cilantro)
15ml/1 tbsp chopped fresh parsley
good pinch of ground cumin
good pinch of cayenne pepper

1 Place the couscous in a bowl and pour over the boiling stock. Stir with a fork and then set aside for 10 minutes for the stock to be absorbed. Fluff up with a fork.

2 Trim the courgettes at both ends then cut into pieces about 2cm/1in long. Slice into fine julienne strips with a sharp knife. Halve the black olives, discarding the stones (pits).

3 Carefully mix the courgettes, olives and almonds into the couscous.

4 Blend together the olive oil, lemon juice, coriander, parsley, cumin and cayenne in a small bowl. Stir into the salad, tossing gently to mix through. Transfer to a large serving dish and serve immediately.

THAI RICE SALAD

THIS IS A LOVELY, SOFT, FLUFFY RICE DISH, PERFUMED WITH LIMES AND FRESH LEMON GRASS. AS WELL AS BEING A GOOD ACCOMPANIMENT FOR A FAMILY SUPPER, IT WOULD BE AN EXCELLENT CHOICE, IN DOUBLE OR EVEN TRIPLE THE QUANTITY, FOR A BARBECUE OR BUFFET TABLE.

SERVES FOUR

INGREDIENTS
2 limes
1 lemon grass stalk
225g/8oz/generous 1 cup brown long
   grain rice
15ml/1 tbsp olive oil
1 onion, chopped
2.5cm/1in piece fresh root ginger,
   peeled and finely chopped
7.5ml/1½ tsp coriander seeds
7.5ml/1½ tsp cumin seeds
750ml/1¼ pints/3 cups
   vegetable stock
60ml/4 tbsp chopped fresh
   coriander (cilantro)
spring onion (scallion) finely sliced,
   and toasted coconut strips,
   to garnish
lime wedges, to serve

1 Pare the limes using a zester or a fine grater, taking care to avoid cutting the bitter pith. Set aside the rind. Finely chop the lower portion of the lemon grass stalk and set aside.

2 Rinse the rice in plenty of cold water until the water runs clear. Tip it into a sieve and drain thoroughly.

COOK'S TIP
You could substitute the finely grated rind of kaffir limes for an authentic Thai flavour, but you will need to use juicier Tahitian or Mexican limes for cutting into wedges to serve.

3 Heat the olive oil in a pan. Add the onion, ginger, spices, lemon grass and lime rind and cook gently over a low heat, stirring occasionally, for about 3 minutes until the onion is soft.

4 Add the drained rice and cook. stirring constantly, for 1 minute, then pour in the stock and bring to the boil. Reduce the heat to very low and cover the pan with a tight-fitting lid. Cook gently for 30 minutes, then check the rice. If it is still crunchy, re-cover and leave for 3–5 minutes more. Remove the pan from the heat when done.

5 Stir in the fresh coriander, fluff up the grains, cover the pan again and leave for about 10 minutes. Transfer to a large serving dish or individual bowls, garnish with strips of spring onion and toasted coconut, and serve with plenty of lime wedges.

CHARGRILLED PEPPER SALAD

THE SIMPLE ADDITION OF FRESH BASIL AND CORIANDER TO THIS PEPPER AND PASTA SALAD GIVE IT LOADS OF FLAVOUR. A LEMON AND PESTO DRESSING BRINGS ALL THE FLAVOURS TOGETHER MAKING THIS A SUPERB SUMMER SIDE SALAD THAT WOULD BE IDEAL FOR AN AL FRESCO MEAL.

SERVES FOUR

INGREDIENTS
    1 large red (bell) pepper
    1 large green (bell) pepper
    250g/9oz/2¼ cups dried
        fusilli tricolore
    1 handful fresh basil leaves
    1 handful fresh coriander
        (cilantro) leaves
    1 garlic clove
    salt and ground black pepper
For the dressing
    30ml/2 tbsp pesto
    juice of ½ lemon
    60ml/4 tbsp extra virgin olive oil

1 Put the peppers under a hot grill (broiler) and grill (broil) them for about 10 minutes, turning frequently until they are charred on all sides. Put the hot peppers in a plastic bag, seal the bag and set aside until the peppers are cool.

2 Meanwhile, bring a large pan of salted water to the boil. Add the pasta and cook according to the instructions on the packet.

4 Rinse the cooled peppers under cold running water. Peel off the skins with your fingers, split the peppers open and pull out the cores. Rub off all the seeds under the running water, then pat dry on kitchen paper.

5 Chop the peppers and add them to the pasta. Put the basil, coriander and garlic on a board and chop them. Add to the pasta and toss well to mix, then taste and adjust the seasoning, if necessary, and serve.

3 Whisk all the dressing ingredients together in a large mixing bowl. Drain the cooked pasta and tip it into the bowl of dressing. Toss well to mix and set aside to cool.

COOK'S TIP
Fusilli tricolore are small, red, white and green pasta spirals.

VEGETARIAN DISHES

Cuisines around the world have been quick to exploit the natural affinity between citrus fruits and vegetables, combining ingredients such as peppers, mushrooms, broccoli and asparagus with lemons, limes, oranges and grapefruit. Citrus fruits, in combination with herbs and spices, breathe new life into otherwise dull pulses, while pasta and rice dishes take on a completely new identity. These fruits also play an important role in vegetarian nutrition, as the presence of vitamin C enables the body to absorb the mineral iron from vegetable sources, which it otherwise couldn't do.

LEMON-FLAVOURED STUFFED CELERIAC

THIS UNUSUAL-LOOKING ROOT VEGETABLE TASTES LIKE SWEET, NUTTY CELERY. IN THIS ROMANIAN RECIPE, ITS CENTRE IS SCOOPED OUT AND MIXED WITH HERBS FOR A DELICIOUS STUFFING, AND IT IS COOKED IN A MIXTURE OF OLIVE OIL AND LEMON-FLAVOURED WATER, GIVING IT EXTRA ZEST.

SERVES FOUR

INGREDIENTS
   4 small celeriac, about
      200–225g/7–8oz each
   juice of 2 lemons
   150ml/¼ pint/⅔ cup olive oil
   lemon wedges and sprigs of flat leaf
      parsley, to garnish
For the stuffing
   6 garlic cloves, finely chopped
   5ml/1 tsp black peppercorns,
      finely crushed
   60–75ml/4–5 tbsp chopped
      fresh parsley
   salt

1 Peel the celeriac carefully with a sharp knife and immediately immerse in a bowl of water mixed with the lemon juice until ready to use.

2 Reserve the lemon water. Scoop out the flesh of each celeriac, leaving a shell about 2cm/¾in thick, in which to put the filling.

3 To make the stuffing, working quickly, chop the scooped out celeriac flesh and mix it with the garlic and peppercorns. Add the chopped parsley and season to taste with salt.

4 Fill the shells with the stuffing and place them in a large pan, making sure they remain upright throughout cooking. Pour in the olive oil and enough lemon water to come halfway up the celeriac.

5 Simmer very gently until the celeriac are tender and nearly all the cooking liquid has been absorbed. Serve the celeriac hot or cold with their juices, and garnish with lemon wedges and sprigs of parsley.

COOK'S TIP
Adding lemon juice to the water helps to prevent the peeled celeriac discolouring.

BEAN AND LEMON STUFFED MUSHROOMS

LARGE FIELD MUSHROOMS HAVE A RICH FLAVOUR AND A MEATY TEXTURE THAT GO WELL WITH THIS FRAGRANT HERB, BEAN AND LEMON STUFFING. THE GARLIC AND PINE NUT ACCOMPANIMENT IS A TRADITIONAL MIDDLE EASTERN DISH WITH A SMOOTH, CREAMY CONSISTENCY.

SERVES FOUR

INGREDIENTS
200g/7oz/1 cup dried or 400g/14oz/
    2 cups drained, canned aduki beans
45ml/3 tbsp olive oil, plus extra
    for brushing
1 onion, finely chopped
2 garlic cloves, crushed
30ml/2 tbsp fresh chopped or 5ml/
    1 tsp dried thyme
8 large field (portabello) mushrooms,
    stalks finely chopped
50g/2oz/1 cup fresh wholemeal
    (whole-wheat) breadcrumbs
juice of 1 lemon
185g/6½oz/generous ¾ cup
    crumbled goat's cheese
salt and ground black pepper
steamed spinach leaves, to serve
For the pine nut paste
50g/2oz/½ cup pine nuts,
    lightly toasted
50g/2oz/1 cup cubed white bread
2 garlic cloves, chopped
about 200ml/7fl oz/scant 1 cup milk
45ml/3 tbsp olive oil
15ml/1 tbsp chopped fresh parsley,
    to garnish (optional)

1 If using dried beans, soak them overnight, then drain and rinse well. Place in a pan, add enough water to cover and bring to the boil. Boil rapidly for 10 minutes, then reduce the heat, cook for 30 minutes, or until tender, then drain. If using canned beans, drain, rinse under cold running water, then drain well again, and set aside.

2 Preheat the oven to 200°C/400°F/ Gas 6. Heat the oil in a large, heavy frying pan, add the onion and garlic and cook over a low heat, stirring frequently, for 5 minutes, or until softened.

3 Add the thyme and the mushroom stalks and cook for a further 3 minutes, stirring occasionally, until tender.

4 Stir in the aduki beans, breadcrumbs and lemon juice, season to taste with salt and pepper, then cook gently for 2–3 minutes, or until heated through. Mash about two-thirds of the beans with a fork or potato masher, leaving the remaining beans whole, then mix thoroughly together.

5 Brush an ovenproof dish and the base and sides of the mushrooms with oil. Top each with a spoonful of the bean mixture, place in the dish, cover with foil and bake for 20 minutes.

6 Remove the foil. Top each mushroom with cheese and bake for 15 minutes more, or until the cheese is melted.

7 To make the pine nut paste, place all the ingredients in a food processor or blender and process until smooth and creamy. Add a little more milk if the mixture appears too thick. Sprinkle with parsley, if using. Serve the mushrooms on a bed of steamed spinach, with the pine nut paste alongside.

PEPPERS FILLED WITH SPICED VEGETABLES

INDIAN SPICES AND LEMON SEASON THE POTATO AND AUBERGINE STUFFING IN THESE COLOURFUL BAKED PEPPERS. THEY ARE EXCELLENT WITH PLAIN RICE AND A LENTIL DHAL, OR THEY CAN BE SERVED WITH SALAD, INDIAN BREADS AND A CUCUMBER AND YOGURT RAITA.

SERVES SIX

INGREDIENTS

6 large evenly shaped red or yellow (bell) peppers
500g/1¼lb waxy potatoes
1 small onion, chopped
4–5 garlic cloves, chopped
5cm/2in piece fresh root ginger, peeled and chopped
1–2 fresh green chillies, seeded and chopped
105ml/7 tbsp water
90ml/6 tbsp groundnut (peanut) oil
1 aubergine (eggplant), cut into 1cm/½in dice
10ml/2 tsp cumin seeds
5ml/1 tsp kalonji seeds (see Cook's Tip)
2.5ml/½ tsp ground turmeric
5ml/1 tsp ground coriander
5ml/1 tsp ground toasted cumin seeds
pinch or two of cayenne pepper
about 45ml/3 tbsp lemon juice
salt and ground black pepper
30ml/2 tbsp chopped fresh coriander (cilantro), to garnish

3 Cook the potatoes in salted boiling water for 10–12 minutes, or until just tender. Drain, cool and peel, then cut into 1cm/½in dice.

4 Put the onion, garlic, ginger and green chillies in a food processor or blender with about 60ml/4 tbsp of the measured water and process to a purée.

5 Heat 45ml/3 tbsp of the oil in a large frying pan, add the aubergine and cook, stirring occasionally, until browned on all sides. Remove from the pan and set aside. Add another 30ml/2 tbsp of the oil to the pan and cook the potatoes until lightly browned. Remove from the pan and set aside.

6 If necessary, add another 15ml/1 tbsp oil to the pan. Add the cumin and kalonji seeds. Cook briefly until the seeds darken, then add the turmeric, coriander and ground cumin. Cook for 15 seconds. Stir in the onion and garlic purée and cook, scraping the pan with a spatula, until it begins to brown.

7 Return the potatoes and aubergines to the pan, season with salt, pepper and a pinch or two of cayenne. Add the remaining water and 30ml/2 tbsp lemon juice and then cook, stirring, until the liquid evaporates. Preheat the oven to 190°C/375°F/Gas 5.

8 Fill the peppers with the potato mixture and place on a lightly greased baking sheet. Brush the peppers with a little oil and bake for 30–35 minutes, until the peppers are cooked through and tender. Leave to cool slightly, then sprinkle with a little more lemon juice, garnish with the chopped coriander and serve immediately.

COOK'S TIP

Kalonji, or nigella as it is sometimes known, is a tiny black seed. It is widely used in Indian cooking, often sprinkled over breads or in potato dishes. It has a mild, slightly nutty flavour and is best toasted for a few seconds in a dry frying pan over a medium heat. This helps to bring out its flavour.

1 Cut the tops off the peppers then remove and discard the seeds. Cut a thin slice off the base, if necessary, to make them stand upright.

2 Bring a large pan of lightly salted water to the boil. Add the peppers and cook for 5–6 minutes. Drain and leave the peppers upside down in a colander.

VEGETABLE FAJITAS

LIME ADDS PIQUANCY AND ITS DISTINCTIVE FLAVOUR TO THE GUACAMOLE SERVED WITH THESE FAJITAS.
FOR EXTRA TANG, WEDGES ARE SQUEEZED OVER THE TORTILLAS BEFORE EATING.

SERVES TWO

INGREDIENTS
  1 onion
  1 red (bell) pepper
  1 green (bell) pepper
  1 yellow (bell) pepper
  1 garlic clove, crushed
  225g/8oz/3¼ cups mushrooms
  90ml/6 tbsp vegetable oil
  30ml/2 tbsp medium chilli powder
  salt and ground black pepper
  coriander (cilantro) sprigs and
    1 lime, cut into wedges, to garnish
  4–6 flour tortillas, warmed, to serve
For the guacamole
  1 ripe avocado
  1 shallot, coarsely chopped
  1 fresh green chilli, seeded and
    coarsely chopped
  juice of 1 lime

1 Slice the onion. Cut the peppers in half, remove the seeds and cut the flesh into strips. Combine the onion and peppers in a bowl. Add the crushed garlic and mix lightly.

2 Remove the mushroom stalks. Save for making stock, or discard. Slice the caps and add to the pepper mixture.

3 Mix the oil and chilli powder in a cup, pour over the vegetable mixture and stir well. Set aside.

4 To make the guacamole, cut the avocado in half and remove the stone (pit) and the peel. Put the flesh into a food processor or blender with the shallot, green chilli and lime juice. Process for 1 minute, or until smooth. Transfer to a small bowl, cover closely with clear film (plastic wrap) and put in the refrigerator to chill until required.

5 Heat a frying pan or wok until very hot. Add the marinated vegetables and stir-fry over a high heat for 5–6 minutes, or until the mushrooms and peppers are just tender. Season to taste with salt and pepper.

6 Spoon a little of the filling on to each tortilla and roll up. Garnish with fresh coriander sprigs and lime wedges and serve immediately with the guacamole.

VEGETABLE STIR-FRY <u>IN</u> LIME DRESSING

THERE IS NOTHING QUITE LIKE CRISP AND SWEET, YOUNG VEGETABLES. HERE, THEY ARE QUICKLY STIR-FRIED TO RETAIN THEIR TEXTURE AND THEN TOSSED IN A ZESTY LIME AND HONEY DRESSING.

SERVES FOUR

INGREDIENTS

15ml/1 tbsp groundnut
(peanut) oil
1 garlic clove, sliced
2.5cm/1in piece fresh root ginger,
peeled and finely chopped
115g/4oz baby carrots
115g/4oz patty pan squash
115g/4oz baby corn
115g/4oz green beans, trimmed
115g/4oz sugar-snap peas, trimmed
115g/4oz young asparagus, cut into
7.5cm/3in pieces
8 spring onions (scallions), cut into
5cm/2in pieces
115g/4oz cherry tomatoes
For the dressing
juice of 2 limes
15ml/1 tbsp clear honey
15ml/1 tbsp soy sauce
5ml/1 tsp sesame oil

1 Heat the groundnut oil in a large frying pan or wok. Add the garlic and chopped root ginger and stir-fry over a high heat for 1 minute, stirring the spices constantly.

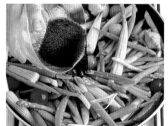

2 Add the baby carrots, patty pan squash, baby corn and green beans and stir-fry for another 3–4 minutes.

3 Add the sugar-snap peas, asparagus, spring onions and cherry tomatoes, and stir-fry for a further 1–2 minutes. Use two wooden spoons or chopsticks to toss the ingredients, so that they cook evenly on all sides.

4 To make the dressing, add the lime juice, honey, soy sauce and sesame oil to a small bowl and stir to mix well. Add the dressing to the frying pan or wok and stir through.

COOK'S TIP
Stir-fries take only moments to cook so prepare this dish at the last minute to retain its crisp texture.

5 Cover the pan or wok and cook the vegetables for 2–3 minutes more, or until they are just tender but still crisp. Transfer to individual bowls or plates and serve immediately.

VARIATION
You can substitute other vegetables, such as baby leeks or fresh peas, but keep a balance of colour and flavour.

CHICKPEA TAGINE WITH PRESERVED LEMON

NUTTY-FLAVOURED CHICKPEAS ARE OFTEN USED IN MOROCCAN COOKING. HERE THEY ARE SLOWLY COOKED WITH TOMATOES AND SPICES, WITH PRESERVED LEMON ADDED JUST BEFORE SERVING.

SERVES FOUR TO SIX

INGREDIENTS
  150g/5oz/¾ cup chickpeas, soaked
    overnight and drained, or 2 × 400g/
    14oz cans chickpeas, drained
  30ml/2 tbsp sunflower oil
  1 large onion, chopped
  1 garlic clove, crushed
  400g/14oz can chopped tomatoes
  350ml/12fl oz/1½ cups
    vegetable stock
  5ml/1 tsp ground cumin
  ¼ preserved lemon
  30ml/2 tbsp chopped fresh
    coriander (cilantro)
  salt and ground black pepper

1 If using dried chickpeas, simmer in plenty of water for 1–1½ hours until tender. Drain.

2 Skin the chickpeas by placing them in a bowl of cold water and rubbing them between your fingers.

3 Heat the oil in a pan and cook the onion and garlic for 8–10 minutes.

4 Add the chickpeas, tomatoes, stock and cumin and stir to mix well. Season well. Bring to the boil and simmer for 30–40 minutes, or until the chickpeas are completely soft and most of the liquid has evaporated.

5 Rinse the preserved lemon and cut away the flesh and pith. Use a sharp knife to cut the peel into slivers, then stir into the chickpeas along with the chopped coriander. Serve immediately with crusty bread.

LEMONY OKRA AND TOMATO TAGINE

IN THIS SPICY VEGETABLE DISH, THE HEAT OF THE CHILLI IS OFFSET BY THE REFRESHING FLAVOUR OF LEMON JUICE. THIS IS A SURPRISINGLY SUBSTANTIAL DISH, AND IDEAL FOR A VEGETARIAN MEAL.

SERVES FOUR

INGREDIENTS
350g/12oz okra
5–6 tomatoes
2 small onions
2 garlic cloves, crushed
1 fresh green chilli, seeded
5ml/1 tsp paprika
small handful of fresh coriander
 (cilantro), plus extra to garnish
30ml/2 tbsp sunflower oil
juice of 1 lemon

4 Thinly slice the second onion and cook in the oil for 5–6 minutes, or until golden brown. Transfer to a plate with a slotted spoon.

5 Reduce the heat and pour in the onion and coriander mixture. Cook for 1–2 minutes, stirring frequently, and then add the okra, tomatoes, lemon juice and about 120ml/4fl oz/½ cup water. Stir well to mix, cover tightly and simmer gently over a low heat for about 15 minutes, or until the okra is tender.

6 Transfer to a warmed serving dish, sprinkle with the fried onion rings, garnish with coriander and serve immediately.

COOK'S TIP
Okra is also known as bhindi, gumbo and ladies' fingers.

1 Trim the okra and then cut them into 1cm/½in lengths. Set aside.

2 Plunge the tomatoes into a bowl of boiling water for 30 seconds, then drain and refresh in cold water. Peel off the skins and coarsely chop the flesh. Set the tomatoes aside.

3 Coarsely chop one of the onions and place it in a food processor or blender with the garlic, green chilli, paprika, fresh coriander and 60ml/4 tbsp water. Process to a paste.

CALIFORNIAN CITRUS FRIED RICE

PINK GRAPEFRUIT ADDS ITS DISTINCTIVE FLAVOUR TO THIS DELICIOUS VEGETABLE, NUT AND CITRUS RECIPE. IT IS IMPORTANT TO MAKE SURE THAT THE COOKED RICE IS COLD BEFORE IT IS FRIED.

SERVES FOUR TO SIX

INGREDIENTS

1 pink grapefruit or Jaffa orange
4 eggs
10ml/2 tsp Japanese rice vinegar
30ml/2 tbsp light soy sauce
about 45ml/3 tbsp groundnut
   (peanut) oil
50g/2oz/½ cup cashew nuts
2 garlic cloves, crushed
6 spring onions (scallions),
   diagonally sliced
2 small carrots, cut into
   julienne strips
225g/8oz asparagus, each spear cut
   diagonally into 4 pieces
175g/6oz/2¼ cups button (white)
   mushrooms, halved
30ml/2 tbsp sake
30ml/2 tbsp water
450g/1lb/4 cups cooked white long
   grain rice
about 10ml/2 tsp sesame oil
thin strips of orange rind, to garnish
For the hot dressing
5ml/1 tsp grated orange rind
30ml/2 tbsp sake
45ml/3 tbsp soy sauce
30ml/2 tbsp freshly squeezed pink
   grapefruit or orange juice
5ml/1 tsp medium or hot
   chilli sauce

2 Beat the eggs with the vinegar and 10ml/2 tsp of the soy sauce. Heat 15ml/1 tbsp of the oil in a wok and cook the eggs until lightly scrambled. Transfer to a plate and set aside.

3 Add the cashew nuts to the wok and stir-fry for 1–2 minutes. Set aside.

4 Heat the remaining oil and add the garlic and spring onions. Cook over a medium heat for 1–2 minutes, or until the onions begin to soften, then add the carrots and stir-fry for 4 minutes.

5 Add the asparagus and cook for 2–3 minutes, then add the mushrooms and stir-fry for 1 minute. Stir in the sake, the remaining soy sauce and the water. Simmer for a few minutes until the vegetables are just tender.

6 Mix together the ingredients for the dressing, then add to the wok and bring to the boil. Add the rice, scrambled eggs and cashew nuts. Toss over a low heat for about 4 minutes until the rice is warmed through. Just before serving, stir in the sesame oil and the grapefruit or orange segments. Garnish with strips of orange rind and serve immediately.

1 Cut a thin slice of peel and pith from each end of the grapefruit or orange. Place cut-side down on a plate and cut off the peel and pith in strips. Remove any remaining pith. Cut out each segment leaving the membrane behind.

SWEET RICE WITH HOT SOUR CHICKPEAS

*LEMON PROVIDES THE SOUR FLAVOURING IN THIS SPICY CHICKPEA DISH FROM INDIA. IT IS SERVED
WITH A SWEET RICE THAT HAS BEEN PERFUMED WITH CLOVES AND CARDAMOM PODS.*

SERVES SIX

INGREDIENTS

225g/8oz tomatoes
350g/12oz/2 cups dried chickpeas,
 soaked overnight and drained
60ml/4 tbsp vegetable oil
1 large onion, very finely chopped
15ml/1 tbsp ground coriander
15ml/1 tbsp ground cumin
5ml/1 tsp ground fenugreek
5ml/1 tsp ground cinnamon
1–2 fresh hot green chillies, seeded
 and thinly sliced
2.5cm/1in piece fresh root ginger,
 peeled and grated
60ml/4 tbsp lemon juice
15ml/1 tbsp chopped fresh
 coriander (cilantro)
salt and ground black pepper
For the rice
 40g/1½oz/3 tbsp ghee or butter
 4 green cardamom pods
 4 cloves
 650ml/22fl oz/2¾ cups boiling water
 350g/12oz/1¾ cups basmati rice,
 soaked for 30 minutes and drained
 5–10ml/1–2 tsp granulated sugar
 5–6 saffron threads, soaked in
 warm water

1 Plunge the tomatoes into boiling water for 30 seconds, then refresh in cold water. Peel off the skins, remove the seeds and chop finely. Set aside.

2 Place the chickpeas in a large pan. Pour in water to cover, bring to the boil, then simmer, covered, for 1–1¼ hours, or until tender, topping up the liquid from time to time. Drain the chickpeas, reserving the cooking liquid.

3 Heat the oil in a pan. Reserve 30ml/ 2 tbsp of the chopped onion and add the remainder to the pan. Cook over a medium heat for 4–5 minutes, stirring.

4 Add the tomatoes to the pan. Cook over a moderately low heat for about 5 minutes, or until they are very soft, stirring and mashing them frequently.

5 Stir in the ground coriander, cumin, fenugreek and cinnamon. Cook for 30 seconds, then add the chickpeas and 350ml/12fl oz/1½ cups of the reserved cooking liquid. Season with salt, then cover and simmer very gently for 15–20 minutes, stirring occasionally and adding more liquid if the chickpeas begin to dry out.

6 While the chickpeas are cooking, melt the ghee or butter in a pan and fry the cardamom pods and cloves for a few minutes. Remove the pan from the heat and, when the fat has cooled a little, pour in the boiling water and stir in the basmati rice. Cover tightly and simmer for 10 minutes.

7 When the rice is fully cooked, add the sugar and saffron liquid and stir thoroughly. Cover the pan again. The rice will keep warm while you finish cooking the chickpeas.

8 In a bowl, mix the reserved chopped onion with the sliced chillies, ginger and lemon juice, then stir the mixture into the chickpeas. Add the chopped coriander, adjust the seasoning, if necessary, and serve with the rice.

LEEK, MUSHROOM AND LEMON RISOTTO

THE DELICIOUS COMBINATION OF LEEKS AND LEMON IS PERFECT IN THIS LIGHT RISOTTO; BROWN CAP
MUSHROOMS PROVIDE ADDITIONAL TEXTURE AND EXTRA FLAVOUR.

SERVES FOUR

INGREDIENTS
  225g/8oz trimmed leeks
  225g/8oz/3 cups brown cap
    (cremini) mushrooms
  30ml/2 tbsp olive oil
  3 garlic cloves, crushed
  75g/3oz/6 tbsp butter
  1 large onion, coarsely chopped
  350g/12oz/1¾ cups risotto rice, such
    as arborio or carnaroli
  1.2 litres/2 pints/5 cups simmering
    vegetable stock
  grated rind of 1 lemon
  45ml/3 tbsp lemon juice
  50g/2oz/⅔ cup freshly grated
    Parmesan cheese
  60ml/4 tbsp mixed chopped fresh
    chives and flat leaf parsley
  salt and ground black pepper

1 Slice the leeks in half lengthways, wash them well and then slice them evenly. Wipe the mushrooms with kitchen paper and chop them coarsely.

2 Heat the oil in a large pan and cook the garlic for 1 minute. Add the leeks, mushrooms and plenty of seasoning and cook over a medium heat for about 10 minutes, or until the leeks have softened and browned. Spoon into a bowl and set aside.

3 Add 25g/1oz/2 tbsp of the butter to the pan. When it has melted, add the onion and cook over a medium heat for 5 minutes, or until it has softened and is golden.

4 Stir in the rice and cook for about 1 minute, or until the grains begin to look translucent and are coated in the fat. Add a ladleful of stock and cook gently, stirring occasionally, until the liquid has been absorbed.

5 Continue to add stock, a ladleful at a time, until all of it has been absorbed, stirring constantly. This will take about 30 minutes. The risotto will become thick and creamy, and the rice should be tender, but not sticky.

6 Just before serving, add the leeks and mushrooms with the remaining butter. Stir in the grated lemon rind and juice. Add the grated Parmesan cheese and the herbs. Adjust the seasoning if necessary and serve immediately.

COOK'S TIP
Risotto rice is a rounder grain than long grain and is capable of absorbing a lot of liquid, which gives it a creamy texture.

TAGLIATELLE <u>WITH</u> BROCCOLI <u>AND</u> SPINACH

IN THIS EXCELLENT VEGETARIAN SUPPER DISH, LEMON JUICE ADDS SHARPNESS TO QUICKLY STEAMED BROCCOLI AND SPINACH. IT MAKES A NUTRITIOUS AND FILLING MEAL AND NEEDS NO ACCOMPANIMENT.

SERVES FOUR

INGREDIENTS

2 heads of broccoli
450g/1lb fresh spinach,
  stalks removed
nutmeg
450g/1lb fresh or dried
  egg tagliatelle
about 45ml/3 tbsp extra virgin
  olive oil
juice of 1 lemon
salt and ground black pepper
freshly shaved Parmesan cheese,
  to serve

1 Put the broccoli in the basket of a steamer, cover and steam over boiling water for 5 minutes.

3 Add a pinch of salt to the water already in the steamer, then fill up with more boiling water. Add the pasta, bring the water back to the boil and cook according to the instructions on the packet. Meanwhile, chop the broccoli and spinach.

4 Drain the pasta. Heat the oil in the pasta pan, add the pasta and chopped vegetables and toss over a medium heat until evenly mixed. Sprinkle with the lemon juice and season well with black pepper. Serve immediately, sprinkled with the Parmesan shavings.

2 Add the spinach leaves to the steamer basket, cover and steam for 3–4 minutes, or until both vegetables are just tender. Towards the end of the cooking time, sprinkle the vegetables with freshly grated nutmeg and season to taste with salt and pepper. Lift out the steamer and put to one side.

VARIATIONS
• For a little extra kick, add a sprinkling of crushed dried chillies with the black pepper in step 2.
• You can add one or two handfuls of toasted pine nuts to the finished dish. They are often served with broccoli and spinach in Italy and taste wonderful.

VERMICELLI WITH LEMON

FRESH AND TANGY, THIS MAKES AN EXCELLENT FIRST COURSE FOR A DINNER PARTY. IT DOES NOT RELY ON FRESH SEASONAL INGREDIENTS, AS LEMONS PROVIDE THE ESSENTIAL FLAVOURING, SO IT IS GOOD AT ANY TIME OF YEAR. IT IS ALSO AN IDEAL CHOICE WHEN YOU ARE PUSHED FOR TIME.

SERVES FOUR

INGREDIENTS

350g/12oz dried vermicelli
juice of 2 large lemons
50g/2oz/¼ cup butter
200ml/7fl oz/scant 1 cup single
  (light) cream
115g/4oz/1⅓ cups freshly grated
  Parmesan cheese
salt and ground black pepper

1 Bring a large pan of lightly salted water to the boil. Add the pasta, bring back to the boil and cook according to the instructions on the packet.

COOK'S TIP
Lemons vary in the amount of juice they yield and are best squeezed at room temperature. On average, a large fresh lemon will yield 60–90ml/4–6 tbsp. The flavour of this dish is quite sharp – you can use less juice if you prefer.

2 While the pasta is cooking, pour the lemon juice into a medium pan. Add the butter and cream, then season with salt and pepper to taste.

3 Bring to the boil, then lower the heat and simmer gently for about 5 minutes, stirring occasionally, until the cream has reduced slightly.

4 Drain the pasta and return it to the pan. Add the grated Parmesan, then taste the sauce for seasoning and adjust if necessary. Pour it over the pasta. Toss quickly over a medium heat until the pasta is evenly coated with the sauce, then divide among four warmed bowls and serve immediately.

VARIATIONS
• Use spaghettini or spaghetti, or even small pasta shapes, such as fusilli, farfalle or orecchiette.
• For an even tangier taste, add a little grated lemon rind to the sauce when you add the butter and the cream to the pan in Step 2.

PENNE WITH ARTICHOKES

ARTICHOKES ARE A VERY POPULAR VEGETABLE IN ITALY, AND ARE OFTEN USED IN SAUCES FOR PASTA. THIS SAUCE IS RICHLY FLAVOURED WITH GARLIC, TOMATOES, WINE AND LEMON JUICE — THE PERFECT DISH TO SERVE AS A FIRST COURSE WHEN GLOBE ARTICHOKES ARE IN SEASON.

SERVES SIX

INGREDIENTS
juice of 1 lemon
2 globe artichokes
30ml/2 tbsp olive oil
1 small fennel bulb, thinly sliced,
  with feathery tops reserved
1 onion, finely chopped
4 garlic cloves, finely chopped
1 handful fresh flat leaf parsley,
  coarsely chopped
400g/14oz can chopped
  plum tomatoes
150ml/¼ pint/⅔ cup dry
  white wine
350g/12oz/3 cups dried penne
10ml/2 tsp capers, chopped
salt and ground black pepper
freshly grated Parmesan cheese,
  to serve

1 Fill a large mixing bowl with cold water and add the juice of half a lemon. To prepare the artichokes, cut or break off the artichoke stalks, then pull off and discard the outer leaves until only the pale inner leaves that are almost white at the base remain.

2 Cut off the tops of these leaves so that the base remains. Cut the base in half lengthways, then prise the hairy choke out of the centre with the tip of the knife and discard. Cut the artichokes lengthways into 5mm/¼in slices, adding them immediately to the bowl of acidulated water to prevent them from discolouring.

3 Bring a large pan of salted water to the boil. Drain the artichokes and add them immediately to the water. Boil for 5 minutes, then drain and set aside.

4 Heat the oil in a large skillet or pan and add the fennel, onion, garlic and parsley. Cook over a low to medium heat, stirring frequently, for 10 minutes, or until the fennel has softened and is lightly coloured.

5 Add the tomatoes and wine, with salt and pepper to taste. Bring to the boil, stirring, then lower the heat, cover and simmer for 10–15 minutes. Stir in the artichokes, replace the lid and simmer for 10 minutes more. Meanwhile, add the pasta to a large pan of lightly salted boiling water and cook according to the instructions on the packet.

6 Drain the pasta, reserving a little of the cooking water. Add the capers to the sauce, stir well, then taste for seasoning. Add the remaining lemon juice.

7 Tip the pasta into a warmed, large serving bowl, pour the sauce over and toss thoroughly to mix, adding a little of the reserved cooking water if you like a thinner sauce. Serve immediately, garnished with the reserved fennel fronds. Hand around a bowl of grated Parmesan separately.

Poultry and Meat Dishes

The tangy sharpness of citrus fruit is the perfect foil for rich meat and poultry dishes, whether in a classic combination, such as duck and orange, or in an unfamiliar guise, such as ham with a fruity clementine sauce. By contrast, it is also ideal for adding zest and piquancy to lighter meats, such as chicken and veal, that can sometimes seem rather bland and unexciting. Citrus fruit is so versatile that it can be used as a single, keynote flavouring, in a subtle partnership with garlic and herbs, or as part of a blend with aromatic spices to give depth and variety to every kind of meat and poultry.

CHICKEN THIGHS WITH LEMON AND GARLIC

THIS RECIPE FEATURES CLASSIC FLAVOURINGS FOR CHICKEN – PUNGENT GARLIC, WHITE WINE AND SCENTED LEMON. DIFFERENT VERSIONS OF THIS SUCCULENT DISH CAN BE FOUND IN BOTH SPAIN AND ITALY. THIS PARTICULAR RECIPE, HOWEVER, IS OF FRENCH ORIGIN.

SERVES FOUR

INGREDIENTS

- 600ml/1 pint/2½ cups chicken stock
- 20 large garlic cloves
- 25g/1oz/2 tbsp butter
- 15ml/1 tbsp olive oil
- 8 chicken thighs
- 1 lemon, peeled, pith removed and thinly sliced
- 30ml/2 tbsp plain (all-purpose) flour
- 150ml/¼ pint/⅔ cup dry white wine
- salt and ground black pepper
- chopped fresh parsley or basil, to garnish

1 Pour the stock into a pan and bring to the boil. Add the garlic, cover and simmer for 40 minutes.

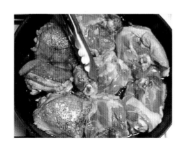

2 Meanwhile, heat the butter and oil in a sauté or frying pan. Add the chicken thighs and cook over a low heat, turning occasionally until golden on all sides. With tongs or a slotted spoon, transfer them to an ovenproof dish. Preheat the oven to 190°C/375°F/Gas 5.

3 Strain the chicken stock and reserve it. Distribute the garlic and lemon slices among the chicken pieces. Add the flour to the fat in the pan in which the chicken was browned, and cook, stirring constantly, for 1 minute. Add the wine, stirring and scraping the base of the pan, then pour in the stock. Cook, still stirring, until the sauce has thickened and is smooth. Season to taste with a little salt and pepper.

4 Pour the sauce over the chicken, cover and transfer to the oven. Cook for 40–45 minutes until the chicken is tender and cooked through. If a thicker sauce is required, lift out the chicken pieces and reduce the sauce by boiling rapidly until it reaches the desired consistency. Sprinkle over the chopped parsley or basil and serve with boiled new potatoes or rice.

VARIATION
Substitute a bitter orange, such as Seville (Temple), for the lemon and dry vermouth for the white wine.

CHICKEN WITH PRESERVED LEMON AND OLIVES

THIS IS ONE OF THE MOST FAMOUS MOROCCAN DISHES. YOU MUST USE PRESERVED LEMON AS FRESH LEMON SIMPLY DOES NOT HAVE THE MELLOW FLAVOUR THAT THIS DISH REQUIRES. FOR A TRULY AUTHENTIC FLAVOUR, USE TAN-COLOURED MOROCCAN OLIVES.

SERVES FOUR

INGREDIENTS

30ml/2 tbsp olive oil
1 Spanish onion, chopped
3 garlic cloves
1cm/½ in piece fresh root ginger,
  peeled and grated, or 2.5ml/½ tsp
  ground ginger
2.5–5ml/½–1 tsp ground cinnamon
pinch of saffron threads
4 chicken quarters, preferably breast
  portions, halved if you like
750ml/1¼ pints/3 cups
  chicken stock
30ml/2 tbsp chopped fresh
  coriander (cilantro)
30ml/2 tbsp chopped fresh parsley
1 preserved lemon
115g/4oz/⅔ cup Moroccan tan olives
salt and ground black pepper
lemon slices and fresh coriander
  (cilantro) sprigs, to garnish

1 Heat the oil in a large flameproof casserole, add the onion and cook over a medium heat, stirring occasionally, for 6–8 minutes until lightly golden.

2 Meanwhile, crush the garlic and blend with the ginger, cinnamon, saffron and a little salt and pepper. Stir into the pan and cook for about 1 minute. Add the chicken and cook over a medium heat for 2–3 minutes, or until golden.

3 Add the stock and herbs, and bring to the boil. Cover and simmer for about 45 minutes until the chicken is tender.

4 Rinse the preserved lemon under cold running water, discard the flesh and cut the peel into small pieces. Stir into the pan with the olives, and simmer for a further 15 minutes, or until the chicken is very tender.

5 Transfer the chicken to a plate and keep warm. Bring the sauce to the boil and cook for 3–4 minutes, or until reduced and fairly thick. Pour it over the chicken and serve, garnished with lemon slices and coriander sprigs.

CITRUS CHICKEN SALAD

THIS LIGHT, ZESTY SALAD MAKES A REFRESHING CHANGE FROM RICH FOOD. IT IS A GOOD CHOICE FOR A POST-CHRISTMAS BUFFET, WHEN COOKED TURKEY CAN BE USED INSTEAD OF CHICKEN.

2 Using a sharp knife, cut a thin slice of peel and pith from each end of two of the oranges. Place them cut side down on a plate and cut off the peel and pith in strips. Remove any bits of remaining pith. Cut out each segment leaving the membrane behind and set aside. Grate the rind and squeeze the juice from one of the remaining oranges and place both in a large bowl.

3 Stir in the Dijon mustard, 5ml/1 tsp of the honey, 60ml/4 tbsp of the oil and seasoning to taste. Mix in the cabbage, carrots, spring onions and celery, then leave to stand for 10 minutes.

4 Meanwhile, squeeze the juice from the remaining orange and mix it with the tarragon and remaining honey and oil. Peel and segment the limes, as for the oranges, and lightly mix the lime segments into the dressing with the reserved orange segments. Season to taste with salt and pepper.

5 Thinly slice the cooled chicken portions and add them to the dressing. Spoon the vegetable salad on to six individual plates and add the chicken mixture, then serve immediately.

SERVES SIX

INGREDIENTS
  120ml/4fl oz/½ cup extra virgin
    olive oil
  6 skinless, boneless chicken
    breast portions
  4 oranges
  5ml/1 tsp Dijon mustard
  15ml/3 tsp clear honey
  300g/11oz/2¾ cups finely shredded
    white cabbage
  300g/11oz carrots, peeled and
    thinly sliced
  2 spring onions (scallions),
    thinly sliced
  2 celery sticks, cut into thin batons
  30ml/2 tbsp chopped fresh tarragon
  2 limes
  salt and ground black pepper

1 Heat 30ml/2 tbsp of the oil in a large, heavy frying pan. Add the chicken breast portions to the pan and cook for 15–20 minutes, or until the chicken is cooked through and golden brown. (If your pan is too small, cook the chicken in two or three batches.) Remove the chicken from the pan and leave to cool.

COOK'S TIP
Seedless navel oranges would be a good choice for this dish, but you could also use easy-to-peel Jaffa or Shamouti oranges or even substitute clementines, satsumas or ortaniques. As most varieties of tangerines are smaller than oranges, you will need five or six of them.

FRAGRANT THAI CHICKEN CURRY

LIMES REALLY BRING OUT THE THAI FLAVOURINGS IN THIS CREAMY CURRY. IT IS QUITE SIMPLE TO MAKE EVEN THOUGH IT INCLUDES A VARIETY OF UNUSUAL INGREDIENTS.

SERVES SIX

INGREDIENTS

    400ml/14oz can unsweetened
      coconut milk
    6 skinless, boneless chicken breast
      portions, thinly sliced
    225g/8oz can bamboo shoots,
      drained and sliced
    30ml/2 tbsp Thai fish sauce
    15ml/1 tbsp soft light brown sugar
For the green curry paste
    4 fresh green chillies, seeded
    1 lemon grass stalk, sliced
    1 small onion, sliced
    3 garlic cloves
    1cm/½in piece galangal or fresh root
      ginger, peeled and chopped
    grated rind of ½ lime
    5ml/1 tsp coriander seeds
    5ml/1 tsp cumin seeds
    2.5ml/½ tsp Thai fish sauce
To garnish
    1 fresh red chilli, seeded
    pared rind of ½ lime
    fresh Thai purple basil or
      coriander (cilantro)
To serve
    175g/6oz/scant 1 cup Thai
      jasmine rice
    pinch of saffron threads
    salt

1 First make the green curry paste. Put the chillies, lemon grass, onion, garlic cloves, galangal or ginger, lime rind, coriander seeds, cumin seeds and fish sauce in a food processor or blender and process until they are reduced to a thick, smooth paste.

2 Bring half the coconut milk to the boil in a large frying pan, then reduce the heat and simmer gently for about 5 minutes, or until reduced by half. Stir in the green curry paste and simmer for a further 5 minutes.

3 Add the sliced chicken to the pan and pour in the remaining coconut milk. Add the bamboo shoots, Thai fish sauce and sugar. Stir well to combine all the ingredients and bring the curry back to simmering point, then simmer gently for about 10 minutes, or until the chicken slices are cooked through. The mixture will look quite grainy or curdled during cooking, but do not worry, as this is quite normal.

4 To make the garnish, cut the chilli, lime rind and basil or coriander into fine strips. Add the rice and saffron to a pan of salted boiling water. Simmer for about 10 minutes, drain, then serve it with the curry and the prepared garnish.

MEDITERRANEAN CHICKEN AND VEGETABLES

LEMON AND THYME ADD A FRAGRANCE TO CHICKEN ROASTED WITH PEPPER, AUBERGINE, FENNEL AND GARLIC IN THIS WONDERFUL FRENCH ALTERNATIVE TO A TRADITIONAL ROAST CHICKEN. FOR ADDITIONAL CITRUS APPEAL, USE LEMON THYME RATHER THAN THE ORDINARY VARIETY.

SERVES FOUR

INGREDIENTS

1.8–2kg/4–4½lb roasting chicken
150ml/¼ pint/⅔ cup extra virgin
   olive oil
½ lemon
few sprigs of fresh thyme
450g/1lb small new potatoes
1 aubergine (eggplant), cut into
   2.5cm/1in cubes
1 red (bell) pepper, seeded
   and quartered
1 fennel bulb, trimmed
   and quartered
8 large garlic cloves, unpeeled
coarse salt and ground black pepper

1 Preheat the oven to 200°C/400°F/ Gas 6. Rub the chicken with some of the oil and pepper. Place the lemon and two thyme sprigs inside it. Transfer to a roasting pan. Roast for 30 minutes.

2 Remove the chicken from the oven and season with salt. Turn it over and baste with the juices. Surround the bird with the potatoes, roll them in the pan juices, and return the pan to the oven.

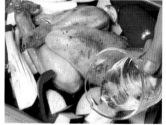

3 After 30 minutes, add the aubergine, red pepper, fennel and garlic cloves to the pan. Drizzle with the remaining oil, and season with salt and pepper. Add the remaining thyme to the vegetables. Return the chicken to the oven, and cook for 30–50 minutes more, basting and turning the vegetables occasionally.

4 To find out if the chicken is cooked, push the tip of a sharp knife between the thigh and breast. If the juices run clear, it is done. Test the vegetables with a fork: they should be tender and just beginning to brown.

5 Serve the chicken and vegetables from the pan, or transfer the vegetables to a serving dish, joint the chicken and place it on top. Serve the skimmed juices in a gravy boat.

GRILLED POUSSINS WITH CITRUS GLAZE

THIS RECIPE IS SUITABLE FOR MANY KINDS OF SMALL BIRDS, INCLUDING PIGEONS, SNIPE AND PARTRIDGES. IT WOULD ALSO WORK WITH QUAIL, BUT DECREASE THE COOKING TIME AND SPREAD THE CITRUS MIXTURE OVER, RATHER THAN UNDER, THE FRAGILE SKIN.

2 Beat the butter in a small bowl with a wooden spoon, then beat in 15ml/1 tbsp of the olive oil, the garlic, thyme, cayenne, salt and pepper, half the lemon and lime rind and 15ml/1 tbsp each of the lemon and lime juice.

3 Using your fingertips, carefully loosen the skin of each poussin breast. With a round-bladed knife or small spatula, spread the butter mixture between the skin and breast meat.

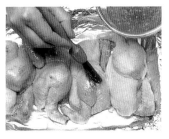

4 Preheat the grill (broiler) and line a grill pan with foil. In a small bowl, mix together the remaining olive oil, lemon and lime juices and the honey. Place the bird halves, skin-side up, on the grill pan and brush with the juice and honey mixture.

5 Grill (broil) for 10–12 minutes, basting twice with the juices. Turn over and grill for 7–10 minutes, basting once, until the juices run clear when the thigh is pierced. Serve with tomato salad, garnished with dill.

SERVES FOUR

INGREDIENTS

2 poussins, about 675g/1½lb each
50g/2oz/¼ cup unsalted (sweet) butter, softened
30ml/2 tbsp olive oil
2 garlic cloves, crushed
2.5ml/½ tsp dried thyme
1.5ml/¼ tsp cayenne pepper, or to taste
grated rind and juice of 1 lemon
grated rind and juice of 1 lime
30ml/2 tbsp clear honey
salt and ground black pepper
fresh dill sprigs, to garnish
tomato salad, to serve

1 Using kitchen scissors, cut along both sides of the backbone of each bird; remove and discard. Cut the birds in half along the breast bone. Using a rolling pin, press down to flatten.

DUCK <u>WITH</u> CUMBERLAND SAUCE

THIS COMBINATION OF DUCK AND ORANGE IS SO GOOD IT SHOULDN'T BE RESERVED FOR SPECIAL OCCASIONS ONLY. SERVE WITH POTATOES AND PEAS FOR A SIMPLE, BUT DELICIOUS, WEEKDAY MEAL.

SERVES EIGHT

INGREDIENTS

    4 minneolas or oranges, segmented, with rind and juice reserved
    2 × 2.25kg/5lb oven-ready ducks, with giblets
    salt and ground black pepper
    fresh parsley sprig, to garnish
For the Cumberland sauce
    30ml/2 tbsp plain (all-purpose) flour
    300ml/½ pint/1¼ cups chicken or duck stock
    150ml/¼ pint/⅔ cup port or red wine
    15ml/1 tbsp redcurrant jelly

1 Preheat the oven to 180°C/350°F/ Gas 4. Tie the minneola or orange rind with string and place it inside the cavities of the two ducks.

2 Place the ducks on a rack in one large or two smaller roasting pans, prick the skin well with a fork or a skewer, season with salt and pepper and cook for 30 minutes per every 450g/1lb (about 2½ hours) until the flesh is tender and the juices run clear.

3 Halfway through the cooking time, pour off the fat from the roasting pan(s) into a heatproof bowl. When the ducks are cooked, transfer them to a carving board, remove the orange rind from the cavities and reserve.

4 To make the sauce, remove any fat from the roasting pan(s), leaving the sediment and juices behind. If using two pans, scrape the sediment and juices into one of them. Sprinkle in the flour and cook over a low heat, stirring constantly, for 2 minutes.

VARIATION
Bigarade sauce is also classically served with duck, but is time-consuming to make. For a speedy version, thinly pare the rinds of 4 Seville (Temple) oranges, cut into thin strips and simmer in a pan of water for 10 minutes, then drain. Squeeze the juice from the oranges. Add the rind and juice in step 5 with the stock, but substitute red Bordeaux wine for the port and lemon juice for the redcurrant jelly. Stir in 5ml/1 tsp tomato purée (paste) and omit the orange segments.

5 Finely chop the reserved orange rind and add to the roasting pan with the stock, port or red wine and redcurrant jelly. Stir well to blend, then bring to the boil and simmer, stirring frequently, for about 10 minutes, then strain into a pan. Add the orange segments with their juices.

6 To carve the ducks, remove the legs and wings, cutting through the joints. Cut the two end joints off the wings and discard them. Cut the breast meat off the carcass in one piece and slice it thinly. Arrange the slices on a warmed serving plate with the legs and the wing joints. Spoon over a little of the hot sauce and serve the rest separately, in a sauce boat. Garnish with parsley and serve immediately.

COOK'S TIP
Cumberland sauce is extremely versatile and can be served with game, ham and mutton, although the latter is rarely available nowadays. It also goes very well with roast goose and turkey.

DUCK WITH ORANGE SAUCE

THIS TRADITIONAL SAUCE OF FRESH ORANGES AND ORANGE LIQUEUR IS ALWAYS A FAVOURITE. AS COMMERCIALLY RAISED DUCKS TEND TO BE MUCH FATTIER THAN WILD DUCKS, INITIAL SLOW COOKING AND PRICKING THE DUCK'S SKIN HELPS TO DRAW OUT EXCESS FAT.

SERVES THREE TO FOUR

INGREDIENTS
2kg/4½lb duck
2 oranges
90g/3½oz/½ cup caster
  (superfine) sugar
90ml/6 tbsp white wine vinegar or
  cider vinegar
120ml/4fl oz/½ cup Grand Marnier or
  other orange liqueur
salt and ground black pepper
watercress and orange slices,
  to garnish

1 Preheat the oven to 150°C/300°F/
Gas 2. Prick the duck's skin all over
with a fork. Season the duck inside and
out with salt and pepper and tie the
legs with string.

2 Place the duck on a rack in a large
roasting pan. Cover with foil and roast
for 1½ hours. With a vegetable peeler,
remove the rind in wide strips from
the oranges, then stack two or three
strips at a time and slice into very thin
julienne strips. Squeeze the juice from
the oranges.

3 Place the sugar and vinegar in a
small, heavy pan and stir to dissolve the
sugar. Boil over a high heat, without
stirring, until the mixture is a rich
caramel colour.

4 Remove the pan from the heat and
add the orange juice, pouring it down
the side of the pan. Swirl to blend, bring
back to the boil and add the orange
rind and liqueur. Simmer for 3 minutes.

5 Remove the duck from the oven and
carefully pour off all the fat from the
pan. Raise the oven temperature to
200°C/400°F/Gas 6.

6 Roast the duck, uncovered, for about
30 minutes, basting three or four times
with the caramel and orange mixture,
until the duck is golden brown and the
juices run clear when the thigh is
pierced with a knife.

7 Pour the juices from the cavity into
the roasting pan and transfer the duck
to a carving board. Cover loosely with
foil and leave to stand for 15 minutes.
Skim the fat from the roasting juices,
and pour the juices into the pan with
the rest of the caramel mixture and
simmer. Serve the duck, with the
sauce, garnished with watercress and
orange slices.

COOK'S TIP
For crisp skin, the duck must be dry
before roasting. Leave, uncovered, in a
cool place for 2 hours before roasting.

PHEASANT WITH LEMON AND SAGE

A POPULAR GAME BIRD, YOUNG PHEASANTS ARE IDEALLY SUITED TO GRILLING AND ROASTING. CITRUS RIND AND SAGE IS TUCKED BENEATH THE SKIN SO THAT THEIR FLAVOURS PERMEATE THE MEAT WHILE IT COOKS. WITH THE MUSTARD AND BRANDY SAUCE ACCOMPANIMENT, THIS IS A TASTY MEAL INDEED.

SERVES FOUR

INGREDIENTS

    2 pheasants, about 450g/
        1lb each
    1 lemon
    60ml/4 tbsp chopped fresh
        sage leaves
    3 shallots
    5ml/1 tsp Dijon mustard
    15ml/1 tbsp brandy or dry sherry
    150ml/¼ pint/⅔ cup crème fraîche
    salt and ground black pepper
    lemon wedges and sage sprigs,
        to garnish

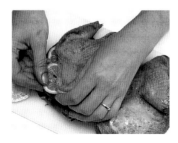

1 Place the pheasants, breast-side up, on a chopping board and cut them in half lengthways, using poultry shears or a sharp knife.

2 Grate the rind from half the lemon and thinly slice the other half. Place the lemon rind and half the chopped sage in a small bowl and mix well. Preheat the grill (broiler) or light the charcoal for a barbecue.

3 Loosen the skin on the breast and legs of the pheasants and push a little of the sage mixture under each. Tuck the lemon slices under the skin, then smooth the skin back firmly.

4 Place each half-pheasant under the grill or on a medium-hot barbecue rack and cook for 25–30 minutes, turning them once.

5 Meanwhile, place the shallots under the grill or on the barbecue and cook for 10–12 minutes, turning occasionally, until the skin is blackened. Peel off the skins, chop the flesh and mash it with the mustard and brandy or sherry. Stir in the crème fraîche, add the remaining sage and season to taste. Garnish the pheasants with lemon wedges and sage sprigs and serve with the sauce.

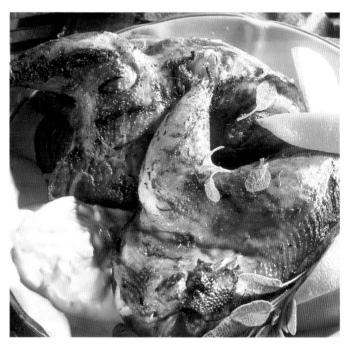

TURKEY PATTIES WITH LIME

MINCED TURKEY, DELICATELY FLAVOURED WITH LIME AND THYME, MAKES DELICIOUSLY LIGHT PATTIES, WHICH ARE IDEAL FOR EASY, MIDWEEK MEALS. SERVE THE PATTIES IN SPLIT AND TOASTED BUNS OR PIECES OF CRUSTY BREAD, WITH CHUTNEY, SALAD LEAVES AND CHUNKY FRIES.

SERVES SIX

INGREDIENTS
    675g/1½lb minced (ground) turkey
    1 small red onion, finely chopped
    grated rind and juice of 1 lime
    small handful of fresh thyme leaves
    15–30ml/1–2 tbsp olive oil
    salt and ground black pepper

VARIATIONS

• Minced (ground) chicken, lamb, pork or beef could be used instead of turkey in these patties.

• You could try chopped oregano, parsley or basil in place of the thyme, and lemon rind instead of lime.

1 Mix together the turkey, onion, lime rind and juice, thyme and seasoning. Cover and chill for up to 4 hours to allow the flavours to infuse (steep), then divide the mixture into six equal portions and shape into round patties.

2 Preheat a griddle pan. Brush the patties with oil, then cook them on the griddle for 10–12 minutes. Turn them over, brush with more oil and cook for 10–12 minutes on the second side, or until cooked through. Serve hot.

TEX-MEX BURGERS WITH LIME GUACAMOLE

MELT-IN-THE-MOUTH GUACAMOLE WITH ITS DISTINCTIVE FLAVOURS OF CHILLI, GARLIC AND LIME, IS THE PERFECT ACCOMPANIMENT TO THESE EASY TEX-MEX BURGERS. SERVE THE BURGERS IN WARMED CORN TORTILLAS FOR A FABULOUS HAND-HELD MEAL.

SERVES FOUR

INGREDIENTS

   500g/1¼lb lean minced
     (ground) beef
   1 small onion, finely chopped
   1 small green (bell) pepper, seeded
     and finely chopped
   1 garlic clove, crushed
   oil, for brushing
   4 fresh tortillas
   salt and ground black pepper
   chopped fresh coriander (cilantro),
     to garnish
   salad, to serve
For the lime guacamole
   2 ripe avocados
   1 garlic clove, crushed
   2 tomatoes, chopped
   juice of 1 lime
   ½ green chilli, seeded and chopped
   30ml/2 tbsp chopped fresh coriander

1 Put the minced beef, onion, green pepper and garlic in a bowl and mix well. Season with salt and pepper.

2 Using your hands, shape the mixture into four large, round burgers and brush them with oil.

COOK'S TIP
The guacamole should be made not more than an hour before it is needed, or it will start to brown. If it has to be left to stand, sprinkle a little extra lime juice over the top and stir just before serving.

3 To make the lime guacamole, cut the avocados in half, remove the stones (pits) and scoop out the flesh.

4 Put in a bowl and mash the avocado flesh roughly. Add the garlic, tomatoes, lime juice, chilli and coriander and mix well. Season with salt and pepper.

5 Cook the burgers on a medium hot barbecue or under the grill (broiler) for 10 minutes, turning once. Heat the tortillas on the barbecue or under the grill for 15 seconds each side and then place some guacamole in the middle and add a burger to each. Garnish with coriander and serve with salad.

Osso Buco with Gremolata

Slow-cooked veal in a rich sauce is served with a zesty gremolata of parsley, lemon and garlic. This rich and hearty dish from Milan is excellent served with boiled rice.

SERVES FOUR

INGREDIENTS

    30ml/2 tbsp plain
      (all-purpose) flour
    4 pieces of osso buco (veal shanks)
    2 small onions
    30ml/2 tbsp olive oil
    1 large celery stick, finely chopped
    1 carrot, finely chopped
    2 garlic cloves, finely chopped
    400g/14oz can chopped tomatoes
    300ml/½ pint/1¼ cups dry
      white wine
    300ml/½ pint/1¼ cups chicken or
      veal stock
    1 strip of thinly pared lemon rind
    2 bay leaves, plus extra to garnish
    salt and ground black pepper
For the gremolata
    30ml/2 tbsp finely chopped fresh flat
      leaf parsley
    finely grated rind of 1 lemon
    1 garlic clove, finely chopped

1 Preheat the oven to 160°C/325°F/ Gas 3. Season the flour with salt and pepper and spread it out in a shallow dish. Add the pieces of osso buco and turn them in the flour until evenly coated. Shake off any excess flour.

2 Slice one of the onions and separate it into rings. Heat the olive oil in a large flameproof casserole, then add the veal pieces and the onion rings. Cook over a medium heat until the veal is browned on both sides. Remove the pieces of veal with tongs and set aside on kitchen paper to drain.

3 Chop the remaining onion and add it to the casserole with the celery, carrot and garlic. Stir, scraping the base of the casserole to incorporate the cooking juices and sediment. Cook over a low heat, stirring frequently, for about 5 minutes, or until the vegetables begin to soften slightly.

4 Add the chopped tomatoes, wine, stock, lemon rind and bay leaves, then season to taste with salt and pepper. Bring to the boil, stirring constantly. Return the veal to the casserole and coat with the sauce. Cover and cook in the oven for 2 hours, or until the veal feels tender when pierced with a fork.

5 To make the gremolata, mix together the chopped parsley, lemon rind and garlic in a small bowl.

6 Remove the casserole from the oven and lift out and discard the strip of lemon rind and the bay leaves. Taste the sauce and adjust the seasoning, if necessary. Sprinkle with the gremolata, garnish with extra bay leaves and serve the osso buco immediately.

VEAL ESCALOPES WITH LEMON

POPULAR IN ITALIAN RESTAURANTS, THIS DISH IS VERY EASY TO MAKE AT HOME. WHITE VERMOUTH AND LEMON JUICE MAKE THE PERFECT SAUCE FOR THE DELICATELY FLAVOURED MEAT.

SERVES FOUR

INGREDIENTS

4 veal escalopes (scallops)
30–45ml/2–3 tbsp plain
  (all-purpose) flour
50g/2oz/¼ cup butter
60ml/4 tbsp olive oil
60ml/4 tbsp Italian dry white
  vermouth or dry white wine
45ml/3 tbsp lemon juice
salt and ground black pepper
lemon wedges, grated lemon rind and
  fresh parsley, to garnish
salad, to serve

VARIATIONS

• Use skinless boneless chicken breast portions instead of the veal. If they are thick, cut them in half before pounding.
• Substitute thin slices of pork fillet (tenderloin) for the veal and use orange juice instead of lemon.

1 Put each veal escalope between two sheets of clear film (plastic wrap) and pound with the side of a rolling pin or the smooth side of a meat mallet until very thin.

2 Cut the pounded escalopes in half or quarters. Season the flour with a little salt and pepper and use it to coat escalopes on both sides. Shake off any excess.

3 Melt the butter with half the oil in a large, heavy frying pan until sizzling. Add as many escalopes as the pan will hold. Cook over a medium to high heat for about 2 minutes on each side until lightly coloured. Remove with a spatula and keep hot. Add the remaining oil to the pan and cook the remaining veal escalopes in the same way.

4 Remove the pan from the heat and add the vermouth or wine and the lemon juice. Stir vigorously to mix well with the pan juices, then return the pan to the heat. Return all the veal escalopes to the pan.

5 Spoon the sauce over the veal. Shake the pan over a medium heat until the escalopes are coated in the sauce and heated through. Serve with a fresh salad, garnished with lemon wedges, lemon rind and sprinkled with parsley.

CIDER-GLAZED HAM WITH CLEMENTINE AND CRANBERRY SAUCE

THIS WONDERFUL CURED HAM GLAZED WITH CIDER IS TRADITIONALLY SERVED WITH CRANBERRY SAUCE FLAVOURED WITH CLEMENTINES, AND IS IDEAL FOR ANY SPECIAL OCCASION MEAL. THERE ARE MANY DIFFERENT VARIETIES OF CIDER AVAILABLE — CHOOSE A DRY ONE FOR A LIGHT, CRISP TASTE.

SERVES EIGHT TO TEN

INGREDIENTS

2kg/4½ lb middle gammon (cured ham) joint
1 large or 2 small onions
about 30 whole cloves
3 bay leaves
10 black peppercorns
1.3 litres/2¼ pints/5⅔ cups medium-dry (hard) cider
45ml/3 tbsp soft light brown sugar
bunch of fresh flat leaf parsley, to garnish (optional)
For the cranberry sauce
350g/12oz/3 cups cranberries
175g/6oz/¾ cup soft light brown sugar
grated rind and juice of 2 clementines
30ml/2 tbsp port

1 Weigh the ham and calculate the cooking time, allowing 20 minutes per 450g/1lb, then place it in a flameproof casserole or pan. Stud the onion or onions with 5–10 of the cloves and add to the casserole or pan with the bay leaves and peppercorns.

2 Add 1.2 litres/2 pints/5 cups of the cider and enough water to just cover the ham. Heat until simmering and then carefully skim off the scum that rises to the surface, using a large spoon or ladle. Start timing the cooking from the moment the stock begins to simmer.

3 Cover with a lid or foil, and simmer gently for the calculated time. Towards the end of the cooking time, preheat the oven to 220°C/425°F/Gas 7.

4 Heat the sugar and remaining cider in a pan, stirring until the sugar has completely dissolved.

5 Simmer for 5 minutes to make a dark, sticky glaze. Remove the pan from the heat and set aside to cool for about 5 minutes.

COOK'S TIPS
• A large stock pot or preserving pan can be used for cooking the ham.
• Leave the ham until it is cool enough to handle before removing the hard rind. Snip off the string using a sharp knife or scissors, then carefully slice off the rind, leaving a thin, even layer of fat. Use a narrow-bladed, sharp knife for the best results – a filleting knife, or a long, slim ham knife would be ideal.

6 Lift out the ham. Slice off the rind to leave a thin layer of fat, then score the fat into a diamond pattern. Place the ham in a roasting pan.

7 Press a clove into the centre of each diamond. Spoon over the glaze and bake for 25 minutes, or until golden.

8 Gently simmer the sauce ingredients in a pan for about 20 minutes, stirring frequently. Serve the ham with the sauce, garnished with parsley, if you like.

LOIN OF PORK WITH CASHEW NUT AND ORANGE STUFFING

THE ORANGES AND CASHEW NUTS ADD CONTRASTING FLAVOURS AND TEXTURES TO THIS DELICIOUS STUFFING, AND COMBINE WELL WITH THE BROWN RICE.

SERVES SIX

INGREDIENTS
 1.3–1.6kg/3–3½lb boned pork loin
 15ml/1 tbsp plain (all-purpose) flour
 300ml/½ pint/1¼ cups dry
  white wine
 salt and ground black pepper
 fresh rosemary sprigs and orange
  slices, to garnish
For the stuffing
 25g/1oz/2 tbsp butter
 1 small onion, finely chopped
 75g/3oz/scant ½ cup brown basmati
  rice, soaked for 30 minutes
 350ml/12fl oz/scant 1½ cups
  chicken stock
 50g/2oz/⅓ cup cashew nuts
 1 orange
 50g/2oz/⅓ cup sultanas
  (golden raisins)

1 First prepare the stuffing. Melt the butter in a frying pan and cook the onion for 2–3 minutes until softened. Drain the rice, add it to the pan and cook for 1 minute, then pour in the stock and bring to the boil. Stir, then lower the heat, cover and simmer for 35 minutes, or until the rice is tender and the liquid has been absorbed. Preheat the oven to 220°C/425°F/Gas 7.

2 Meanwhile, open out the pork loin and cut two lengthways slits through the meat, but without cutting right through. Turn the meat over. Remove any excess fat, but leave a good layer.

3 Spread out the cashew nuts for the stuffing in a roasting pan and roast for 2–4 minutes, or until golden. Set aside to cool, then chop coarsely in a food processor or blender. Leave the oven switched on.

4 Grate 5ml/1 tsp of the orange rind into a bowl. Using a sharp knife, cut a thin slice of peel and pith from each end of the orange. Place the orange cut side down on a plate and cut off the peel and pith in strips. Remove any remaining pith. Cut out each segment leaving the membrane behind. Squeeze the remaining juice from the membrane. Chop the segments coarsely.

5 Add the chopped orange segments to the cooked rice and stir in the orange rind, roast cashew nuts and sultanas. Season well with salt and pepper, then stir in 15–30ml/1–2 tbsp of the reserved orange juice. Do not worry if the rice does not bind – it should have a fairly loose consistency.

6 Spread a generous layer of stuffing along the centre of the pork. Put any leftover stuffing in a heatproof bowl.

7 Roll up the loin and firmly tie with kitchen string. Rub salt and pepper into the meat and place it in a roasting pan. Cook for 15 minutes, then lower the oven temperature to 180°C/350°F/Gas 4. Roast for 2–2¼ hours more, or until the juices run clear. Heat any extra stuffing in the covered bowl alongside the meat for the final 15 minutes.

8 Transfer the meat to a serving plate and keep warm. Stir the flour into the juices remaining in the roasting pan, cook for 1 minute, then stir in the white wine. Bring to the boil, stirring until thickened, then strain into a gravy boat.

9 Remove the string from the meat before carving. Stud the pork with the rosemary and garnish with the orange slices. Serve with the gravy and any extra stuffing.

SPICY VENISON CASSEROLE WITH ORANGES AND CRANBERRIES

LOW IN FAT BUT HIGH IN FLAVOUR, VENISON IS AN EXCELLENT CHOICE FOR HEALTHY, YET RICH, CASSEROLES. CRANBERRIES AND ORANGE BRING A FESTIVE FRUITINESS TO THIS SPICY RECIPE. IT IS DELICIOUS SERVED WITH SMALL BAKED POTATOES AND GREEN VEGETABLES.

2 Meanwhile, mix the ground allspice with the flour and either spread the mixture out on a large plate or place in a large plastic bag. Toss a few pieces of venison at a time (to prevent them from becoming soggy) in the flour mixture until they are all lightly coated.

3 When the onion and celery are softened, remove from the casserole using a slotted spoon and set aside. Add the venison pieces to the casserole in batches and cook until browned and sealed on all sides.

4 Add the cranberries, orange rind and juice to the casserole, pour in the beef or venison stock, and stir well. Return the vegetables and all the venison to the casserole and heat until simmering, then cover tightly and reduce the heat. Simmer, stirring occasionally, for about 45 minutes, or until the meat is tender.

5 Season the venison casserole to taste with salt and pepper before serving.

VARIATIONS
• Farmed venison is increasingly easy to find and is available from good butchers and many supermarkets. It makes a rich stew, but lean pork or braising steak could be used in place of the venison.
• You could replace the cranberries with pitted and halved ready-to-eat prunes and, for an extra rich flavour, use stout instead of half the meat stock.

SERVES FOUR

INGREDIENTS
  30ml/2 tbsp olive oil
  1 onion, chopped
  2 celery sticks, sliced
  10ml/2 tsp ground allspice
  15ml/1 tbsp plain
   (all-purpose) flour
  675g/1½lb stewing venison, cubed
  225g/8oz fresh or frozen cranberries
  grated rind and juice of 1 orange
  900ml/1½ pints/3¾ cups beef or
   venison stock
  salt and ground black pepper

1 Heat the olive oil in a flameproof casserole. Add the onion and celery and cook for 5 minutes until softened.

LAMB TAGINE WITH ARTICHOKES AND PRESERVED LEMON

A TAGINE IS A SLOWLY SIMMERED STEW TRADITIONALLY COOKED IN AN EARTHENWARE POT CALLED A TAGINE. IN THIS RECIPE, THE MEAT IS MARINATED IN A BLEND OF FLAVOURS BEFORE COOKING, THEN PRESERVED LEMON AND ARTICHOKES ARE ADDED TO PROVIDE THEIR DISTINCTIVE FLAVOURS.

SERVES FOUR TO SIX

INGREDIENTS
675g/1½ lb leg of lamb, trimmed and
    cut into cubes
2 onions, very finely chopped
2 garlic cloves, crushed
60ml/4 tbsp chopped fresh parsley
60ml/4 tbsp chopped fresh
    coriander (cilantro)
good pinch of ground ginger
5ml/1 tsp ground cumin
90ml/6 tbsp olive oil
350–400ml/12–14fl oz/1½–1⅔ cups
    water or stock
1 preserved lemon
400g/14oz can artichoke hearts,
    drained and halved
15ml/1 tbsp chopped fresh mint,
    plus extra sprigs to garnish
1 egg, beaten (optional)
salt and ground black pepper
couscous, to serve

3 Rinse the preserved lemon under cold water, discard the flesh and cut the peel into pieces. Stir into the meat and simmer for a further 15 minutes, then add the artichoke hearts and mint.

4 Simmer for a few minutes. If you wish to thicken the sauce, remove the pan from the heat and stir in some or all of the egg. Garnish with mint and serve with couscous.

1 Place the meat in a shallow dish. Mix together the onions, garlic, parsley, coriander, ginger, cumin, seasoning and olive oil. Stir into the meat, cover with clear film (plastic wrap) and set aside to marinate for 3–4 hours or overnight.

2 Heat a large, heavy pan and add the meat and marinade. Cook over a high heat for 5–6 minutes, then stir in enough water or stock to just cover it. Bring to the boil, cover and simmer for 45–60 minutes, or until the meat is just tender.

FISH AND SHELLFISH

Pan-fried fish garnished with slices or wedges of lemon is almost a culinary cliché — although no less delicious for that — and is a clear indication of the perfect affinity between fish and citrus fruits. Freshly squeezed juice makes tangy marinades, and including slices of lemon, lime or orange in oven-baked fish parcels is one of the easiest ways to add extra flavour and piquancy. Adding fruit, rind or juice to fish and shellfish stews and curries balances both richness and spiciness. Fish is a popular choice for the health-conscious, and cooking it with citrus fruits is the ideal way of preventing its delicate flesh from drying out without the addition of oil, butter or other fats.

PAPER-WRAPPED AND STEAMED RED SNAPPER

THIS JAPANESE RECIPE USES AN ORIGAMI PACKET TO SEAL IN THE FLAVOURS OF ASPARAGUS, SPRING ONIONS AND LIME. YOU COULD MAKE A SIMPLER VERSION BY FOLDING THE BAKING PARCHMENT IN HALF LENGTHWAYS AND DOUBLE FOLDING THE THREE OPEN EDGES TO SEAL.

SERVES FOUR

INGREDIENTS

4 small red snapper fillets, no greater
  than 18 × 6cm/7 × 2½in each
8 asparagus spears, hard
  ends discarded
4 spring onions (scallions)
60ml/4 tbsp sake
grated rind of ½ lime
½ lime, thinly sliced
salt
5ml/1 tsp shoyu, to serve (optional)

1 Lightly sprinkle the red snapper fillets with salt on both sides and leave in the refrigerator for 20 minutes. Preheat the oven to 180°C/350°F/Gas 4.

2 To make the origami parcels, cut out rectangles of baking parchment measuring about 38 × 30cm/15 × 12in. Use two pieces for each fish for extra thickness. Lay them out on a work surface. Fold up one-third of the paper and turn back 1cm/½in from one end to make a flap.

3 Fold 1cm/½in in from the other end to make another flap. Fold the top edge down to fold over the first flap, interlock the two flaps to form a long rectangle.

4 At each end, fold the top corners down diagonally, then fold the bottom corners up to meet the opposite folded edge to make a triangle. Press flat. Repeat to make four parcels.

5 Cut 2.5cm/1in from the tip of the asparagus. Slice the asparagus stems and spring onions diagonally into ovals. Par-boil the tips for 1 minute in lightly salted water and drain. Set aside.

6 Carefully open the parcels. Place the spring onion and asparagus slices inside. Sprinkle with a little salt, top with the fish, add more salt and some sake, then add the grated lime rind. Refold the parcels.

7 Pour hot water into a deep roasting pan, fitted with a wire rack, to 1cm/½in below the rack. Place the parcels on the rack. Cook in the oven for 20 minutes. Check that the fish is opaque by carefully unfolding a parcel from one triangular side.

8 Transfer the parcels to plates. Unfold both triangular ends on the plate and lift open the middle a little. Insert a thin slice of lime and place two asparagus tips on top. Serve immediately, asking the guests to open their own parcels. A little shoyu can be added, if you like.

ASIAN FISH ᴇɴ PAPILLOTE

THE AROMATIC SMELL THAT WAFTS OUT OF THESE FISH PARCELS AS YOU OPEN THEM IS DELICIOUSLY TEMPTING. LIME IS INCLUDED IN THE ASIAN FLAVOURINGS, WHICH PERFECTLY COMPLEMENT THE SUBTLE TASTE OF SALMON.

SERVES FOUR

INGREDIENTS

- 2 courgettes (zucchini)
- 2 carrots
- 6 spring onions (scallions)
- 2.5cm/1in piece fresh root ginger, peeled
- 1 lime
- 2 garlic cloves, thinly sliced
- 30ml/2 tbsp Thai fish sauce
- 5–10ml/1–2 tsp clear sesame oil
- 4 salmon fillets, about 200g/ 7oz each
- ground black pepper
- rice, to serve

VARIATION

Thick fillets of hake, halibut, hoki and fresh or undyed smoked haddock and cod can all be used for this dish.

1 Slice the courgettes, carrots and spring onions into batons and set aside. Cut the root ginger into batons and put them in a bowl. Using a zester, pare the lime. Add the pared rind and garlic to the ginger. Squeeze the lime juice.

2 Place the fish sauce into a bowl and stir in the lime juice and sesame oil.

3 Preheat the oven to 220°C/425°F/ Gas 7. Cut out four rounds of baking parchment, with a diameter of 40cm/ 16in. Season the fish with pepper. Lay a fillet on one side of each paper round, about 3cm/1¼in off centre. Sprinkle a quarter of the ginger mixture over each and pile a quarter of the vegetable batons on top. Spoon a quarter of the Thai fish sauce mixture over the top.

4 Fold the bare side of the baking parchment over the salmon and roll the edges of the parchment over to seal each parcel very tightly.

5 Place the salmon parcels on a baking sheet and cook for about 10 minutes, depending on the thickness of the fillets. Put the parcels on plates and serve with rice.

GREEN FISH CURRY

ANY FIRM-FLESHED FISH CAN BE USED FOR THIS DELICIOUS CURRY, WHICH GAINS ITS RICH FLAVOUR FROM A MIXTURE OF FRESH HERBS, SPICES AND LIME. EXOTIC FISH, SUCH AS MAHI-MAHI, HOKI OR SWORDFISH, OR HUMBLER FISH, SUCH AS COLEY, ALL WORK WELL.

SERVES FOUR

INGREDIENTS

4 garlic cloves, coarsely chopped
5cm/2in piece fresh root ginger,
   peeled and coarsely chopped
2 fresh green chillies, seeded and
   coarsely chopped
grated rind and juice of 1 lime
5–10ml/1–2 tsp shrimp
   paste (optional)
5ml/1 tsp coriander seeds
5ml/1 tsp Chinese
   five-spice powder
75ml/6 tbsp sesame oil
2 red onions, finely chopped
900g/2lb hoki fillets, skinned
400ml/14fl oz/1⅔ cups canned
   coconut milk
45ml/3 tbsp Thai fish sauce
50g/2oz/2 cups fresh coriander
   (cilantro) leaves
50g/2oz/2 cups fresh basil leaves
6 spring onions (scallions),
   coarsely chopped
150ml/¼ pint/⅔ cup sunflower or
   groundnut (peanut) oil
sliced fresh green chilli and finely
   chopped fresh coriander (cilantro),
   to garnish
cooked basmati or Thai fragrant rice
   and lime wedges, to serve

1 First make the curry paste. Combine the garlic, ginger, chillies, lime juice and shrimp paste, if using, in a food processor. Add the spices, with half the sesame oil. Process to a paste, then spoon into a bowl, cover and set aside.

2 Heat a wok or large, shallow pan, and pour in the remaining sesame oil. When it is hot, stir-fry the red onions over a high heat for 2 minutes. Add the fish and stir-fry for 1–2 minutes to seal the fillets on all sides.

3 Lift out the red onions and fish with a slotted spoon and put them on a plate. Add the curry paste to the wok or pan and fry for 1 minute, stirring constantly.

4 Return the hoki fillets and onions to the pan, pour in the coconut milk and bring to the boil. Lower the heat, add the Thai fish sauce and simmer gently for 5–7 minutes until the fish is cooked through and tender.

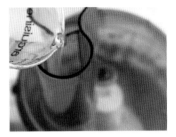

5 Meanwhile, process the herbs, spring onions, lime rind and sunflower or groundnut oil to a coarse paste in a food processor. Stir into the fish curry. Garnish with chilli and coriander and serve with rice and lime wedges.

SEAFOOD LAKSA

A LAKSA IS A MALAYSIAN STEW OF FISH, POULTRY, MEAT OR VEGETABLES WITH NOODLES. AUTHENTIC LAKSAS CONTAIN HOT FLAVOURINGS — SPICES AND FIERY CHILLIES, ACCENTUATED BY FRESH LIMES — BUT ARE COOLED BY THE COCONUT MILK AND THE NOODLES.

SERVES FOUR TO FIVE

INGREDIENTS

450g/1lb large raw prawns (shrimp)
  (about 20)
3 medium-hot fresh red
  chillies, seeded
4–5 garlic cloves
5ml/1 tsp mild paprika
10ml/2 tsp fermented shrimp paste
25ml/1½ tbsp chopped fresh
  root ginger
250g/9oz small red shallots
25g/1oz fresh coriander (cilantro)
  (preferably with roots)
45ml/3 tbsp groundnut (peanut) oil
5ml/1 tsp fennel seeds, crushed
2 fennel bulbs, cut into thin wedges
600ml/1 pint/2½ cups fish stock
300g/11oz thin vermicelli
  rice noodles
450ml/¾ pint/scant 2 cups
  coconut milk
juice of 1–2 limes
30–45ml/2–3 tbsp Thai fish sauce
450g/1lb firm white fish fillet
small bunch of fresh basil
2 spring onions (scallions), sliced

1 Peel the prawns if necessary. Make a shallow cut down the centre of the curved back of each prawn. Remove the black vein with the point of a cocktail stick (toothpick) or the tip of a knife. Rinse the prawns well.

2 Process the chillies, garlic, paprika, shrimp paste, ginger and two shallots to a paste in a blender or food processor. Remove the roots and stems from the coriander and add them to the paste; chop the leaves. Add 15ml/1 tbsp of the oil to the paste and process again.

3 Heat the remaining oil in a pan. Add the remaining shallots, the fennel seeds and fennel wedges. Cook until lightly browned, then add 45ml/3 tbsp of the paste and stir-fry for 1–2 minutes. Pour in the fish stock and bring to the boil, then simmer for 8–10 minutes.

4 Cook the noodles according to the packet instructions. Drain and set aside.

5 Add the coconut milk and the juice of 1 lime to the pan of shallots. Stir in 30ml/2 tbsp of the Thai fish sauce.

6 Bring to a simmer and taste, adding a little more spice paste, lime juice or fish sauce as necessary. Cut the fish into chunks and add to the pan. Cook for 2–3 minutes, then add the prawns and cook until they turn pink. Chop most of the basil and add to the pan with the reserved chopped coriander leaves.

7 Divide the noodles among four or five bowls, then ladle in the stew. Sprinkle with spring onions and the remaining whole basil leaves. Serve immediately.

VARIATION

This dish can also be made with any firm-fleshed white fish. Try monkfish, halibut or snapper.

FISH WITH SPINACH AND LIME

FRESH HERBS AND LIME WITH PIQUANT PAPRIKA MARINATE THE FISH IN THIS TASTY RECIPE. USE FRESH SPINACH, BOTH FOR FLAVOUR AND TEXTURE.

SERVES FOUR

INGREDIENTS

5 tomatoes
675g/1½lb white fish, such as
   haddock, cod, sea bass or monkfish
sunflower oil, for frying
500g/1¼lb potatoes, sliced
1 onion, chopped
1–2 garlic cloves, crushed
375g/13oz fresh spinach, chopped
lime wedges, to garnish
For the charmoula
6 spring onions (scallions), chopped
10ml/2 tsp fresh thyme
60ml/4 tbsp chopped fresh parsley
30ml/2 tbsp chopped fresh
   coriander (cilantro)
10ml/2 tsp paprika
generous pinch of cayenne pepper
60ml/4 tbsp olive oil
grated rind of 1 lime and 60ml/
   4 tbsp lime juice
salt

1 Plunge the tomatoes into boiling water for 30 seconds, then refresh in cold water. Peel off the skins, remove the seeds and chop the flesh. Cut the fish into pieces, discarding any skin and bones, and place in a shallow dish.

2 Blend together the ingredients for the charmoula and season well with salt. Pour over the fish, stir to mix and leave in a cool place, covered with clear film (plastic wrap), for 2–4 hours.

3 Heat about 5mm/¼in oil in a large, heavy pan and fry the potatoes until cooked through and golden. Drain on kitchen paper.

4 Pour off all but 15ml/1 tbsp of the oil and add the chopped onion, garlic and tomatoes. Cook over a low heat for 5–6 minutes, stirring occasionally, until the onion is soft. Place the potatoes on top and then pile the chopped spinach into the pan.

5 Place the pieces of fish on top of the spinach and pour over all the marinade. Cover the pan tightly and steam for 15–18 minutes. After about 8 minutes, carefully stir the contents of the pan, so that the fish at the top is distributed throughout the dish. Re-cover the pan and continue cooking, but check the contents occasionally – the dish is ready once the fish is tender and opaque and the spinach has wilted.

6 Serve immediately on individual serving plates, garnished with wedges of lime.

COD CARAMBA

LIME ADDS SHARPNESS TO THE FRESH FLAVOURS IN THIS COLOURFUL MEXICAN DISH, WITH ITS
CONTRASTING CRUNCHY TOPPING AND TENDER FISH FILLING.

SERVES FOUR TO SIX

INGREDIENTS
2 tomatoes
450g/1lb cod fillets
225g/8oz smoked cod fillets
300ml/½ pint/1¼ cups fish stock
50g/2oz/¼ cup butter
1 onion, sliced
2 garlic cloves, crushed
1 green (bell) pepper, seeded
   and diced
1 red (bell) pepper, seeded and diced
2 courgettes (zucchini), diced
115g/4oz/⅔ cup drained canned or
   thawed frozen corn kernels
juice of 1 lime
Tabasco sauce
salt, ground black pepper and
   cayenne pepper
For the topping
   75g/3oz tortilla chips
   50g/2oz/½ cup grated
      Cheddar cheese
   coriander (cilantro) sprigs, to garnish
   lime wedges, to serve

1 Plunge the tomatoes into boiling water for 30 seconds, then refresh in cold water. Peel off the skins, remove the seeds and chop the flesh. Set aside.

2 Lay the fish in a shallow pan and pour over the fish stock. Bring to the boil, lower the heat, cover and poach for about 8 minutes, or until the flesh flakes easily when tested with the tip of a sharp knife. Leave to cool slightly, then remove the skin and separate the flesh into large flakes. Keep hot.

3 Melt the butter in a pan, add the onion and garlic and cook over a low heat, stirring frequently, for 5 minutes until soft. Add the diced peppers, stir and cook for 2 minutes. Stir in the courgettes and cook for 3 minutes more, until the vegetables are tender.

4 Stir in the corn and tomatoes, then add lime juice and Tabasco sauce to taste. Season with salt, black pepper and cayenne. Cook for a couple of minutes to heat the corn and tomatoes, then stir in the fish and transfer to a dish that can safely be used under the grill (broiler).

VARIATION
This dish can also be made with other white fish such as haddock.

5 Preheat the grill. Make the topping by crushing the tortilla chips with a rolling pin, then mix in the cheese. Add cayenne pepper to taste and sprinkle over the fish. Place the dish under the grill until the topping is crisp and brown. Garnish with coriander sprigs and lime wedges and serve immediately.

Thai Prawn Salad with Garlic Dressing and Frizzled Shallots

In this intensely flavoured salad, sweet prawns and fresh mango are partnered with a sweet-sour lime and garlic dressing accentuated with the hot taste of chilli. The crisp frizzled shallots are a traditional addition to Thai salads.

SERVES FOUR TO SIX

INGREDIENTS
    675g/1½lb medium-size raw
        prawns (shrimp)
    finely shredded rind of 1 lime
    ½ fresh red chilli, seeded and
        finely chopped
    30ml/2 tbsp olive oil, plus extra
        for brushing
    1 ripe but firm mango
    2 carrots, cut into long,
        thin shreds
    10cm/4in piece cucumber, sliced
    1 small red onion, halved and
        thinly sliced
    a few sprigs of fresh
        coriander (cilantro)
    a few sprigs of fresh mint
    45ml/3 tbsp roasted peanuts,
        coarsely chopped
    4 large shallots, thinly sliced and
        fried until crisp in 30ml/2 tbsp
        groundnut (peanut) oil
    salt and ground black pepper
For the dressing
    1 large garlic clove, chopped
    10–15ml/2–3 tsp caster
        (superfine) sugar
    juice of 2 limes
    15–30ml/1–2 tbsp Thai fish sauce
    1 fresh red chilli, seeded
    5–10ml/1–2 tsp light rice vinegar

1 Peel the prawns and remove the heads, but leave the tails intact. Make a shallow cut down the centre of the curved back of each prawn. Pull out the black vein with the point of a cocktail stick (toothpick) or the tip of the knife, then rinse the prawns thoroughly in cold water.

COOK'S TIP
Removing the vein that runs along the back of prawns (shrimp) is to prevent it from spoiling the flavour. It is not toxic or dangerous.

2 Place the prawns in a glass or china dish and add the lime rind and chilli. Season with salt and pepper and spoon the oil over them. Toss to mix, cover with clear film (plastic wrap) and leave to marinate for 30–40 minutes.

3 To make the dressing, place the chopped garlic in a mortar with 10ml/2 tsp caster sugar and pound with a pestle until smooth, then gradually work in the juice of 1½ limes and about 15ml/1 tbsp of the Thai fish sauce.

4 Transfer the dressing to a small jug (pitcher). Finely chop half the red chilli and add it to the dressing. Taste the dressing and add more sugar, lime juice, Thai fish sauce and rice vinegar to taste.

5 Cut the mango in two either side of the stone (pit). Trim any flesh from the stone. Peel the remaining pieces and cut the flesh into very fine strips.

6 Put the mango, carrots, cucumber and onion and half the dressing in a large bowl and toss thoroughly to mix. Arrange the salad on individual plates or in bowls.

7 Heat a ridged, cast-iron griddle pan or heavy frying pan until very hot. Brush with a little oil, then sear the prawns for 2–3 minutes on each side, until they turn pink and are patched with brown on the outside. Arrange the prawns on the salads.

8 Sprinkle the remaining dressing over the salads and then sprinkle with the sprigs of coriander and mint. Finely shred the remaining chilli and sprinkle it over the salads with the peanuts and crisp-fried shallots. Serve immediately.

SCOTTISH SALMON WITH HERB BUTTER

COOKING SALMON IN A PARCEL SEALS IN ALL THOSE LOVELY FLAVOURS AND JUICES. IT IS IDEAL WHEN USING A SUBTLE DILL AND LEMON BUTTER THAT IMPARTS A DELICATE FRAGRANCE TO THE FISH.

2 Spoon the butter on to a small piece of baking parchment and then roll up, smoothing with your hands into a sausage shape. Twist the ends tightly, wrap in clear film (plastic wrap) and put in the freezer for 20 minutes until firm.

3 Meanwhile, preheat the oven to 190°C/375°F/Gas 5. Cut out four squares of foil large enough to encase the salmon steaks, and grease lightly. Place a salmon steak in the centre of each one.

SERVES FOUR

INGREDIENTS
   50g/2oz/¼ cup butter, softened
   finely grated rind of ½ small lemon
   15ml/1 tbsp lemon juice
   15ml/1 tbsp chopped fresh dill
   4 salmon steaks
   2 lemon slices, halved
   4 fresh dill sprigs
   salt and ground black pepper
   new potatoes and sugar snap peas,
     to serve

COOK'S TIP
Other fresh herbs could be used to flavour the butter – try mint, fennel fronds, lemon balm, parsley or oregano instead of the dill.

1 Place the butter, grated lemon rind, lemon juice and chopped dill in a small bowl, then season to taste with salt and plenty of black pepper. Mix together with a fork until thoroughly blended and smooth.

4 Remove the butter from the freezer and slice into eight rounds. Place two rounds on top of each salmon steak with a halved lemon slice in the centre and a sprig of dill on top. Lift up the edges of the foil and firmly crinkle them together until well sealed.

5 Lift the parcels on to a baking sheet and bake for about 20 minutes. When cooked, place the unopened parcels on warmed plates. Open the parcels and slide the fish and its juices on to the plates. Serve immediately.

PAN-FRIED RED MULLET <u>WITH</u> CITRUS

RED MULLET IS POPULAR ALL OVER THE MEDITERRANEAN. THIS ITALIAN RECIPE COMBINES IT WITH
ORANGES AND LEMONS, WHICH GROW IN ABUNDANCE THERE.

SERVES FOUR

INGREDIENTS

2 oranges, such as Navelina
4 red mullet or snapper, about
    225g/8oz each, filleted
90ml/6 tbsp olive oil
10 black peppercorns, crushed
1 lemon
30ml/2 tbsp plain
    (all-purpose) flour
15g/½oz/1 tbsp butter
2 drained canned anchovies,
    chopped
60ml/4 tbsp shredded fresh basil
salt and ground black pepper

1 Using a sharp knife, cut the peel and pith from one of the oranges, then slice the flesh into rounds. Squeeze the juice from the other orange into a small bowl, cover and set aside.

4 Carefully lift the fish out of the marinade, and pat dry with kitchen paper. Reserve the marinade and orange slices. Season the fish on both sides with salt and pepper, then dust lightly with flour.

5 Heat 45ml/3 tbsp of the marinade in a frying pan. Add the fish and cook for 2 minutes on each side. Remove from the pan and keep warm. Discard the marinade that is left in the pan.

6 Melt the butter in the pan with any of the remaining original marinade. Add the anchovies and cook over a low heat until completely softened.

7 Stir in the orange and lemon juice, then check and adjust the seasoning if necessary. Simmer until the sauce has slightly reduced. Stir in the basil. Pour the sauce over the fish, garnish with the reserved orange slices and the lemon slices, and serve immediately.

2 Place the fish fillets in a shallow dish in a single layer. Pour over the olive oil and sprinkle with the crushed black peppercorns. Lay the orange slices on top of the fish. Cover the dish and leave to marinate in the refrigerator for at least 4 hours.

3 Halve the lemon. Cut the skin and pith from one half using a small sharp knife and slice thinly and reserve. Squeeze the juice from the other half.

VARIATION

If you prefer, use other fish fillets for this dish, such as lemon sole, monkfish, haddock or hake.

SALMON FISHCAKES

THE SECRET OF A GOOD FISHCAKE IS TO MAKE IT WITH FRESHLY PREPARED FISH AND POTATOES, HOME-MADE BREADCRUMBS AND PLENTY OF INTERESTING FLAVOURINGS — WHOLEGRAIN MUSTARD, FRESH HERBS AND LEMON ARE THE PERFECT COMBINATION.

SERVES FOUR

INGREDIENTS
  450g/1lb cooked salmon fillet
  450g/1lb freshly cooked
    potatoes, mashed
  25g/1oz/2 tbsp butter, melted
  10ml/2 tsp wholegrain mustard
  15ml/1 tbsp each chopped fresh dill
    and chopped fresh parsley
  grated rind and juice of ½ lemon
  15g/½oz/2 tbsp plain
    (all-purpose) flour
  1 egg, lightly beaten
  150g/5oz/2 cups dried breadcrumbs
  60ml/4 tbsp sunflower oil
  salt and ground black pepper
  rocket (arugula) leaves, chives and
    lemon wedges, to garnish

1 Flake the cooked salmon, discarding any skin and bones. Put the flesh in a bowl with the mashed potato, melted butter and wholegrain mustard, and mix well. Stir in the dill and parsley, lemon rind and juice. Season to taste with salt and pepper.

2 Divide the mixture into eight portions and shape each into a ball, then flatten into a thick disc. Coat the fishcakes first in flour, then in egg and finally in breadcrumbs, making sure that they are evenly coated.

3 Heat the oil in a frying pan until it is very hot. Fry the fishcakes in batches until golden brown and crisp all over. As each batch is ready, drain on kitchen paper and keep hot. Garnish with rocket leaves, chives and lemon wedges and serve immediately.

VARIATION
Almost any fresh white or hot-smoked fish is suitable; smoked cod and haddock are particularly good.

PAN-FRIED SOLE WITH LEMON

THE DELICATE FLAVOUR AND TEXTURE OF SOLE IS BROUGHT OUT IN THIS SIMPLE, CLASSIC RECIPE USING TART CAPERS AND LEMON JUICE. LEMON SOLE IS USED HERE BECAUSE IT IS EASIER TO OBTAIN — AND LESS EXPENSIVE — THAN DOVER SOLE.

SERVES TWO

INGREDIENTS
    30–45ml/2–3 tbsp plain
      (all-purpose) flour
    4 lemon sole fillets
    45ml/3 tbsp olive oil
    50g/2oz/¼ cup butter
    60ml/4 tbsp lemon juice
    30ml/2 tbsp rinsed bottled capers
    salt and ground black pepper
    fresh flat leaf parsley and lemon
      wedges, to garnish

COOK'S TIP
It is important to cook the pan juices to the right colour after removing the fish. Too pale, and they will taste insipid, too dark, and they may taste bitter. Take great care not to be distracted at this point so that you can watch the colour of the juices change to a golden brown.

1 Season the flour with salt and pepper. Coat the fish evenly on both sides. Put the oil and half the butter in a large pan and heat until foaming. Add two sole fillets and fry over a medium heat for 2–3 minutes on each side.

2 Lift out the sole fillets with a spatula and place on a warmed serving platter. Keep hot. Fry the remaining sole fillets.

3 Remove the pan from the heat and add the lemon juice and remaining butter. Return to a high heat and stir until the juices are sizzling and are turning golden brown. Remove from the heat and stir in the capers.

4 Pour the pan juices over the sole and season. Garnish with the parsley and lemon wedges and serve immediately.

MONKFISH <u>WITH</u> CITRUS MARINADE

A MEATY FISH THAT KEEPS ITS SHAPE WELL, MONKFISH IS IDEAL FOR COOKING ON A BARBECUE OR GRILL. A TRIO OF CITRUS FRUITS IMPART THEIR DELICATE FLAVOURS TO PEPPERED MONKFISH FILLETS.

2 Turn and repeat on the other side, to remove the second fillet. Repeat on the second tail to produce four fillets in all. Lay the fillets out flat.

3 Cut two slices from each fruit and arrange them over two of the fillets. Add a few sprigs of thyme and season well. Finely grate the rind from the remaining fruit and sprinkle it over the fish.

4 Lay the other two fillets on top and tie them firmly at intervals, with fine cotton string. Place in a wide dish.

5 Squeeze the juice from the fruit, mix it with the oil, and season. Spoon over the fish. Cover and leave to marinate for 1 hour, turning and spooning the marinade over it occasionally.

SERVES FOUR

INGREDIENTS
  2 monkfish tails, about 350g/
    12oz each
  1 lime
  1 lemon
  2 Valencia or blood oranges
  handful of fresh thyme sprigs
  30ml/2 tbsp olive oil
  15ml/1 tbsp mixed peppercorns,
    coarsely crushed
  salt and ground black pepper

VARIATION
You can also use this marinade for monkfish kebabs.

1 Remove any skin or membrane from the monkfish tails. Cut carefully down one side of the backbone, sliding the knife between the bone and flesh, and remove the fillet on one side.

6 Drain the fish, pat dry with kitchen paper and sprinkle with the crushed peppercorns. Reserve the marinade. Cook the fish on a medium-hot barbecue, or under a grill (broiler), for about 20 minutes, basting with the marinade and turning occasionally.

GRILLED HALIBUT WITH SAUCE VIERGE

TOMATOES, CAPERS, ANCHOVIES, HERBS AND LEMON MAKE A VIBRANT SAUCE THAT IS PERFECT FOR HALIBUT, BUT IT IS ALSO SO VERSATILE IT WILL SUIT ANY THICK WHITE FISH FILLETS.

SERVES FOUR

INGREDIENTS

105ml/7 tbsp olive oil
2.5ml/½ tsp fennel seeds
2.5ml/½ tsp celery seeds
5ml/1 tsp mixed peppercorns
5ml/1 tsp fresh thyme
   leaves, chopped
5ml/1 tsp fresh rosemary
   leaves, chopped
5ml/1 tsp fresh oregano or marjoram
   leaves, chopped
675–800g/1½–1¾lb middle cut of
   halibut, about 3cm/1¼in thick, cut
   into four pieces
coarse sea salt
shredded lettuce and lemon wedges,
   to serve
For the sauce
2 tomatoes
105ml/7 tbsp extra virgin olive oil
juice of 1 lemon
1 garlic clove, finely chopped
5ml/1 tsp small capers
2 drained canned anchovy
   fillets, chopped
5ml/1 tsp chopped fresh chives
15ml/1 tbsp shredded fresh
   basil leaves
15ml/1 tbsp chopped fresh chervil

1 Plunge the tomatoes into boiling water for 30 seconds, then refresh in cold water. Peel off the skins, remove the seeds and dice the flesh. Set aside.

2 Heat a ridged griddle or preheat the grill (broiler) to high. Brush the griddle or grill pan with a little of the olive oil.

3 Meanwhile, mix the fennel and celery seeds with the peppercorns in a mortar. Crush with a pestle, and then stir in sea salt to taste. Spoon the mixture into a large, flat dish and stir in the herbs and the remaining olive oil.

VARIATION
Try turbot, brill and John Dory, or even humbler fish, like cod or haddock, with this sauce.

4 Add the halibut pieces to the olive oil and herb mixture, turning them to coat thoroughly, then arrange them with the dark skin uppermost on the oiled griddle or grill pan. Cook or grill (broil) for about 7 minutes, turning once, or until the fish is cooked through and the skin has browned.

5 Combine all the sauce ingredients, except the fresh herbs, in a pan and heat gently until warm but not hot. Stir in the chives, basil and chervil.

6 Place the halibut on four plates and spoon the sauce over the fish. Serve with the lettuce and lemon wedges.

SPICED FISH BARBECUED THAI-STYLE

THAI SPICES AND LIME FLAVOUR RED MULLET OR SNAPPER, WHICH IS THEN WRAPPED IN BANANA LEAVES AND COOKED ON THE BARBECUE. IT MAKES A TASTY AND COLOURFUL MAIN COURSE. HOWEVER, IF BANANA LEAVES ARE NOT AVAILABLE, USE A DOUBLE LAYER OF FOIL INSTEAD.

SERVES FOUR

INGREDIENTS
    4 red mullet or snapper, about
        350g/12oz each
    banana leaves
    1 lime
    1 garlic clove, thinly sliced
    2 spring onions (scallions),
        thinly sliced
    30ml/2 tbsp Thai red curry paste
    60ml/4 tbsp coconut milk

1 Scale the fish by holding the tail and scraping the scales away from the tail, using a knife. Slit the belly below the head and remove the guts. Rinse thoroughly under cold water.

4 Grate the rind and squeeze the juice from the remaining half-lime and mix with the curry paste and coconut milk. Spoon over the fish.

5 Wrap the leaves over the fish to enclose them completely. Tie firmly with kitchen string and cook on a medium-hot barbecue for about 15–20 minutes.

2 Cut several deep slashes in the side of each fish with a sharp knife. Place each fish on a layer of banana leaves.

3 Thinly slice half the lime and tuck the slices into the slashes in the fish, with slivers of garlic. Sprinkle the spring onions over the fish.

SEA BASS <u>WITH</u> CITRUS FRUIT

THIS BEAUTIFUL, STEELY GREY FISH HAS JUSTIFIABLY BECOME A FIRM FAVOURITE WITH BOTH RESTAURANT CHEFS AND HOME COOKS IN RECENT YEARS. IN THIS FRENCH RECIPE, ITS DELICATE FLAVOUR IS COMPLEMENTED BY CITRUS FRUITS AND FRUITY OLIVE OIL.

<u>SERVES SIX</u>

INGREDIENTS

1 small grapefruit
1 orange
1 lemon
1 sea bass, about 1.3kg/3lb, cleaned
   and scaled
6 fresh basil sprigs
6 fresh dill sprigs
plain (all-purpose) flour,
   for dusting
45ml/3 tbsp olive oil
4–6 shallots, peeled
   and halved
60ml/4 tbsp dry white wine
15g/½oz/1 tbsp butter
salt and ground black pepper

1 With a vegetable peeler, remove the rind from the citrus fruits. Cut into thin julienne strips, cover and set aside.

2 Using a sharp knife, cut a thin slice of pith from each end of the fruits. Place cut side down on a plate and cut off the pith. Cut out the segments from the grapefruit and orange leaving the membrane behind, and set aside for the garnish. Slice the lemon thickly.

3 Preheat the oven to 190°C/375°F/ Gas 5. Wipe the fish dry inside and out and season the cavity with salt and pepper. Make three diagonal slashes on each side. Reserve a few basil and dill sprigs for the garnish and fill the cavity with the remaining herbs, the lemon and half the julienne strips of rind.

4 Dust the fish lightly with flour. In a roasting pan or flameproof casserole large enough to hold the fish, heat 30ml/2 tbsp of the olive oil over a medium-high heat. Add the fish and cook for about 1 minute, or until the skin just crisps and browns on one side. Add the shallot halves.

5 Place the fish in the oven and bake for about 15 minutes, then carefully turn the fish over and stir the shallots. Drizzle the fish with the remaining oil and bake for a further 10–15 minutes, or until the flesh is opaque throughout.

6 Carefully transfer the fish to a heated serving dish and remove and discard the cavity stuffing. Keep warm.

7 Pour off any excess oil and add the wine and 30–45ml/2–3 tbsp of the fruit juices to the pan. Bring to the boil over a high heat, stirring constantly. Stir in the remaining strips of rind and boil for 2–3 minutes, then whisk in the butter. Spoon the shallots and sauce around the fish and garnish with the reserved dill and basil and fruit segments. Serve.

TARTS
AND PIES

Small wonder that so many triumphs of the pastry chef's art are tarts and pies with tangy citrus fillings that contrast superbly with the rich, crisp crusts. Eggs, soft cheeses, cream, nuts and chocolate are just some of the ingredients that partner deliciously with lemons, oranges and limes. Dishes range from international classics and family favourites such as lemon and almond tart and Key lime pie to contemporary dishes such as a citrus and peach leaf pie. There are also recipes that feature wonderful orange-flavoured pastry.

LEMON TARTLETS

THESE CLASSIC FRENCH TARTLETS ARE ONE OF THE MOST DELICIOUS DESSERTS THERE IS. A RICH LEMON CURD IS ENCASED IN A CRISP PASTRY CASE AND DECORATED WITH CARAMELIZED LEMON SLICES.

MAKES TWELVE

INGREDIENTS
6 eggs, beaten
350g/12oz/1½ cups caster
   (superfine) sugar
115g/4oz/½ cup butter
grated rind and juice of 4 lemons
icing (confectioners') sugar,
   for dusting (optional)
175ml/6fl oz/¾ cup double (heavy)
   cream, to serve
For the pastry
225g/8oz/2 cups plain
   (all-purpose) flour
115g/4oz/½ cup chilled
   butter, diced
30ml/2 tbsp icing (confectioners')
   sugar
1 egg, beaten
5ml/1 tsp vanilla extract (essence)
15ml/1 tbsp chilled water
For the topping
2 lemons, well-scrubbed
75ml/5 tbsp apricot jam

1 Preheat the oven to 200°C/400°F/ Gas 6. To make the pastry, sift the flour into a large mixing bowl. Using your fingertips, lightly rub the butter into the flour until the mixture resembles fine breadcrumbs. Add the icing sugar and stir well to mix.

2 Add the egg, vanilla essence and most of the chilled water, then work to a soft dough. Add a few more drops of water if necessary. Knead quickly and lightly, while still in the bowl, until a smooth dough forms.

3 Lightly butter 12 × 10cm/4in tartlet tins (muffin pans). Roll out the pastry on a lightly floured work surface to a thickness of 3mm/⅛in.

4 Using a 10cm/4in fluted pastry (cookie) cutter, cut out 12 rounds and press them into the tartlet tins. Prick the bases all over with a fork and then transfer the tins to a baking sheet.

5 Line the pastry cases with baking parchment and fill with baking beans. Bake the pastry cases for 10 minutes. Remove the paper and beans and set the tins aside while you make the filling.

6 Put the eggs, sugar and butter into a pan, and stir over a low heat until all the sugar has dissolved. Add the lemon rind and juice, and continue cooking, stirring constantly, until the lemon curd has thickened slightly.

7 Pour the lemon curd mixture into the pastry cases. Bake for 15 minutes, or until the curd filling is almost set.

8 Prepare the topping while the lemon tartlets are cooking. Cut the lemons into 12 slices, then cut the slices in half.

9 Push the jam through a fine sieve then transfer to a small pan and heat. Place two lemon slices in the centre of each tartlet, overlapping them if you wish. Lightly brush the top of the tartlet with the sieved jam, then put under the grill (broiler) and heat for 5 minutes, or until the top is caramelized and golden. Serve with cream, if you wish.

COOK'S TIP
If you are short of time, simply dust the top with icing (confectioners') sugar.

LEMON CURD TARTS

THESE TASTY LITTLE TARTS, FROM THE NORTH OF ENGLAND, HAVE A LIGHT CHEESE FILLING THAT SITS ON A TANGY LAYER OF LEMON CURD, ENCASED IN LIGHT-AS-AIR PASTRY. THEY ARE ESPECIALLY DELICIOUS IF YOU USE HOME-MADE LEMON CURD.

MAKES TWENTY-FOUR

INGREDIENTS

225g/8oz/1 cup curd
   (farmer's) cheese
2 eggs, beaten
75g/3oz/6 tbsp caster
   (superfine) sugar
5ml/1 tsp finely grated lemon rind
50g/2oz/¼ cup currants
60ml/4 tbsp lemon curd
crème fraîche, to serve

For the pastry

275g/10oz/2½ cups plain
   (all-purpose) flour
2.5ml/½ tsp salt
150g/5oz/10 tbsp chilled
   butter, diced
about 60ml/4 tbsp chilled water

1 To make the pastry, put the flour, salt and butter in a bowl. Rub the butter into the flour with your fingertips until the mixture resembles breadcrumbs. Mix in the water and knead lightly to form a firm dough. Wrap in clear film (plastic wrap) and chill for 30 minutes.

2 Preheat the oven to 180°C/350°F/ Gas 4. On a lightly floured surface, roll out the pastry thinly, then stamp out 24 rounds using a 7.5cm/3in plain pastry (cookie) cutter and use to line patty or tartlet tins (muffin pans). Chill in the refrigerator or set aside in a cool place until required.

3 Beat the curd cheese with the eggs, sugar and lemon rind. Add the currants and mix in. Place 2.5ml/½ tsp of the lemon curd in the base of each tartlet case. Spoon on the filling, flatten the tops and bake for 35–40 minutes, or until just turning golden.

4 Serve the tarts warm or cold, topped with crème fraîche.

CLASSIC LEMON TART

THIS IS ONE DISH WHERE THE COLOUR OF THE YOLKS MAKES A REAL DIFFERENCE TO THE COLOUR OF THE TART — THE YELLOWER THE BETTER. THIS SIMPLE TART CAN BE SERVED WARM OR CHILLED AND DECORATED WITH EXTRA LEMON RIND. IT IS VERY LEMONY, SO SERVE WITH CREAM OR ICE CREAM.

SERVES EIGHT

INGREDIENTS

150g/5oz/1¼ cups plain
  (all-purpose) flour, sifted
50g/2oz/½ cup hazelnuts, toasted
  and finely ground
175g/6oz/scant 1 cup caster
  (superfine) sugar
115g/4oz/½ cup chilled unsalted
  (sweet) butter, softened
4 eggs
finely grated rind of 2 lemons and
  at least 175ml/6fl oz/¾ cup
  lemon juice
150ml/¼ pint/⅔ cup double
  (heavy) cream
thinly pared and shredded lemon
  rind, to decorate

1 Mix together the flour, nuts and 25g/1oz/2 tbsp of the sugar, then gently work in the butter and, if necessary, 15–30ml/1–2 tbsp chilled water to make a soft dough. Chill for 10 minutes.

2 Roll out the dough on a floured work surface and use to line a 20cm/8in loose-based flan tin (tart pan). Ease the pastry into the tins with your fingers, if necessary. Chill for 20 minutes. Preheat the oven to 200°C/400°F/Gas 6.

3 Line the pastry case (pie shell) with baking parchment or foil, fill with baking beans, and bake for about 15 minutes. Remove the paper or foil and beans, and cook for a further 5–10 minutes, or until the base is crisp.

4 Beat together the eggs, lemon rind and juice, the remaining sugar and the cream until thoroughly blended. Pour into the pastry case and bake for about 30 minutes, or until just set.

LEMON AND ALMOND TART

THIS REFRESHING, TANGY TART HAS A RICH, CREAMY LEMON FILLING SET OFF BY A CARAMELIZED SUGAR TOPPING. SERVE WARM OR COLD WITH A SPOONFUL OF CRÈME FRAÎCHE OR NATURAL YOGURT.

SERVES EIGHT TO TEN

INGREDIENTS
  2 eggs
  50g/2oz/¼ cup golden caster
    (superfine) sugar
  finely grated rind and juice of
    4 lemons
  2.5ml/½ tsp vanilla
    essence (extract)
  50g/2oz/½ cup ground almonds
  120ml/4fl oz/½ cup single
    (light) cream
For the pastry
  225g/8oz/2 cups plain
    (all-purpose) flour
  75g/3oz/¾ cup icing (confectioners')
    sugar, plus extra for the topping
  130g/4½oz/9 tbsp butter, diced
  1 egg, beaten
  a pinch of salt

1 Preheat the oven to 180°C/350°F/ Gas 4. To make the pastry, sift together the flour and icing sugar into a large bowl. Add the diced butter and rub it in with your fingertips until the mixture resembles fine breadcrumbs. Add the beaten egg and salt, then mix to a smooth dough.

2 Turn out the dough on to a lightly floured work surface. Knead lightly and form into a smooth flat round. Wrap the dough in clear film (plastic wrap) and chill for at least 15 minutes.

VARIATION
Substitute 2–3 oranges for the lemons and ground hazelnuts for the almonds.

3 Roll out the dough thinly on a lightly floured surface and use to line a 23cm/ 9in loose-based flan tin (tart pan). Prick the pastry base with a fork and chill for about 15 minutes.

4 Line the pastry case (pie shell) with baking parchment or foil. Add baking beans to cover the base of the pastry case and bake blind for 10 minutes. Remove the parchment or foil and the beans and return the pastry case to the oven for 10 minutes more, or until it is light golden.

COOK'S TIPS
• Baking beans are used to prevent the base of the tart from bubbling up unevenly during cooking. Kitchenware stores sell ceramic and metal baking beans, though you can also use any dried beans such as kidney beans. Keep them especially for the purpose and retain after cooking as they are reusable.
• When buying vanilla essence (extract), look for the word pure on the label to be sure that it has not been diluted with syrup. Avoid artificial vanilla essence.

5 Meanwhile, make the filling. Beat the eggs with the sugar until the mixture leaves a thin ribbon trail on the surface. Gently stir in the lemon rind and juice, vanilla essence, almonds and cream.

6 Carefully pour the filling into the pastry case and level the surface. Bake for about 25 minutes, or until the filling is just set.

7 Heat the grill (broiler) to high. Sift a thick layer of icing sugar over the tart and grill (broil) until it caramelizes. Decorate the tart with a little extra sifted icing sugar before serving warm or cold.

FRESH ORANGE TART

GRATED ORANGE RIND GIVES THIS RICH SHORTCRUST PASTRY ITS WONDERFUL COLOUR AND FLAVOUR. A CREAMY CUSTARD FILLING AND FRESH ORANGE TOPPING TURN IT INTO A SOPHISTICATED DESSERT.

SERVES NINE

INGREDIENTS
    2 eggs, plus 2 egg yolks
    150g/5oz/¾ cup caster
      (superfine) sugar
    150ml/¼ pint/⅔ cup single
      (light) cream
    finely grated rind and juice of
      1 orange
    6–8 oranges
    fresh mint sprigs, to decorate
For the pastry
    175g/6oz/1½ cups plain
      (all-purpose) flour
    90g/3½oz/7 tbsp butter, diced
    15ml/1 tbsp caster
      (superfine) sugar
    finely grated rind of 1 orange
    1 egg yolk
    about 10ml/2 tsp orange juice

1 To make the pastry, sift the flour and rub in the butter. Add the sugar and orange rind and mix in. Beat the egg yolk with the orange juice, then add to the dry ingredients and mix to a dough.

2 Lightly knead the dough. Roll out and use to line a 20cm/8in square fluted tart tin (pan). Chill for 30 minutes.

3 Put a baking sheet in the oven and preheat to 200°C/400°F/Gas 6. Prick the pastry case (pie shell) all over with a fork and line with foil and baking beans. Place on the hot baking sheet and bake blind for 12 minutes. Remove the foil and beans and bake the pastry for a further 5 minutes.

4 Whisk the eggs, yolks and sugar in a bowl until foamy. Whisk in the cream, followed by the orange rind and juice. Pour into the pastry case and bake for 30–35 minutes, or until firm. Remove from the oven and leave to cool on a wire rack while still in the tin.

5 Using a sharp knife, cut a thin slice of peel and pith from both ends of each orange. Place cut-side down on a plate and cut off the peel and pith in strips. Remove any remaining pith. Cut out each segment leaving the membrane behind. Arrange the segments in rows on top of the tart. Chill until ready to serve, then carefully remove the tart from the tin and decorate with sprigs of fresh mint.

ORANGE SWEETHEART TART

STUNNING TO LOOK AT AND DELECTABLE TO EAT, THIS TART HAS A CRISP SHORTCRUST PASTRY CASE,
SPREAD WITH APRICOT JAM AND FILLED WITH FRANGIPANE, THEN TOPPED WITH TANGY ORANGE SLICES.

SERVES EIGHT

INGREDIENTS
  200g/7oz/1 cup sugar
  250ml/8fl oz/1 cup fresh orange
    juice, strained
  2 large navel oranges
  75g/3oz/½ cup blanched almonds
  50g/2oz/¼ cup butter
  1 egg
  15ml/1 tbsp plain (all-purpose) flour
  45ml/3 tbsp apricot jam
For the pastry
  175g/6oz/1½ cups plain
    (all-purpose) flour
  2.5ml/½ tsp salt
  75g/3oz/6 tbsp chilled butter, diced
  45ml/3 tbsp chilled water

1 To make the pastry, sift the flour and salt into a mixing bowl. Add the butter and rub in with your fingertips until the mixture resembles fine breadcrumbs. Sprinkle over the water and mix to a dough. Knead the dough on a lightly floured surface for a few seconds until smooth. Wrap the dough in clear film (plastic wrap) and chill for at least 30 minutes.

2 After the pastry has rested, roll it out on a floured surface to a thickness of about 5mm/¼in. Use to line a 20cm/8in heart-shaped tart tin (pan). Trim the pastry edges and chill again for a further 30 minutes.

3 Preheat the oven to 200°C/400°F/ Gas 6, with a baking sheet placed in the centre. Line the pastry case (pie shell) with baking parchment or foil and fill with baking beans. Bake blind for 10 minutes. Remove the parchment or foil and beans and cook for 10 minutes more, or until it is light and golden.

4 Put 150g/5oz/¾ cup of the sugar into a heavy pan and pour in the orange juice. Bring to the boil, stirring until the sugar has dissolved, then boil steadily for about 10 minutes, or until the liquid is thick and syrupy.

5 Cut the unpeeled oranges into 5mm/ ¼in slices. Add to the syrup. Simmer for 10 minutes, or until glazed. Transfer the slices to a wire rack to dry. When cool, cut in half. Reserve the syrup.

6 Grind the almonds finely in a food processor. With an electric mixer, cream the butter and remaining sugar until light. Beat in the egg and 30ml/2 tbsp of the orange syrup. Stir in the almonds, then add the flour.

7 Melt the jam over a low heat, then brush it evenly over the inside of the pastry case. Pour in the ground almond mixture. Bake for 20 minutes, or until set. Leave to cool in the tin.

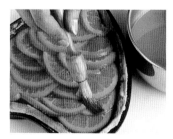

8 Starting at the top of the heart shape and working down to the point, arrange the orange slices on top of the tart in an overlapping pattern, cutting them to fit. Boil the remaining syrup until thick and brush on top to glaze. Leave to cool.

RICOTTA AND CITRUS CHEESECAKE TART

CHEESECAKE FILLINGS ARE EXCELLENT MADE WITH RICOTTA CHEESE BECAUSE RICOTTA HAS A GOOD, FIRM TEXTURE. HERE IT IS ENRICHED WITH EGGS AND CREAM AND ENLIVENED WITH TANGY ORANGE AND LEMON RIND TO MAKE A SICILIAN-STYLE DESSERT.

SERVES EIGHT

INGREDIENTS

450g/1lb/2 cups low-fat ricotta
  cheese
120ml/4fl oz/½ cup double
  (heavy) cream
2 eggs
1 egg yolk
75g/3oz/6 tbsp caster
  (superfine) sugar
finely grated rind of 1 orange
finely grated rind of 1 lemon
thinly pared and shredded orange
  and lemon rind, to decorate
For the pastry
175g/6oz/1½ cups plain
  (all-purpose) flour
45ml/3 tbsp caster
  (superfine) sugar
pinch of salt
115g/4oz/½ cup chilled butter, diced
1 egg yolk

1 To make the pastry, sift the flour, sugar and salt on to a clean, cold work surface. Make a well in the centre and put the diced butter and egg yolk into it. Gradually work the flour into the diced butter and egg yolk, mixing with your fingertips until fully incorporated.

VARIATIONS
Add 50–115g/2–4oz/⅓–⅔ cup finely chopped candied peel to the filling in step 3, or 50g/2oz/⅓ cup plain (semisweet) chocolate chips. For a really rich dessert, you can add both candied peel and some grated plain chocolate.

2 Gather the dough together in your hand, reserve about a quarter for the lattice, then gently press the rest into a 23cm/9in fluted tart tin (pan) with a removable base. Chill the pastry case (pie shell) for 30 minutes and wrap and chill the reserved dough.

3 Meanwhile, preheat the oven to 190°C/375°F/Gas 5 and make the filling. Put the ricotta cheese, cream, eggs, egg yolk, sugar and orange and lemon rinds into a large bowl, and beat together until evenly mixed.

COOK'S TIPS
• The trick to making successful pastry, whatever the type, is to handle it as little and as lightly as possible.
• Use cold utensils. A marble rolling pin is ideal or buy one that can be filled with iced water.
• Don't skip the process of resting the reserved dough in the refrigerator. This will make it easier to roll out and to use as decorative lattice strips without it breaking apart.

4 Prick the base of the pastry case, then line with baking parchment or foil and fill with baking beans. Bake blind for 15 minutes, then transfer to a wire rack, remove the parchment or foil and beans and leave the tart shell to cool completely in the tin.

5 Spoon the cheese and cream filling evenly into the pastry case and level the surface. Roll out the reserved dough and cut into strips about 1cm/½in wide. Arrange the strips across the top of the filling in a lattice pattern, sticking them in place at the edges with a little water.

6 Bake for 30–35 minutes, or until golden and set. Transfer to a wire rack and leave to cool, then remove the side of the tin, leaving the cheesecake on the tin base. Carefully slide on to a serving platter and serve decorated with orange and lemon rind.

LEMONY TREACLE TART

THIS OLD-FASHIONED FAVOURITE IS ALWAYS POPULAR AND IS ESPECIALLY LOVED BY CHILDREN, WITH ITS MELT-IN-THE-MOUTH SHORTCRUST PASTRY CASE, GLORIOUSLY STICKY LEMON AND GOLDEN SYRUP FILLING AND PRETTY TWISTED LATTICE TOPPING.

SERVES FOUR TO SIX

INGREDIENTS
   250g/9oz/generous ¾ cup golden
      (light corn) syrup
   about 75g/3oz/1½ cups fresh
      white breadcrumbs
   grated rind of 1 lemon
   30ml/2 tbsp lemon juice
   custard, to serve
For the pastry
   150g/5oz/1¼ cups plain
      (all-purpose) flour
   2.5ml/½ tsp salt
   130g/4½oz/9 tbsp chilled butter,
      diced
   45–60ml/3–4 tbsp chilled water

1 To make the pastry, sift the flour and salt into a mixing bowl. Rub in the butter with your fingertips until the mixture resembles fine breadcrumbs.

5 Remove the syrup from the heat and stir in the breadcrumbs and lemon rind. Leave to stand for 10 minutes, then add more breadcrumbs if the mixture is too thin. Stir in the lemon juice. Spread the mixture evenly over the pastry case.

6 Roll out the pastry trimmings and cut into 10–12 thin strips.

7 Twist the strips into spirals. Lay half of them across the filling. Arrange the remaining strips at right angles to form a lattice. Press the ends on to the rim and trim off any excess pastry. Bake for 10 minutes, then lower the temperature to 190°C/375°F/Gas 5. Bake for about 15 minutes more until golden. Serve warm with custard.

2 With a fork, stir in enough water to bind the dough. Gather into a ball, knead until smooth then wrap in clear film (plastic wrap) and chill for 20 minutes.

3 On a lightly floured surface, roll out the pastry to a thickness of 3mm/⅛in. Transfer to a 20cm/8in fluted flan tin (tart pan), easing it into the tin with your fingers. Trim off any overhang. Chill the pastry case (pie shell) for 20 minutes. Reserve the pastry trimmings.

4 Put a baking sheet in the oven and preheat to 200°C/400°F/Gas 6. Warm the syrup in a pan until it melts.

LEMON MERINGUE PIE

CRISP SHORTCRUST IS FILLED WITH A MOUTH-WATERING LEMON FILLING AND HEAPED WITH SOFT GOLDEN-TOPPED MERINGUE. THIS CLASSIC OPEN TART NEVER FAILS TO PLEASE. POPULAR WITH ADULTS AND CHILDREN, IT IS A CLASSIC SUNDAY LUNCH DESSERT.

SERVES SIX

INGREDIENTS
   3 large (US extra large) egg yolks
   30ml/2 tbsp caster (superfine) sugar
   grated rind and juice of 1 lemon
   25g/1oz/½ cup white breadcrumbs
   250ml/8fl oz/1 cup milk
For the pastry
   115g/4oz/1 cup plain
     (all-purpose) flour
   pinch of salt
   25g/1oz/2 tbsp chilled butter
   25g/1oz/2 tbsp lard or white
     vegetable fat
   15ml/1 tbsp caster (superfine) sugar
   about 15ml/1 tbsp iced water
For the topping
   3 large (US extra large) egg whites
   115g/4oz/generous ½ cup caster
     (superfine) sugar

1 To make the pastry, sift the flour and salt into a bowl. Using your fingertips, rub in the butter and lard. Stir in the sugar and add enough iced water to make a soft dough.

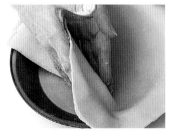

2 Roll out the pastry on a lightly floured surface and use to line a deep 21cm/8½in pie plate. Chill until required.

3 Meanwhile, make the filling. Place the egg yolks, sugar, lemon rind and juice, breadcrumbs and milk in a bowl, mix lightly and leave to soak for 1 hour.

4 Preheat the oven to 200°C/400°F/Gas 6. Beat the filling until smooth and pour into the pastry case (pie shell). Bake for 20 minutes, or until the filling has just set and the pastry is golden. Cool on a wire rack for 30 minutes, or until a skin has formed on the surface. Lower the oven temperature to 180°C/350°F/Gas 4.

5 Make the topping. Whisk the egg whites in a grease-free bowl until they form stiff peaks. Whisk in the sugar a spoonful at a time to form a glossy meringue. Spoon on top of the set lemon filling, spreading to the rim of the pastry case. Swirl the meringue slightly.

6 Bake the pie for 20–25 minutes, or until the meringue is crisp and golden brown. Leave the pie to cool on a wire rack for 10 minutes before serving.

KEY LIME PIE

THIS SPLENDID TART WITH ITS RICH LIME FILLING IS ONE OF AMERICA'S FAVOURITES. AS THE NAME SUGGESTS, IT ORIGINATED IN THE FLORIDA KEYS.

SERVES TEN

INGREDIENTS

4 eggs, separated
400g/14oz can condensed milk
grated rind and juice of 3 limes
a few drops of green food
  colouring (optional)
30ml/2 tbsp caster (superfine) sugar
thinly pared lime rind and fresh mint
  leaves, to decorate
For the pastry
225g/8oz/2 cups plain
  (all-purpose) flour
115g/4oz/½ cup chilled butter, diced
30ml/2 tbsp caster (superfine) sugar
2 egg yolks
pinch of salt
30ml/2 tbsp chilled water
For the topping
300ml/½ pint/1¼ cups double
  (heavy) cream
2–3 limes, thinly sliced

1 To make the pastry, sift the flour into a mixing bowl, add the butter and rub in with your fingertips until the mixture resembles fine breadcrumbs. Add the sugar, egg yolks, salt and water, then mix to a soft dough.

COOK'S TIP
You can make the pastry in a food processor, but you must take care not to overprocess the dough. Process the flour, butter and sugar first, then add the egg yolks and water. Use the pulse button and process for a few seconds at a time; switch off the motor the moment the dough gathers together.

2 Roll out the pastry on a lightly floured surface and use to line a deep 21cm/8½in fluted flan tin (tart pan), allowing the excess pastry to hang over the edge. Prick the pastry base with a fork and chill for at least 30 minutes.

3 Preheat the oven to 200°C/400°F/Gas 6. Trim off the excess pastry from around the edge of the pastry case (pie shell) using a sharp knife. If using a metal flan tin, you can just roll over the rim with a rolling pin. Line the pastry case with baking parchment or foil and baking beans.

4 Bake the pastry case blind for about 10 minutes. Remove the parchment or foil and beans and return the pastry case to the oven for 10 minutes more.

5 Meanwhile, beat the egg yolks in a large bowl until light and creamy, then beat in the condensed milk, with the lime rind and juice, until thoroughly combined. Add the food colouring, if using, and continue to beat until the mixture is thick.

6 In a grease-free bowl, whisk the egg whites to stiff peaks. Whisk in the caster sugar, then fold into the lime mixture.

7 Lower the oven temperature to 160°C/325°F/Gas 3. Pour the lime filling into the pastry case, smoothing the top. Bake for 20–25 minutes until it has set and is turning brown. Cool, then chill.

8 Whip the cream for the topping and spoon it around the edge of the pie. Cut each lime slice from the centre to the edge, then twist it and arrange between the spoonfuls of cream. Decorate with lime rind and mint leaves.

PEACH LEAF PIE <u>WITH</u> ORANGE PASTRY

CONCENTRIC CIRCLES OF ORANGE-FLAVOURED PASTRY LEAVES TOP THIS SPECTACULAR PIE, WHICH IS FILLED WITH FRESH, LIGHTLY SPICED PEACHES WITH A HINT OF LEMON.

SERVES EIGHT

INGREDIENTS
  1.2kg/2½lb ripe peaches
  juice of 1 lemon
  115g/4oz/½ cup granulated sugar
  45ml/3 tbsp cornflour (cornstarch)
  1.5ml/¼ tbsp freshly grated nutmeg
  2.5ml/½ tsp ground cinnamon
  1 egg, beaten with 15ml/1 tbsp
    water, to glaze
  25g/1oz/2 tbsp butter, diced
  custard or cream, to serve (optional)
For the pastry
  225g/8oz/2 cups plain
    (all-purpose) flour
  pinch of salt
  115g/4oz/½ cup cold
    butter, diced
  pinch of ground cloves
  finely grated rind of 1 orange
  25g/1oz/2 tbsp caster
    (superfine) sugar
  2 egg yolks
  10ml/2 tsp fresh orange juice

1 To make the pastry, sift the flour and salt into a mixing bowl. Add the diced butter and rub it into the flour with your fingertips until the mixture resembles fine breadcrumbs. Add the ground cloves, grated orange rind and sugar and stir into the flour mixture.

2 Mix the egg yolks with the orange juice and add to the bowl. Knead lightly to form a smooth dough. Gather the dough into two balls, one slightly larger than the other. Wrap separately in clear film (plastic wrap) and chill for at least 40 minutes. Meanwhile, put a baking sheet in the oven and preheat to 220°C/425°F/Gas 7.

COOK'S TIP
When cooking the pie, placing it on a preheated baking sheet helps to make the pastry case (pie shell) crisp on the base. The moisture from the filling might otherwise cause the pastry to become soggy and unappetizing.

3 Drop a few peaches at a time into a large pan of boiling water, leave for 20 seconds, then transfer to a bowl of cold water. When cool, peel off the skins. Slice the peaches and mix with the lemon juice, sugar, cornflour and spices. Set aside.

4 On a lightly floured surface, roll out the larger piece of pastry to a thickness of 3mm/⅛in. Use to line a 23cm/9in pie plate. Chill until required.

5 Roll out the second piece of pastry thinly and cut out leaf shapes about 7.5cm/3in long. Mark veins with a knife.

6 Lightly brush the base of the pastry case (pie shell) with egg glaze. Add the peach mixture, piling it into a dome in the centre. Dot with the butter.

7 To assemble the pie top, start from the outside edge. Make a ring of pastry leaves around the edge attaching each leaf to the pastry base with a dab of egg glaze. Place a second ring of leaves above the first, staggering the positions. Continue with rows of leaves until the pie is completely covered. Brush with egg glaze.

8 Place the pie on the hot baking sheet and bake for about 10 minutes. Lower the oven temperature to 180°C/350°F/Gas 4 and continue to bake for about 40 minutes more, or until the pastry topping is golden. Serve the pie hot, with custard or cream, if you like.

VARIATION
Substitute other stone fruits for peaches, such as nectarines, apricots, plums or damsons. These are all usually sweet enough without adding sugar.

BLUEBERRY AND CITRUS PIE

ORANGE AND LEMON IMPART A FRAGRANT QUALITY TO BERRIES, AND HERE THE CITRUS IS FURTHER COMPLEMENTED BY CINNAMON, MAKING THIS A WARMLY FLAVOURED PIE. BOTH AMERICAN BLUEBERRIES AND EUROPEAN BLUEBERRIES OR BILBERRIES CAN BE USED. SERVE WITH A DOLLOP OF CREAM.

SERVES SIX

INGREDIENTS
800g/1¾lb/7 cups blueberries
75g/3oz/6 tbsp caster
   (superfine) sugar, plus extra
   for sprinkling
45ml/3 tbsp cornflour (cornstarch)
grated rind and juice of ½ orange
grated rind of ½ lemon
2.5ml/½ tsp ground cinnamon
15g/½oz/1 tbsp butter, diced
1 egg, beaten
For the pastry
275g/10oz/2½ cups plain
   (all-purpose) flour
pinch of salt
75g/3oz/6 tbsp butter, diced
50g/2oz/¼ cup white vegetable
   fat (shortening)
60–75ml/4–5 tbsp chilled water

1 To make the pastry, sift the flour and salt into a bowl. Rub in the butter and vegetable fat with your fingertips until the mixture resembles fine breadcrumbs.

2 Sprinkle over most of the water and mix to a soft dough. Add more water if necessary. Knead lightly. Wrap in clear film (plastic wrap) and chill in the refrigerator for at least 30 minutes.

3 Preheat the oven to 200°C/400°F/ Gas 6. Roll out half the pastry and use to line a 23cm/9in pie dish, allowing the excess pastry to overhang the edge.

4 In a bowl, mix the blueberries, caster sugar, cornflour, orange rind and juice, lemon rind and cinnamon. Spoon evenly into the pastry case and dot the top with the butter.

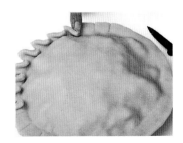

5 Roll out the remaining pastry for a lid. Trim off the excess. Cut the rim at 2.5cm/1in intervals. Fold each section over on itself to form triangles. Re-roll the trimmings and cut out decorations. Attach them to the pastry lid with some beaten egg, glaze with egg and sprinkle with caster sugar. Bake for 30 minutes, or until golden. Serve warm or cold.

APPLE AND ORANGE PIE

TANGY ORANGES AND MELT-IN-THE MOUTH APPLES ARE TOPPED WITH A CRISP CRUST IN THIS SATISFYING PIE THAT IS SIMPLE TO MAKE. PERFECT FOR A FAMILY DESSERT AT THE WEEKEND, IT IS ALSO SPECIAL ENOUGH FOR AN INFORMAL SUPPER PARTY.

SERVES FOUR TO SIX

INGREDIENTS
    3 navel oranges
    1kg/2¼lb cooking apples, peeled,
       cored and thickly sliced
    30ml/2 tbsp demerara (raw) sugar
    beaten egg, to glaze
    caster (superfine) sugar,
       for sprinkling
For the pastry
    275g/10oz/2½ cups plain
       (all-purpose) flour
    2.5ml/½ tsp salt
    150g/5oz/10 tbsp chilled
       butter, diced
    about 40ml/4 tbsp chilled water

1 To make the pastry, sift the flour and salt into a large bowl. Rub in the butter with your fingertips, until the mixture resembles fine breadcrumbs. Mix in the water and knead lightly to form a firm dough. Wrap the dough in clear film (plastic wrap) and chill for at least 30 minutes.

2 Roll out the pastry on a lightly floured work surface to a round 2cm/¾in larger than the top of a 1.2 litre/2 pint/5 cup pie dish. Cut off a narrow strip around the edge of the pastry and firmly attach it to the rim of the pie dish with a little cold water.

COOK'S TIP
Use any excess pastry to make leaves for decorating the pie, marking the veins with the blade of a knife.

3 Preheat the oven to 190°C/375°F/ Gas 5. Using a sharp knife, cut a thin slice of peel and pith from both ends of each orange. Place cut side down on a plate and cut off the peel and pith in strips. Remove any bits of remaining pith. Cut out each segment leaving the membrane behind. Squeeze the remaining juice from the membrane.

4 Mix together the orange segments and juice, the apples and sugar in the pie dish. Place a pie funnel in the centre of the dish.

VARIATIONS
• Substitute 2 pink grapefruit for the oranges and double the quantity of sugar.
• Replace the cooking apples with firm pears such as Conference.

5 Dampen the pastry strip on the rim of the dish and cover with the pastry. Press the edges to the pastry strip.

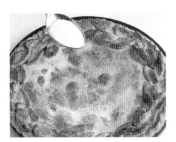

6 Brush the top with beaten egg to glaze, then bake for 35 minutes, or until golden. Sprinkle the pie with caster sugar before serving.

MINCE PIES WITH ORANGE WHISKY BUTTER

MINCEMEAT GETS THE LUXURY TREATMENT WITH THE ADDITION OF GLACÉ CITRUS PEEL, CHERRIES AND WHISKY TO MAKE A MARVELLOUS FILLING FOR THESE TRADITIONAL FESTIVE PIES. SERVING THEM WITH A SPOONFUL OF WHISKY BUTTER IS PURE INDULGENCE.

MAKES TWELVE TO FIFTEEN

INGREDIENTS
    225g/8oz/²⁄₃ cup mincemeat
    50g/2oz/¼ cup glacé (candied) citrus
      peel, chopped
    50g/2oz/¼ cup glacé (candied)
      cherries, chopped
    30ml/2 tbsp whisky
    1 egg, beaten or a little milk
    icing (confectioners') sugar,
      for dusting
For the pastry
    1 egg yolk
    5ml/1 tsp grated orange rind
    15ml/1 tbsp caster (superfine) sugar
    10ml/2 tsp chilled water
    225g/8oz/2 cups plain
      (all-purpose) flour
    150g/5oz/10 tbsp butter, diced
For the orange whisky butter
    75g/3oz/6 tbsp butter, softened
    175g/6oz/1½ cups icing
      (confectioners') sugar, sifted
    30ml/2 tbsp whisky
    5ml/1 tsp grated orange rind

1 To make the pastry, lightly beat the egg yolk in a bowl, then add the grated orange rind, caster sugar and water and mix together. Cover and set aside. Sift the flour into a separate mixing bowl.

VARIATIONS
• Use either puff or filo pastry instead of shortcrust for a change.
• Replace the whisky in both the filling and the flavoured butter with Cointreau or brandy, if you like.

2 Using your fingertips, rub the diced butter into the flour until the mixture resembles fine breadcrumbs. Stir in the egg mixture and mix to a dough. Wrap in clear film (plastic wrap) and chill for 30 minutes.

3 Mix together the mincemeat, glacé peel and cherries, then add the whisky.

4 Roll out three-quarters of the pastry. With a fluted pastry (cookie) cutter stamp out rounds and line 12–15 patty tins (muffin pans). Re-roll the trimmings thinly and stamp out star shapes.

5 Preheat the oven to 200ºC/400ºF/ Gas 6. Spoon a little filling into each pastry case (pie shell) and top with a star shape. Brush with a little beaten egg or milk and bake for 20–25 minutes, or until golden. Leave to cool.

6 Meanwhile, make the orange whisky butter. Place the softened butter, icing sugar, whisky and grated orange rind in a bowl and beat with a wooden spoon until light and fluffy.

7 To serve, lift off each pastry star, pipe a whirl of whisky butter on top of the filling, then replace the star. Lightly dust the mince pies with a little icing sugar.

COOK'S TIP
There is a wide range of small, shaped pastry (cookie) cutters available from kitchenware stores and special seasonal packs with a festive theme also include stars and Christmas trees. While metal cutters are usually the wiser buy, as these will be used only annually, cheaper plastic cutters are fine.

CAKES, BREADS AND BISCUITS

From light-as-air sponge cakes to rich dried fruit mixtures and from melt-in-the-mouth cookies to speciality breads, citrus fruits take a starring role. While it is sometimes used in other dishes, candied peel really comes into its own among baking recipes, where its unique flavour and texture make it an essential ingredient in celebration cakes and luxury teabreads. The fruits themselves can be used in a variety of ways. An indulgent, lemon and lime flavoured sponge cake or a fabulous chocolate and orange marmalade teabread are sure to prove irresistible. Cakes and biscuits subtly flavoured with orange or lemon make wonderful treats for a well-earned break in a busy day.

RICH LEMON POPPY-SEED CAKE

THE CLASSIC COMBINATION OF POPPY SEEDS AND LEMON IS USED FOR THIS TANGY CAKE, WHICH HAS A DELICIOUS LEMON CURD AND FROMAGE FRAIS FILLING.

SERVES EIGHT

INGREDIENTS
  350g/12oz/1½ cups unsalted (sweet)
    butter, plus extra for greasing
  350g/12oz/1¾ cups golden caster
    (superfine) sugar
  45ml/3 tbsp poppy seeds
  20ml/4 tsp grated lemon rind
  70ml/4½ tbsp lemon curd
  6 eggs, separated
  120ml/4fl oz/½ cup semi-skimmed
    (low-fat) milk
  350g/12oz/3 cups self-raising
    (self-rising) flour
  icing (confectioners') sugar,
    to decorate
For the filling
  150g/5oz/½ cup luxury lemon curd
  150ml/¼ pint/⅔ cup fromage frais

1 Butter and lightly flour two 23cm/9in springform cake tins (pans). Preheat the oven to 180°C/350°F/Gas 4.

2 Cream together the butter and caster sugar in a mixing bowl with a wooden spoon until light and fluffy. Alternatively, you can use a hand-held electric whisk.

3 Add the poppy seeds, lemon rind, lemon curd and egg yolks and beat well, then add the milk and mix well. Gently fold in the flour until combined.

4 Whisk the egg whites until they form soft peaks. Fold the egg whites into the cake mixture until just combined. Divide the cake mixture evenly between the prepared tins.

5 Bake for 40–45 minutes, or until a skewer inserted into the centre of the cakes comes out clean.

6 Leave the cakes to cool in the tins for about 5 minutes, then remove from the tins and leave to cool completely on wire racks.

7 To finish, place one cake upside down on a serving plate. Spread evenly with the lemon curd for the filling and spoon the fromage frais generously over the lemon curd. Put the second cake on top, right way up, press down gently, then dust with a light coating of icing sugar before serving.

MADEIRA CAKE <u>WITH</u> LEMON SYRUP

THIS SUGAR-CRUSTED CAKE IS SOAKED IN A LEMON SYRUP, SO THAT IT STAYS MOIST AND IS INFUSED WITH A TANGY CITRUS FLAVOUR. SERVE IT SLICED WITH MORNING COFFEE OR AFTERNOON TEA.

SERVES TEN

INGREDIENTS
  250g/9oz/1 cup butter, softened,
    plus extra for greasing
  225g/8oz/generous 1 cup caster
    (superfine) sugar
  5 eggs
  275g/10oz/2½ cups plain (all-
    purpose) flour, sifted
  30ml/2 tbsp baking powder
  salt
For the sugar crust
  60ml/4 tbsp lemon juice
  15ml/1 tbsp golden (light corn) syrup
  30ml/2 tbsp sugar

1 Preheat the oven to 180°C/350°F/ Gas 4. Lightly grease a 1kg/2¼lb loaf tin (pan). Beat the butter and sugar until light and creamy, then gradually beat in the eggs.

2 Mix the sifted flour, baking powder and salt, and gently fold into the egg mixture. Spoon into the prepared tin, level the top and bake for 1¼ hours, or until a skewer pushed into the middle comes out clean.

3 Remove the cake from the oven and, while still warm and in the tin, use a skewer to pierce it several times.

4 To make the sugar crust, warm the lemon juice and syrup, add the sugar and immediately spoon over the cake. Chill for several hours or overnight.

MARMALADE TEABREAD

ORANGE MARMALADE AND CINNAMON GIVE THIS MOIST TEABREAD A DELICIOUSLY WARM FLAVOUR. IT IS SURE TO BE POPULAR WITH THE WHOLE FAMILY.

SERVES EIGHT

INGREDIENTS
90g/3½oz/7 tbsp butter or
   margarine, plus extra
   for greasing
200g/7oz/1¾ cups plain
   (all-purpose) flour
5ml/1 tsp baking powder
6.25ml/1¼ tsp ground cinnamon
50g/2oz/4 tbsp soft light
   brown sugar
60ml/4 tbsp chunky
   orange marmalade
1 egg, beaten
about 45ml/3 tbsp milk
50g/2oz/½ cup icing
   (confectioners') sugar
about 15ml/1 tbsp warm water
thinly pared and shredded orange and
   lemon rind, to decorate

1 Preheat the oven to 160°C/325°F/ Gas 3. Butter a 900ml/1½ pint/3¾ cup loaf tin (pan), then line the base with greased baking parchment.

2 Sift the flour, baking powder and cinnamon into a large bowl, then rub in the butter with your fingertips until the mixture resembles fine breadcrumbs. Stir in the sugar.

3 Mix together the marmalade, egg and most of the milk, then stir into the bowl to make a soft dropping (pourable) consistency, adding a little more milk if necessary.

4 Transfer the mixture to the tin and bake for about 1¼ hours until firm to the touch. Leave the cake to cool for 5 minutes, then turn on to a wire rack.

5 Carefully peel off the lining paper and leave the cake to cool completely.

6 When the cake is cold, make the icing. Sift the icing sugar into a bowl and mix in the water a little at a time to make a thick glaze. Drizzle the icing over the top of the cake and decorate with the orange and lemon rinds.

ORANGE MARMALADE CHOCOLATE LOAF

DO NOT BE ALARMED AT THE AMOUNT OF CREAM IN THIS RECIPE — IT REPLACES BUTTER TO MAKE A MOIST DARK CAKE, TOPPED WITH A BITTER-SWEET STICKY MARMALADE TOPPING.

SERVES EIGHT

INGREDIENTS
  butter, for greasing
  115g/4oz cooking chocolate
    (unsweetened), broken into squares
  3 eggs
  175g/6oz/scant 1 cup caster
    (superfine) sugar
  175ml/6fl oz/¾ cup sour cream
  200g/7oz/1¾ cups self-raising
    (self-rising) flour
For the filling and glaze
  185g/6½oz/⅔ cup bitter
    orange marmalade
  115g/4oz plain (semisweet)
    chocolate, broken into squares
  60ml/4 tbsp sour cream
  thinly pared and shredded orange
    rind, to decorate

1 Preheat the oven to 180°C/350°F/ Gas 4. Lightly grease a 1kg/2¼lb loaf tin (pan) with butter, then line the base with a piece of baking parchment. Melt the chocolate in a heatproof bowl over a pan of hot water.

2 Combine the eggs and sugar in a separate mixing bowl. Using a hand-held electric mixer, beat the mixture until it is thick and creamy, then stir in the sour cream and chocolate. Sprinkle over the flour and fold in evenly.

COOK'S TIP
When melting chocolate over hot water, do not allow the base of the bowl to touch the surface of the water, which should be barely simmering.

3 Pour the mixture into the prepared tin and bake for about 1 hour, or until well risen and firm to the touch. Cool for a few minutes in the tin, then turn out on to a wire rack and leave the loaf to cool completely.

4 Make the filling. Spoon two-thirds of the marmalade into a small pan and melt over a low heat. Melt the chocolate in a heatproof bowl over a pan of hot water and stir it into the marmalade with the sour cream.

5 Slice the cake across into three layers and sandwich back together with about half the marmalade filling. Spread the rest evenly over the top of the cake and leave to set. Spoon the remaining marmalade over the cake and sprinkle with shredded orange rind, to decorate.

VARIATION
The filling is also delicious made with other marmalades such as kumquat.

LEMON AND LIME SYRUP CAKE

THIS CAKE IS PERFECT FOR BUSY COOKS AS IT CAN BE MIXED IN MOMENTS AND NEEDS NO ICING. THE SIMPLE TANGY LIME TOPPING TRANSFORMS IT INTO A FABULOUSLY MOIST CAKE.

SERVES EIGHT

INGREDIENTS
225g/8oz/1 cup butter, softened,
  plus extra for greasing
225g/8oz/2 cups self-raising
  (self-rising) flour
5ml/1 tsp baking powder
225g/8oz/generous 1 cup caster
  (superfine) sugar
4 eggs, beaten
grated rind of 2 lemons
30ml/2 tbsp lemon juice
For the topping
  finely pared rind of 1 lime
  juice of 2 limes
  150g/5oz/¾ cup caster
  (superfine) sugar

VARIATION
Use lemon rind and juice instead of lime for the topping if you like. You will need only one large lemon.

1 Preheat the oven to 160°C/325°F/ Gas 3. Grease and line a 20cm/8in round cake tin (pan). Sift the flour and baking powder into a bowl. Add the caster sugar, butter and eggs and beat until the mixture is smooth and creamy.

2 Beat in the lemon rind and juice. Spoon the mixture into the tin, smooth the surface and gently indent the top with the back of a spoon.

3 Bake for 1¼–1½ hours, or until the cake is golden on top and spongy when lightly pressed, and a skewer inserted in the centre comes out clean.

4 Meanwhile, mix the ingredients for the topping together. As soon as the cake is cooked, remove it from the oven and pour the topping evenly over the surface. Leave the cake to cool fully in the tin before removing and serving.

MOIST ORANGE AND ALMOND CAKE

THE KEY TO THIS RECIPE IS TO COOK THE ORANGE SLOWLY FIRST, SO THAT IT IS COMPLETELY TENDER BEFORE IT IS BLENDED. DO NOT USE A MICROWAVE TO SPEED THINGS UP.

SERVES EIGHT

INGREDIENTS
  1 large Valencia or Navelina orange
  butter, for greasing
  3 eggs
  225g/8oz/generous 1 cup caster
    (superfine) sugar
  5ml/1 tsp baking powder
  225g/8oz/2 cups ground almonds
  25g/1oz/¼ cup plain
    (all-purpose) flour
  icing (confectioners') sugar,
    for dusting

1 Pierce the orange with a skewer. Put it in a deep pan and pour over water to cover it. Bring to the boil, then cover and simmer for 1 hour until the skin is soft. Drain, then cool.

2 Preheat the oven to 180°C/350°F/Gas 4. Lightly grease a 20cm/8in round cake tin (pan) and line it with baking parchment. Cut the cooled orange in half and discard all the pips (seeds). Place the orange, peel, skin and all, in a food processor or blender and purée until smooth and pulpy.

3 In a bowl, whisk the eggs and sugar until thick. Fold in the baking powder, almonds and flour. Fold in the purée.

4 Pour into the prepared tin, level the surface and bake for 1 hour, or until a skewer inserted into the middle comes out clean. Cool the cake in the tin for 10 minutes, then turn out on to a wire rack, peel off the lining paper and cool completely. Dust the top liberally with icing sugar and serve.

COOK'S TIP
To make a delicious dessert, serve the cake with a little whipped cream and, if you are after extra colour, tuck orange slices underneath it just beforehand. For a special treat, serve the cake with spiced poached kumquats.

SICILIAN RICOTTA CAKE

ORANGE LIQUEUR AND GLACÉ CITRUS PEEL MAKE THIS TRADITIONAL CAKE OF LAYERED RICOTTA
CHEESE TRULY IRRESISTIBLE AND THE PERFECT CHOICE FOR A DINNER PARTY DESSERT. START
PREPARATIONS THE DAY BEFORE, AS THE CAKE NEEDS TO BE CHILLED.

SERVES EIGHT TO TEN

INGREDIENTS
    675g/1½lb/3 cups ricotta cheese
    finely grated rind of 1 orange
    150g/5oz/¾ cup vanilla sugar
    75ml/5 tbsp Cointreau or other
        orange liqueur
    115g/4oz/½ cup glacé (candied)
        citrus peel
    8 trifle sponge cakes
    60ml/4 tbsp freshly squeezed
        orange juice
    extra glacé (candied) citrus peel,
        to decorate

1 Push the ricotta cheese through a
sieve into a bowl with a wooden spoon,
add the orange rind, vanilla sugar and
15ml/1 tbsp of the liqueur and beat well
to mix. Transfer about one-third of the
mixture to another bowl, cover and chill
until ready to serve.

2 Finely chop the citrus peel and beat
into the remaining ricotta cheese
mixture until evenly mixed. Set aside.

3 Line the base of a 1.2 litre/2 pint/
5 cup loaf tin (pan) with baking
parchment. Cut the trifle sponge cakes
in half horizontally. Arrange four pieces
of sponge side by side in the base of
the loaf tin and sprinkle with 15ml/
1 tbsp each of liqueur and orange juice.

4 Spread one-third of the ricotta and
fruit mixture evenly over the sponge
layer. Cover with four more pieces of
sponge and sprinkle with another 15ml/
1 tbsp each of orange liqueur and
orange juice as before.

COOK'S TIP
Baking parchment, sometimes called
non-stick baking paper, has largely
replaced greaseproof (waxed) paper for
lining cake and loaf tins (pans). It is
made from paper and contains heat-
resistant silicon, giving it an extremely
effective non-stick surface. Although
more expensive than greaseproof paper,
it is more efficient and is especially
useful with mixtures containing a high
proportion of sugar.

5 Repeat with the alternate layers of
ricotta mixture and sponge until all
the ingredients are used, soaking the
sponge pieces with liqueur and orange
juice each time, and ending with a
soaked-sponge layer. Cover the cake
with a piece of baking parchment.

6 Cut a piece of thin cardboard to fit
inside the tin, place on top of the
baking parchment and weigh down
evenly. (Use a couple of cans of fruit or
tomatoes.) Chill for 24 hours.

7 To serve, remove the weights,
cardboard and baking parchment and
run a palette knife (metal spatula)
between the sides of the cake and the
tin. Place a large serving plate on top
of the tin, then invert the two, holding
them firmly together, so that the cake is
upside down on the plate. Peel off the
lining parchment.

8 Spread the chilled ricotta mixture
over the cake to cover it completely,
then decorate the top with citrus peel,
cut into fancy shapes. Serve chilled.

VARIATIONS
• Use mandarin or tangerine juice
instead of orange and replace the orange
liqueur with Mandarine Napoléon.
• Add 25g/1oz/¼ cup finely chopped
pistachio nuts and 30ml/2 tbsp chopped
glacé (candied) cherries to the ricotta
mixture in step 2.
• Add 30ml/2 tbsp chopped stem
(preserved) ginger in step 2.

CHOCOLATE ORANGE MARQUISE

HERE IS A CAKE FOR PEOPLE WHO ARE PASSIONATE ABOUT CHOCOLATE. THE RICH, DENSE FLAVOUR IS
ACCENTUATED BY FRESH ORANGE TO MAKE IT A TRULY DELECTABLE TREAT.

3 Remove from the heat and stir in the chocolate until melted, then add the butter, piece by piece, until melted.

4 Whisk the eggs with the remaining sugar in a large bowl, until the mixture is pale and very thick. Add the orange rind, then lightly fold the chocolate mixture into the egg mixture. Sift the flour over the top and fold in.

5 Pour the mixture into the prepared tin. Place in a roasting pan, transfer to the oven, then pour hot water into the roasting pan to reach about halfway up the sides of the cake tin.

6 Bake for 1 hour, or until the cake is firm to the touch. Remove the tin from the roasting pan and cool for 20 minutes. Invert the cake on a baking sheet, place a serving plate upside down on top, then carefully turn plate and baking sheet over together so that the cake is transferred to the plate. Dust with a little icing sugar, decorate with strips of orange rind and serve slightly warm or chilled.

SERVES SIX TO EIGHT

INGREDIENTS
  225g/8oz/1 cup unsalted (sweet)
    butter, diced, plus extra for greasing
  200g/7oz/1 cup caster
    (superfine) sugar
  60ml/4 tbsp freshly squeezed
    orange juice
  350g/12oz dark (bittersweet)
    chocolate, broken into squares
  5 eggs
  finely grated rind of 1 orange
  45ml/3 tbsp plain (all-purpose) flour
  icing (confectioners') sugar and finely
    pared strips of orange rind,
    to decorate

COOK'S TIP
It is not necessary to heat the chocolate to melt it. This will make it grainy.

1 Preheat the oven to 180°C/350°F/ Gas 4. Grease a 23cm/9in layer cake tin (pan) with a depth of 6cm/2½in. Line the base of the tin with a sheet of baking parchment.

2 Place 90g/3½oz/½ cup of the sugar in a pan. Add the orange juice and stir over a low heat until dissolved.

SEMOLINA AND NUT HALVA

A TRADITIONAL SEMOLINA PASTRY FROM THE EASTERN MEDITERRANEAN, HALVA IS DELICATELY FLAVOURED WITH ORANGE, AND A FRAGRANT, SPICY SYRUP MAKES IT BEAUTIFULLY MOIST.

SERVES TEN

INGREDIENTS
115g/4oz/½ cup unsalted (sweet) butter, softened
115g/4oz/generous ½ cup caster (superfine) sugar
finely grated rind of 1 orange, plus 30ml/2 tbsp juice
3 eggs
175g/6oz/1 cup semolina
10ml/2 tsp baking powder
115g/4oz/1 cup ground hazelnuts
50g/2oz/⅓ cup unblanched hazelnuts, toasted and chopped
50g/2oz/⅓ cup blanched almonds, toasted and chopped
thinly pared and shredded rind of 1 orange
For the syrup
350g/12oz/1¾ cups caster (superfine) sugar
2 cinnamon sticks, halved
juice of 1 lemon
60ml/4 tbsp orange flower water

1 Preheat the oven to 220°C/425°F/ Gas 7. Grease and line the base of a deep 23cm/9in square cake tin (pan).

2 Lightly cream the butter in a bowl. Add the sugar, orange rind and juice, eggs, semolina, baking powder and hazelnuts and beat until smooth.

5 Bring to the boil and boil rapidly, without stirring, for 5 minutes. Pour half the syrup into a bowl and add the lemon juice and orange flower water to it. Pour over the halva. Reserve the remainder of the syrup in the pan.

6 Leave the halva in the tin until the syrup is absorbed, then turn it out on to a plate and cut diagonally into diamond-shaped portions. Sprinkle with the nuts.

3 Turn into the prepared tin and level the surface. Bake for 20–25 minutes, or until just firm and golden. Remove from the oven and leave to cool in the tin on a wire rack.

4 To make the syrup, put the sugar in a small, heavy pan with 550ml/18fl oz/ 2½ cups water and the cinnamon sticks. Heat gently, stirring, until the sugar has dissolved completely.

7 Boil the remaining syrup until slightly thickened, then pour it over the halva. Sprinkle the shredded orange rind over the cake and serve with lightly whipped or clotted cream.

LEMON ROULADE WITH LEMON CURD CREAM

THIS FEATHER-LIGHT ROULADE FILLED WITH A RICH FRESH LEMON CURD CREAM MAKES A MARVELLOUS TEA-TIME DESSERT. FRESH LEMON CURD IS THE KEY TO ITS SPECIAL FLAVOUR, BUT IT CAN BE MADE AHEAD, STORED IN SEALED, STERILIZED JARS AND KEPT IN THE REFRIGERATOR.

MAKES EIGHT SLICES

INGREDIENTS
    butter, for greasing
    4 eggs, separated
    115g/4oz/generous ½ cup caster
      (superfine) sugar
    finely grated rind of 2 lemons
    5ml/1 tsp pure vanilla
      essence (extract)
    25g/1oz/¼ cup ground almonds
    40g/1½oz/⅓ cup plain (all-purpose)
      flour, sifted
    45ml/3 tbsp icing (confectioners')
      sugar, for dusting
For the filling
    300ml/½ pint/1¼ cups double
      (heavy) cream
    60ml/4 tbsp fresh lemon curd (see
      Cook's Tip)

1 Preheat the oven to 190°C/375°F/
Gas 5. Grease a 33 × 23cm/13 × 9in
Swiss roll tin (jelly roll pan) and line
with baking parchment.

2 In a large bowl, beat the egg yolks
with half the caster sugar until light and
foamy. Beat in the lemon rind and
vanilla essence, then lightly fold in the
ground almonds and flour using a large
metal spoon or spatula.

VARIATION
Substitute orange rind for the roulade
and orange curd for the cream filling.
Use the rind of three oranges, but the
juice of only two to make the fresh
orange curd in the same way.

3 Whisk the egg whites until they form
stiff peaks. Gradually whisk in the
remaining caster sugar to form a stiff
meringue. Stir half the mixture into the
egg yolk mixture and fold in the rest.

4 Pour into the tin, level the surface
with a palette knife (metal spatula) and
bake for 10 minutes, or until risen and
spongy to the touch. Cover loosely with
a sheet of baking parchment and a
damp dishtowel. Leave to cool.

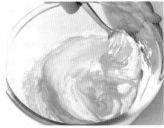

5 To make the filling, whip the cream;
then lightly fold in the lemon curd.

6 Sift the icing sugar over a piece of
baking parchment. Turn the sponge out
on to it and trim the edges. Peel off the
lining paper and spread the lemon curd
cream over the surface of the sponge,
leaving a border.

7 Using the paper underneath as a
guide, roll up the sponge from one of
the long sides. Keep it wrapped in the
baking parchment for 1 minute to allow
the shape to set. Remove the paper and
transfer the roulade to a serving platter,
with the seam underneath and serve.

COOK'S TIP
To make fresh lemon curd, put the
grated rind and juice of 3 lemons into
a pan with 115g/4oz/generous ½ cup
caster (superfine) sugar. Bring to the
boil, stirring to dissolve the sugar. Stir
in 15ml/1 tbsp cornflour (cornstarch)
mixed to a paste with 15ml/1 tbsp water.
Remove from the heat and whisk in
2 egg yolks. Return to a low heat, whisk
for 2 minutes and remove from the heat.
Gradually whisk in 50g/2oz/¼ cup butter.

LIGHT JEWELLED FRUIT CAKE

FULL OF NUTS, CANDIED PEEL, FRESH CITRUS RIND AND DRIED FRUITS, THIS MOIST CAKE MAKES IDEAL CHRISTMAS FARE. DECORATE IT WITH A PRETTY RIBBON, IF YOU LIKE.

SERVES SIX TO EIGHT

INGREDIENTS

115g/4oz/½ cup currants
115g/4oz/⅔ cup sultanas
  (golden raisins)
225g/8oz/1 cup quartered glacé
  (candied) cherries
50g/2oz/⅓ cup finely chopped mixed
  candied peel
30ml/2 tbsp rum, brandy or sherry
225g/8oz/1 cup butter
225g/8oz/generous 1 cup caster
  (superfine) sugar
finely grated rind of 1 orange
finely grated rind of 1 lemon
4 eggs
50g/2oz/½ cup chopped almonds
50g/2oz/½ cup ground almonds
225g/8oz/2 cups plain
  (all-purpose) flour
50g/2oz/⅓ cup whole
  blanched almonds
30ml/2 tbsp apricot jam, warmed

3 Preheat the oven to 160°C/325°F/ Gas 3. In a large bowl, whisk the butter, sugar and orange and lemon rinds together until they are light and fluffy. Beat in the eggs, one at a time.

4 Add the chopped almonds, ground almonds, soaked fruits (with their liquid) and the flour, and mix to make a soft dropping (pourable) consistency. Spoon into the tin. Bake for 30 minutes.

5 Gently arrange the whole almonds in a pattern on top of the cake. Do not press them into the cake or they will sink during cooking. Return the cake to the oven and cook for a further 1½–2 hours, or until the centre is firm to the touch. Let the cake cool in the tin for 30 minutes, then remove it and let it cool completely on a wire rack. Remove the paper and brush the top with a little warmed apricot jam.

1 Soak the currants, sultanas, glacé cherries and the mixed peel in the rum, brandy or sherry in a large bowl. Cover with clear film (plastic wrap) and leave for a few hours but ideally overnight.

2 Grease and line a 20cm/8in round or an 18cm/7in square cake tin with a double thickness of baking parchment.

COOK'S TIP
This cake can be stored for up to two weeks. Do not remove the paper before cooling as it helps to keep the cake moist. Store in an airtight container.

PANETTONE

THIS ITALIAN BREAD IS A WELL-LOVED CHRISTMAS TREAT. IT IS SURPRISINGLY LIGHT EVEN THOUGH THE DOUGH IS RICH WITH BUTTER, CANDIED PEEL AND DRIED FRUIT.

SERVES SIX TO EIGHT

INGREDIENTS
  150g/5oz/10 tbsp butter, softened,
    plus extra for greasing
  400g/14oz/3½ cups unbleached
    strong white bread flour, plus extra
    for kneading and dusting
  2.5ml/½ tsp salt
  15g/½oz fresh yeast
  120ml/4fl oz/½ cup lukewarm milk
  2 eggs
  2 egg yolks
  75g/3oz/6 tbsp caster
    (superfine) sugar
  oil, for greasing
  115g/4oz/⅔ cup mixed chopped
    candied peel
  75g/3oz/generous ½ cup raisins
  melted butter, for brushing

1 Using a double layer of baking parchment, line and butter a 15cm/6in deep cake tin (pan) or soufflé dish. Extend the paper 7.5cm/3in above the top of the tin or dish.

2 Sift the flour and salt together into a large bowl. Make a well in the centre. Cream the yeast with 60ml/4 tbsp of the milk, then mix in the remainder.

3 Pour the yeast mixture into the well in the centre of the flour, add the whole eggs and mix in sufficient flour to make a thick batter. Sprinkle a little of the remaining flour over the top and leave in a warm place for about 30 minutes to "sponge" – when the yeast begins to bubble through the flour covering.

4 Add the egg yolks and sugar and mix to a soft dough. Work in the butter, then turn out on to a lightly floured surface and knead for about 5 minutes, or until smooth and elastic. Place in a lightly oiled bowl, cover with oiled clear film (plastic wrap) and leave to rise, in a warm place, for 1½–2 hours, or until doubled in bulk.

5 Knock back (punch down) the dough and turn out on to a lightly floured surface. Gently knead in the candied peel and raisins. Shape into a ball and place in the prepared tin or dish. Cover with lightly oiled clear film and leave to rise in a slightly warm place for 1 hour, or until doubled in size.

COOK'S TIP
Once the dough has been enriched with butter, do not leave to rise in too warm a place or the loaf will become greasy.

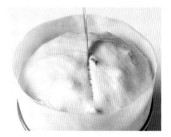

6 Meanwhile, preheat the oven to 190°C/375°F/Gas 5. Brush the surface of the dough with melted butter and cut a cross in the top using a sharp knife. Bake for 20 minutes, then reduce the oven temperature to 180°C/350°F/Gas 4. Brush the top with butter again and bake for a further 25–30 minutes, or until golden. Cool in the tin or dish for 5–10 minutes, then turn out on to a wire rack to cool.

LEMON AND MACADAMIA BREAD

*THE BUTTERY TASTE OF MACADAMIA NUTS COMBINES WELL WITH THE TANGY FLAVOUR OF THE LEMON
RIND AND YOGURT IN THIS DELICIOUS BREAD.*

MAKES ONE LOAF

INGREDIENTS
- 40g/1½oz/3 tbsp butter, plus extra
  for greasing and brushing
- 500g/1¼lb/5 cups unbleached
  strong white bread flour, plus
  extra for dusting
- 4ml/¾ tsp salt
- 7.5ml/1½ tsp dried yeast
- 50g/2oz/¼ cup caster
  (superfine) sugar
- 120ml/4fl oz/½ cup lukewarm milk
- 1 egg
- 175ml/6fl oz/¾ cup lemon yogurt
- 40g/1½oz/¼ cup macadamia nuts,
  roughly chopped
- 15ml/1 tbsp finely grated organic
  lemon rind

1 Line and grease a 15cm/6in cake tin
(pan), extending the paper 5cm/2in
above the rim, or line and grease a
900g/2lb loaf tin (pan).

2 Sift the flour and salt into a bowl and
make a well in the centre.

3 Mix together the yeast, 5ml/1 tsp of
the sugar and the lukewarm milk in a
bowl and pour into the well. Gradually
mix in enough of the surrounding flour
to make a thick batter. Sprinkle a little
of the remaining flour over the top to
cover and leave in a warm place for
20–30 minutes to "sponge" – when the
yeast begins to bubble through the
flour covering.

4 Add the egg, butter, yogurt and the
remaining sugar to the batter, and mix
in the remaining flour to make a dough.
Knead for 10 minutes, or until smooth
and elastic. Cover and leave in a slightly
warm place to rise for 1–1½ hours, or
until doubled in bulk.

5 Knock back (punch down) the dough
and turn out on to a lightly floured
surface. Gently knead in the nuts and
grated rind. Shape the dough into a ball
if using a cake tin, or a long roll if using
a loaf tin, and place in the tin. Cover
and leave to rise for 30–60 minutes,
or until doubled in size.

6 Meanwhile, preheat the oven to
190°C/375°F/Gas 5. Brush with melted
butter and bake for 50 minutes, or until
golden brown and sounding hollow
when tapped. Cool on a wire rack.

COOK'S TIP
Knocking back (punching down) the
dough after the first rising helps to
disperse the air bubbles produced by the
yeast evenly through it. Simply punch it
with your fist.

ORANGE AND CORIANDER BRIOCHES

THE WARM, SPICY FLAVOUR OF CORIANDER COMBINES PARTICULARLY WELL WITH ORANGE IN THESE
DAINTY, INDIVIDUAL BRIOCHES, WHICH WOULD MAKE A WONDERFUL MID-MORNING SNACK.

MAKES TWELVE

INGREDIENTS
    oil, for greasing
    225g/8oz/2 cups strong white
        bread flour
    10ml/2 tsp easy-blend (rapid-rise)
        dried yeast
    2.5ml/½ tsp salt
    15ml/1 tbsp caster (superfine) sugar
    10ml/2 tsp coriander seeds,
        coarsely ground
    grated rind of 1 orange
    2 eggs, beaten
    50g/2oz/¼ cup unsalted (sweet)
        butter, melted
    1 small egg, beaten, to glaze
    thinly pared and shredded orange
        rind, to decorate (optional)

1 Grease 12 individual brioche tins
(pans). Sift the flour into a bowl and stir
in the yeast, salt, sugar, coriander seeds
and orange rind. Make a well in the
centre, pour in 30ml/2 tbsp lukewarm
water, the eggs and melted butter and
beat to make a soft dough.

2 Turn on to a lightly floured surface
and knead for about 5 minutes, or until
smooth and elastic. Return to the clean,
oiled bowl, cover with clear film (plastic
wrap) and leave in a warm place for
1 hour, or until doubled in bulk.

3 Turn on to a floured surface, knead
briefly and roll into a sausage. Cut into
12 pieces. Break off a quarter of each
piece. Shape the larger pieces into balls
and place in the tins.

4 With the floured handle of a wooden
spoon, press a hole in each dough ball.
Shape each small piece of dough into a
little plug and press into the holes.

COOK'S TIP
These individual brioches look especially
attractive if they are made in special
brioche tins. However, they can also be
made in bun or muffin tins (pans) or as a
single loaf in a large brioche tin.

5 Place the brioche tins on a baking
sheet. Cover with lightly oiled clear film
and leave in a warm place until the
dough rises almost to the top of the
tins. Preheat the oven to 220°C/425°F/
Gas 7. Brush the brioches with beaten
egg and bake for 15 minutes, or until
golden brown. Sprinkle over extra
shreds of orange rind to decorate, if you
like, and serve the brioches warm with
plenty of butter.

CLEMENTINE SHORTBREAD FINGERS

LIGHT AND MOUTHWATERING, THESE CITRUS SHORTBREADS ARE A REAL TEA-TIME TREAT. MADE WITH CLEMENTINES THEY MAKE SUBTLY SWEET FESTIVE FARE.

MAKES EIGHTEEN

INGREDIENTS
   115g/4oz/½ cup unsalted (sweet)
      butter, plus extra for greasing
   50g/2oz/¼ cup caster (superfine)
      sugar, plus extra for sprinkling
   finely grated rind of 4 clementines
   175g/6oz/1½ cups plain
      (all-purpose) flour, plus extra
      for dusting

VARIATION
Substitute the grated rind of one Ugli
fruit for the clementine rind and sprinkle
the shortbread fingers well with sugar
before baking.

1 Preheat the oven to 190°C/375°F/
Gas 5 and grease a large baking sheet
with butter. Beat together the butter and
sugar until soft and creamy, then beat
in the clementine rind.

COOK'S TIP
The shortbread fingers will keep in an
airtight container for up to 2 weeks.

2 Gradually add the flour and gently
pull the dough together to form a soft
ball. Roll out the dough on a lightly
floured surface to about 1cm/½in thick.

3 Cut into fingers, sprinkle over a little
extra sugar and put on to the baking
sheet. Prick with a fork and bake for
20 minutes, or until light golden brown.

CINNAMON AND ORANGE TUILES

THESE DELIGHTFUL FRENCH BISCUITS ARE GENTLY AROMATIC WITH THE ADDITION OF CINNAMON AND ORANGE. DIP THEM IN GOOD QUALITY CHOCOLATE FOR AN ELEGANT FINISHING TOUCH.

MAKES FIFTEEN

INGREDIENTS
    2 egg whites
    90g/3½oz/½ cup caster
        (superfine) sugar
    7.5ml/1½ tsp ground cinnamon
    finely grated rind of 1 orange
    50g/2oz/½ cup plain
        (all-purpose) flour
    75g/3oz/6 tbsp butter, melted
For the dipping chocolate
    75g/3oz Belgian plain
        (semisweet) chocolate
    45ml/3 tbsp milk
    75–90ml/5–6 tbsp double (heavy)
        or whipping cream

1 Preheat the oven to 200°C/400°F/ Gas 6. Line three large baking trays with baking parchment.

2 Whisk the egg whites to soft peaks, then whisk in the sugar until smooth and glossy. Add the cinnamon and orange rind, sift over the flour and fold in with the melted butter. Add 15ml/ 1 tbsp freshly boiled water.

3 Place 5 spoonfuls of the mixture on each tray. Flatten and bake, one tray at a time, for about 7 minutes, or until golden. Cool briefly, then remove with a spatula and roll around the handle of a wooden spoon. Cool on a rack.

4 To make the dipping chocolate, place the chocolate in a small pan and pour in the milk. Heat very gently, stirring constantly, until the chocolate has melted and the mixture is smooth, then stir in the cream.

5 Dip one or both ends of the biscuits (cookies) in the chocolate and leave to cool on wire racks.

COOK'S TIP
If you have not made these before, cook only one or two at a time until you get the hang of it. If they harden too quickly to allow you time to roll them, return the baking sheet to the oven for a few seconds, then try rolling them again.

HOT DESSERTS

When people think about hot fruit desserts, citrus fruits do not immediately spring to mind, so the recipes featured here will probably come as a delightful surprise. There are, of course, traditional favourites — crêpes flambéed in orange liqueur are still a popular offering in Parisian-style bistros, while children never cease to enjoy the apparently magical surprise of a reversible sponge pudding swimming in a lovely, lemony syrup. However, there are lots of unexpected treats in store, from compôtes and Scotch pancakes to familiar rice puddings given a tangy citrus makeover.

KUMQUAT AND GOLDEN GINGER COMPÔTE

WARM, SPICY AND FULL OF SUN-RIPENED KUMQUATS, APRICOTS AND SULTANAS — THIS DELIGHTFUL DESSERT WILL ADD A NOTE OF CHEER ON A DREARY WINTER'S DAY.

SERVES FOUR

INGREDIENTS
200g/7oz/2 cups kumquats
200g/7oz/scant 1 cup
  dried apricots
30ml/2 tbsp sultanas (golden raisins)
400ml/14fl oz/1⅔ cups water
1 orange, such as Valencia
2.5cm/1in piece fresh root
  ginger, peeled
4 cardamom pods, lightly crushed
4 cloves
about 30ml/2 tbsp clear honey
15ml/1 tbsp flaked (sliced)
  almonds, toasted

1 Wash the kumquats, and, if they are large, cut them in half. Place them in a pan with the apricots, sultanas and water. Bring to the boil.

2 Thinly pare the orange rind and add to the pan. Grate in the root ginger and add the cardamom pods and cloves.

3 Reduce the heat, cover and simmer gently, stirring occasionally, for about 30 minutes, or until the fruit is tender.

4 Squeeze the juice from the orange and add to the pan with honey to taste. Sprinkle with almonds and serve warm.

COOK'S TIP
For ready-to-eat dried apricots, reduce the water to 300ml/½ pint/1¼ cups, and add them for the last 5 minutes.

CITRUS FLAMBÉ WITH PISTACHIO PRALINE

A FRUIT FLAMBÉ MAKES A DRAMATIC FINALE FOR A DINNER PARTY. TOPPING THIS REFRESHING CITRUS DESSERT WITH CRUNCHY PISTACHIO PRALINE MAKES IT EXTRA SPECIAL.

SERVES FOUR

INGREDIENTS

    4 oranges
    2 ruby grapefruit
    2 limes
    50g/2oz/¼ cup butter
    50g/2oz/¼ cup light muscovado
      (brown) sugar
    45ml/3 tbsp Cointreau
    fresh mint sprigs, to decorate
For the pistachio praline
    oil, for greasing
    115g/4oz/generous ½ cup caster
      (superfine) sugar
    50g/2oz/⅓ cup pistachio nuts

1 First, make the pistachio praline. Brush a baking sheet lightly with oil. Place the caster sugar and pistachio nuts in a small, heavy pan and cook gently, swirling the pan occasionally until the sugar has melted.

2 Continue to cook over a fairly low heat until the nuts start to pop and the sugar has turned a dark golden colour. Pour on to the oiled baking sheet and set aside to cool. Using a sharp knife, chop the praline into coarse chunks.

COOK'S TIP
If preferred, use a rolling pin or toffee hammer to break up the praline.

VARIATION
Use unskinned almonds instead of pistachio nuts for the praline.

3 Cut a thin slice of peel and pith from each end of the citrus fruits. Place cut side down on a plate and cut off the peel and pith. Remove any remaining pith. Cut out each segment leaving the membrane behind. Squeeze the remaining juice from the membrane.

4 Heat the butter and muscovado sugar together in a heavy frying pan until the sugar has melted and the mixture is golden. Strain the citrus juices into the pan and continue to cook, stirring occasionally, until the juice has reduced and is syrupy.

5 Add the orange, grapefruit and lime segments and warm through without stirring. Pour over the Cointreau and carefully set it alight. As soon as the flames die down, spoon the fruit flambé into serving dishes. Sprinkle some praline over each portion and decorate with mint sprigs. Serve immediately.

ORANGES IN HOT COFFEE SYRUP

THIS RECIPE MAKES A MOUTHWATERING DESSERT AND ALSO WORKS WELL WITH MOST CITRUS FRUITS; TRY SWEET CLEMENTINES AS AN ALTERNATIVE TO THE ORANGES.

SERVES SIX

INGREDIENTS
  6 medium oranges
  200g/7oz/1 cup sugar
  50ml/2fl oz/¼ cup cold water
  100ml/3½fl oz/scant ½ cup
    boiling water
  100ml/3½fl oz/scant ½ cup fresh
    strong brewed coffee
  50g/2oz/⅓ cup pistachio nuts,
    chopped (optional)

COOK'S TIP
Choose a pan in which the oranges will just fit in a single layer.

1 Finely pare the rind from one orange, shred and reserve the rind. Peel the remaining oranges. Cut each orange crossways into slices, then re-form and hold in place with a cocktail stick (toothpick) through the centre.

2 Put the sugar and cold water in a pan. Heat gently, stirring constantly, until the sugar dissolves, then bring to the boil and cook until the syrup turns pale gold.

3 Remove from the heat and carefully pour the boiling water into the pan. Return to the heat until the syrup has dissolved in the water. Stir in the coffee.

4 Add the oranges and the shredded rind to the coffee syrup. Simmer for 15–20 minutes, turning the oranges once during cooking. Sprinkle with pistachio nuts, if using, and serve hot.

FIGS AND PEARS IN HONEY

A STUNNINGLY SIMPLE DESSERT USING FRESH FIGS AND PEARS SCENTED WITH THE WARM FRAGRANCES OF CINNAMON AND CARDAMOM AND DRENCHED IN A LEMON AND HONEY SYRUP.

SERVES FOUR

INGREDIENTS
  1 lemon
  90ml/6 tbsp clear honey
  1 cinnamon stick
  1 cardamom pod
  2 pears
  8 fresh figs, halved

COOK'S TIPS
• Leave the peel on the pears or discard, depending on your preference.
• Figs vary in colour from pale green and yellow to dark purple. When buying, look for firm fruit without any bruises or blemishes. A ripe fig will yield gently in your hand without pressing.
• It is best to use pale green or light beige cardamom pods, rather than the coarser dark brown ones.

1 Pare the rind from the lemon using a zester. Alternatively, use a vegetable peeler and then cut into very thin strips.

2 Place the lemon rind, honey, cinnamon stick, cardamom pod and 350ml/12fl oz/1½ cups water in a heavy pan and boil, uncovered, for about 10 minutes until reduced by about half.

3 Cut the pears into eighths, discarding the cores. Place in the syrup, add the figs and simmer for about 5 minutes, or until the fruit is tender.

4 Transfer the fruit to a serving bowl. Continue cooking the liquid until syrupy, then discard the cinnamon stick and pour over the figs and pears. Serve.

CRÊPES WITH ORANGE SAUCE

THIS IS ONE OF THE BEST-KNOWN FRENCH DESSERTS AND IS EASY TO DO AT HOME. YOU CAN MAKE THE CRÊPES IN ADVANCE, AND THEN COAT THEM IN THE TANGY ORANGE SAUCE AT THE LAST MINUTE.

SERVES SIX

INGREDIENTS
  115g/4oz/1 cup plain
    (all-purpose) flour
  1.5ml/¼ tsp salt
  25g/1oz/2 tbsp caster
    (superfine) sugar
  2 eggs, lightly beaten
  about 250ml/8fl oz/1 cup milk
  about 60ml/4 tbsp water
  30ml/2 tbsp orange flower water,
    Cointreau or orange liqueur
  25g/1oz/2 tbsp unsalted (sweet)
    butter, melted, plus extra for frying
For the sauce
  75g/3oz/6 tbsp unsalted
    (sweet) butter
  50g/2oz/¼ cup caster
    (superfine) sugar
  grated rind and juice of
    1 large orange, such as Jaffa
  grated rind and juice of 1 lemon
  150ml/¼ pint/⅔ cup freshly
    squeezed orange juice
  60ml/4 tbsp Cointreau or orange
    liqueur, plus more for flaming
    (optional)
  brandy, for flaming (optional)
  orange segments, to decorate

1 Sift the flour, salt and sugar into a large bowl. Make a well in the centre and pour in the eggs. Beat the eggs, gradually incorporating the flour.

2 Whisk in the milk, water and orange flower water or liqueur to make a very smooth batter. Strain into a jug (pitcher) and set aside for 20–30 minutes.

3 Heat an 18–20cm/7–8in crêpe pan (preferably non-stick) over a medium heat. If the crêpe batter has thickened, add a little more water or milk to thin it. Stir the melted butter into the batter.

4 Brush the hot pan with a little extra melted butter and pour in about 30ml/2 tbsp of batter. Quickly tilt and rotate the pan to cover the base evenly with a thin layer of batter. Cook for about 1 minute, or until the top is set and the base is golden. With a metal spatula, lift the edge to check the colour, then carefully turn over the crêpe and cook for 20–30 seconds, just to set. Tip out on to a plate.

5 Continue cooking the crêpes, stirring the batter occasionally and brushing the pan with a little more melted butter as and when necessary. Place a sheet of clear film (plastic wrap) or baking parchment between each crêpe as they are stacked to prevent them from sticking. (The crêpes can be prepared ahead to this point – put them in a plastic bag and chill until ready to use.)

6 To make the sauce, melt the butter in a large frying pan over a medium-low heat, then stir in the sugar, orange and lemon rind and juice, the additional orange juice and the orange liqueur.

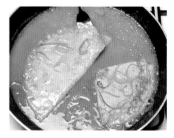

7 Place a crêpe in the pan browned-side down, swirling gently to coat with the sauce. Fold it in half, then in half again to form a triangle, and push to the side of the pan. Continue heating and folding the crêpes until all are warm and covered with the sauce.

8 To flame the crêpes, heat 30–45ml/2–3 tbsp each of orange liqueur and brandy in a small pan over a medium heat. Remove the pan from the heat, carefully ignite the liquid with a match then pour evenly over the crêpes. Sprinkle over the orange segments and serve immediately.

COOK'S TIP
Cointreau is the world's leading brand of orange liqueur. It is colourless and flavoured with a mixture of bitter orange peel and sweet oranges.

CHOCOLATE AND ORANGE SCOTCH PANCAKES

YOU ARE SURE TO ADORE THESE FABULOUS BABY PANCAKES IN A RICH, CREAMY ORANGE LIQUEUR SAUCE. SERVE THEM STRAIGHT FROM THE PAN TO ENJOY THEM AT THEIR BEST.

SERVES FOUR

INGREDIENTS

115g/4oz/1 cup self-raising
(self-rising) flour
30ml/2 tbsp cocoa powder
(unsweetened)
2 eggs
50g/2oz plain (semisweet) chocolate,
broken into squares
200ml/7fl oz/scant 1 cup milk
finely grated rind of 1 orange
30ml/2 tbsp orange juice
butter or oil, for frying
chocolate curls, to decorate
For the sauce
2 large oranges
25g/1oz/2 tbsp unsalted
(sweet) butter
40g/1½oz/3 tbsp soft light
brown sugar
225g/8oz/1 cup crème fraîche
30ml/2 tbsp Grand Marnier

1 Sift the flour and cocoa powder into a large mixing bowl and make a well in the centre. Add the eggs and beat well, gradually incorporating the surrounding dry ingredients as you work to make a smooth batter.

2 Put the chocolate into a heavy pan and pour in the milk. Heat gently, stirring constantly, until the chocolate has melted, then beat the mixture into the batter until smooth and bubbly.

3 Finally, stir the finely grated orange rind and the orange juice into the chocolate mixture.

4 Heat a heavy frying pan or griddle pan. Grease with butter or oil. Drop 2 tablespoons of batter at a time on to the hot surface. When the pancakes are lightly browned underneath and bubbly on top, flip them over to cook the other side. Slide on to a plate and keep hot.

5 Make the sauce. Pare and shred the rind of 1 orange and set aside. Using a sharp knife, peel the second orange, carefully remove all the pith from both oranges, then finely slice the oranges into sections.

6 Heat the butter and sugar in a wide, shallow pan over low heat, stirring until the sugar dissolves. Stir in the crème fraîche and heat gently.

7 Add the pancakes and orange slices to the sauce, heat very gently for about 2 minutes, then top with the liqueur. Carefully transfer to a large serving plate, sprinkle with the reserved orange rind and decorate with the chocolate curls. Serve the pancakes immediately.

SYRUPY BRIOCHE SLICES WITH ICE CREAM

KEEP A FEW INDIVIDUAL BRIOCHE BUNS IN THE FREEZER TO MAKE THIS SUPER FIVE-MINUTE DESSERT.
FOR A SLIGHTLY TARTER TASTE, USE LEMON INSTEAD OF ORANGE RIND.

SERVES FOUR

INGREDIENTS
    butter, for greasing
    finely grated rind and juice of
        1 orange, such as Navelina or blood
        orange
    50g/2oz/¼ cup caster
        (superfine) sugar
    90ml/6 tbsp water
    1.5ml/¼ tsp ground cinnamon
    4 brioche buns
    15ml/1 tbsp icing
        (confectioners') sugar
    400ml/14fl oz/1⅔ cups vanilla
        ice cream

1 Lightly grease a gratin dish and set aside. Put the orange rind and juice, sugar, water and cinnamon in a heavy pan. Heat gently, stirring constantly, until the sugar has dissolved, then boil rapidly, without stirring, for 2 minutes, until thickened and syrupy.

2 Remove the orange syrup from the heat and pour it into a shallow heatproof dish. Preheat the grill (broiler). Cut each brioche vertically into three thick slices. Dip one side of each slice in the hot syrup and arrange in the gratin dish, syrupy sides down. Reserve the remaining syrup. Grill (broil) the brioche until lightly toasted.

VARIATION
Substitute the same amount of ground cardamom for the cinnamon.

3 Using tongs, turn the brioche slices over and dust well with icing sugar. Grill for about 3 minutes more, or until they are just beginning to caramelize around the edges.

4 Transfer the hot brioche to serving plates and top with scoops of vanilla ice cream. Spoon the remaining syrup over them and serve immediately.

COOK'S TIP
You could also use slices of a larger brioche, rather than buns, or madeleines, sliced horizontally in half. These are traditionally flavoured with lemon or orange flower water, making them especially tasty.

STICKY PEAR PUDDING <small>WITH</small> ORANGE CREAM

CLOVES ADD A DISTINCTIVELY FRAGRANT FLAVOUR TO THIS HAZELNUT, PEAR AND COFFEE PUDDING.
ACCOMPANIED BY A TANGY ORANGE CREAM, IT MAKES A HEAVENLY DESSERT.

SERVES SIX

INGREDIENTS
115g/4oz/½ cup unsalted (sweet)
 butter, softened, plus extra
 for greasing
30ml/2 tbsp ground coffee,
 hazelnut-flavoured if possible
15ml/1 tbsp near-boiling water
50g/2oz/⅓ cup hazelnuts, toasted
 and skinned (see Cook's Tip)
4 ripe pears
juice of ½ orange
115g/4oz/generous ½ cup golden
 caster (superfine) sugar, plus an
 extra 15ml/1 tbsp for baking
2 eggs, beaten
50g/2oz/½ cup self-raising
 (self-rising) flour, sifted
pinch of ground cloves
8 whole cloves (optional)
45ml/3 tbsp maple syrup
fine strips of pared orange rind,
 to decorate
For the orange cream
300ml/½ pint/1¼ cups
 whipping cream
15ml/1 tbsp icing (confectioners')
 sugar, sifted
finely grated rind of
 ½ orange

1 Preheat the oven to 180°C/350°F/
Gas 4. Lightly grease a 20cm/8in loose-
based sandwich tin (layer pan) with
butter. Put the ground coffee in a small
bowl and pour the hot water over. Leave
to infuse (steep) for about 4 minutes,
then strain through a fine sieve or
coffee filter paper.

2 Grind the hazelnuts in a coffee
grinder until fine. Peel, halve and core
the pears. Thinly slice across the pear
halves part of the way through. Brush
with orange juice.

3 Beat the butter and the 115g/4oz/
generous ½ cup caster sugar together
in a large bowl until very light and fluffy.
Gradually beat in the eggs, then fold in
the flour, ground cloves, hazelnuts and
coffee. Spoon the mixture into the tin
and level the surface.

4 Pat the pears dry, then arrange them
in the sponge mixture, flat-side down.

5 Press one whole clove into each pear
half, if using, then brush the pears with
15ml/1 tbsp maple syrup.

6 Lightly sprinkle the pears with the
15ml/1 tbsp caster sugar, then bake for
45–50 minutes, or until firm.

7 While the sponge is cooking, make
the orange cream. Whip the cream,
icing sugar and orange rind until soft
peaks form. Spoon into a serving dish
and chill until needed.

8 Allow the sponge to cool for about
10 minutes in the tin, then remove and
place on a serving plate. Lightly brush
with the remaining maple syrup before
decorating with orange rind and serving
warm with the orange cream.

COOK'S TIP
To toast and skin hazelnuts, spread out
in a grill (broiler) pan and toast under
a hot grill for 3–4 minutes, turning them
frequently until well browned. Put the
nuts in a dishtowel and rub off the skins.
Cool before grinding.

APRICOTS WITH CITRUS ALMOND PASTE

TAKE ADVANTAGE OF THE SHORT APRICOT SEASON BY MAKING THIS CHARMING APRICOT AND ALMOND DESSERT, DELICATELY SCENTED WITH LEMON JUICE AND ORANGE FLOWER WATER.

2 Place the ground almonds, icing sugar, orange flower water, butter and almond essence in a bowl and blend together to make a smooth paste.

3 Wash the apricots and then make a slit in the flesh and ease out the stone (pit). Take small pieces of the almond paste, roll into balls and press one into each of the apricots.

4 Arrange the stuffed apricots in a shallow ovenproof dish and carefully pour the sugar syrup around them. Cover with foil and bake in the oven for 25–30 minutes.

5 Serve the apricots with a little of the syrup, and decorated with sprigs of fresh mint.

COOK'S TIP
Always use a heavy pan when making syrup and stir constantly with a wooden spoon until the sugar has completely dissolved. Do not let liquid come to the boil before it has dissolved, or the result will be grainy.

SERVES SIX

INGREDIENTS
75g/3oz/6 tbsp caster
   (superfine) sugar
30ml/2 tbsp lemon juice
300ml/½ pint/1¼ cups water
115g/4oz/1 cup ground almonds
50g/2oz/½ cup icing
   (confectioners') sugar
a little orange flower water
25g/1oz/2 tbsp unsalted (sweet)
   butter, melted
2.5ml/½ tsp almond
   essence (extract)
900g/2lb fresh apricots
fresh mint sprigs,
   to decorate

1 Preheat the oven to 180°C/350°F/ Gas 4. Place the sugar, lemon juice and water in a small pan and bring to the boil, stirring occasionally until the sugar has all dissolved. Simmer gently for 5–10 minutes to make a thin syrup.

CREAMY LEMON RICE

THIS IS A BAKED RICE PUDDING WITH A DIFFERENCE, BEING SUBTLY FLAVOURED WITH LEMON. IT IS WONDERFUL SERVED WARM OR COLD WITH FRESH FRUIT.

SERVES FOUR

INGREDIENTS

15g/½oz/1 tbsp butter, cut into
    small pieces, plus extra for greasing
50g/2oz/scant ¼ cup short grain
    white rice
600ml/1 pint/2½ cups milk
25g/1oz/2 tbsp caster
    (superfine) sugar
finely grated rind of 1 lemon
thinly pared and shredded orange
    and lemon rind, to decorate
To serve
225g/8oz prepared fresh fruit, such
    as strawberries or pineapple
90ml/6 tbsp crème fraîche (optional)

1 Grease a 900ml/1½ pint/3¾ cup ovenproof dish. Add the rice and pour in the milk. Set aside for 30 minutes, to allow the rice to soften a little. Preheat the oven to 150°C/300°F/Gas 2.

2 Add the caster sugar, grated lemon rind and diced butter to the rice and milk and stir gently to mix. Bake the pudding for 2–2½ hours, until the top is light golden brown.

3 Decorate with shredded orange and lemon rind and serve warm or hot with the fresh fruit. Alternatively, leave the pudding to cool completely, remove and discard the skin, then chill. Fold in the crème fraîche, if using, and decorate with the shredded citrus rinds just before serving with the fruit.

VARIATION
Replace half the milk with cream.

COCONUT RICE PUDDINGS
WITH GRILLED ORANGES

STICKY RICE PUDDING IS A SPECIALITY OF MANY SOUTH-EAST ASIAN COUNTRIES. IN THESE DELIGHTFUL LITTLE DESSERTS, THAI JASMINE RICE IS COOKED WITH RICH AND CREAMY COCONUT MILK, THEN SERVED WITH GOLDEN GRILLED ORANGES.

SERVES FOUR

INGREDIENTS

2 oranges, such as Valencia
175g/6oz/scant 1 cup jasmine rice
400ml/14fl oz/1⅔ cup coconut milk
2.5ml/½ tsp freshly grated nutmeg, plus extra for sprinkling
large pinch of salt
60ml/4 tbsp golden caster (superfine) sugar
oil, for greasing
orange peel twists, to decorate

1 Using a sharp knife, cut away the peel and pith from the oranges, then cut the flesh into rounds. Set aside.

2 Rinse and drain the rice. Place in a pan, cover with water, and bring to the boil. Cook for 5 minutes, until the grains are just beginning to soften. Place the rice in a muslin-lined (cheesecloth-lined) steamer, then make a few holes in the muslin to allow the steam to get through. Steam the rice for 15 minutes, or until tender.

3 Put the steamed rice in a heavy pan with the coconut milk, nutmeg, salt and sugar and cook over a low heat until the mixture begins to simmer. Simmer for about 5 minutes, or until the mixture is thick and creamy, stirring frequently to prevent the rice from sticking.

4 Spoon the rice mixture into four lightly oiled 175ml/6fl oz/¾ cup dariole moulds or ramekins and leave to cool.

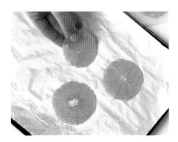

5 Preheat the grill (broiler) to high. Line a baking tray or the grill rack with foil and place the orange slices on top. Sprinkle the oranges with a little grated nutmeg, then grill (broil) for 6 minutes, or until lightly golden, turning the slices halfway through cooking.

6 When the rice mixture is completely cold, run a knife around the edge of the moulds or ramekins and turn out the rice. Decorate with orange peel twists and serve with the warm orange slices.

DATE, FIG AND ORANGE PUDDING

WARM UP COLD WINTER DAYS WITH THIS SATISFYING STEAMED PUDDING OF RICH DRIED FRUITS AND
REFRESHING ORANGE ENLIVENED WITH A DASH OF ORANGE LIQUEUR. FOR EXTRA SELF-INDULGENCE,
SERVE IT WITH A LITTLE WHIPPED CREAM OR CUSTARD.

SERVES SIX

INGREDIENTS
  2 oranges
  115g/4oz/scant 1 cup stoned
    (pitted), ready-to-eat dried
    dates, chopped
  115g/4oz/²/₃ cup ready-to-eat dried
    figs, chopped
  30ml/2 tbsp Cointreau or orange
    liqueur (optional)
  175g/6oz/¾ cup unsalted (sweet)
    butter, plus extra for greasing
  175g/6oz/¾ cup soft light
    brown sugar
  3 eggs
  75g/3oz/²/₃ cup self-raising
    (self-rising) wholemeal
    (whole-wheat) flour
  115g/4oz/1 cup unbleached self-
    raising (self-rising) flour
  30ml/2 tbsp golden (light corn)
    syrup (optional)

1 Thinly pare a few pieces of rind from one orange and cut it into fine strips and reserve. Grate the rind from the remaining oranges and squeeze out the juice. Put the grated rind and juice in a pan. Add the chopped dates and figs and the orange liqueur, if using. Cook, covered, over a low heat for 8–10 minutes, or until the fruit is soft.

2 Leave the fruit mixture to cool, then transfer to a food processor or blender and process until fairly smooth. Press through a sieve to remove the fig seeds, if you like.

3 Cream the butter and sugar until pale and fluffy, then beat in the fruit purée. Beat in the eggs, then fold in the flours.

4 Grease a 1.5 litre/2½ pint/6 cup pudding bowl, and pour in the golden syrup, if using. Spoon in the pudding mixture. Cover the top with baking parchment, with a pleat folded down the centre, and then with pleated foil, and tie down with string.

5 Place the bowl in a large pan, and pour in enough water to come halfway up the sides of the bowl. Cover and steam for 2 hours. Check the water occasionally and top up if necessary. Serve decorated with the reserved orange rind.

SURPRISE LEMON PUDDING

ALTHOUGH ALL THE INGREDIENTS ARE MIXED TOGETHER, DURING COOKING A TANGY LEMON SAUCE FORMS BENEATH A LIGHT TOPPING, MAKING THIS LEMON PUDDING A TASTY SURPRISE.

SERVES FOUR

INGREDIENTS
  75g/3oz/6 tbsp butter
  175g/6oz/¾ cup soft light
    brown sugar
  4 eggs, separated
  grated rind and juice of 4 lemons
  50g/2oz/½ cup self-raising
    (self-rising) flour
  120ml/4fl oz/½ cup milk

VARIATION
This pudding is also delicious made with oranges instead of lemons.

1 Preheat the oven to 180°C/350°F/ Gas 4. Butter an 18cm/7in soufflé dish and stand it in a roasting pan.

2 Beat the butter and sugar together in a large bowl until pale and very fluffy. Beat in one egg yolk at a time, beating well after each addition and gradually beating in the lemon rind and juice until well mixed; do not worry if the mixture curdles a little.

3 Sift the flour and stir it into the lemon mixture until well mixed, then gradually stir in the milk.

4 Whisk the egg whites in a separate bowl until stiff, but not dry, then lightly, but thoroughly, fold into the lemon mixture in three batches. Carefully pour the mixture into the soufflé dish, then pour boiling water into the roasting pan.

5 Bake the pudding in the middle of the oven for 45 minutes, or until golden on top. Dust with icing (confectioners') sugar and serve immediately.

COOK'S TIP
When whisking egg whites, use a grease-free bowl and make sure that there are no traces of yolk.

APPLE AND KUMQUAT SPONGE PUDDINGS

THE INTENSE FLAVOUR OF KUMQUATS MAKES THESE DAINTY PUDDINGS SPECIAL. SERVED WITH MORE KUMQUATS IN A CREAMY SAUCE, THIS IS A DESSERT THAT IS SURE TO PLEASE.

SERVES EIGHT

INGREDIENTS
    150g/5oz/10 tbsp butter, at room
      temperature, plus extra for greasing
    175g/6oz cooking apples, peeled and
      thinly sliced
    75g/3oz kumquats, thinly sliced
    150g/5oz/¾ cup golden caster
      (superfine) sugar
    2 eggs
    115g/4oz/1 cup self-raising
      (self-rising) flour
For the sauce
    75g/3oz kumquats, thinly sliced
    75g/3oz/6 tbsp caster
      (superfine) sugar
    250ml/8fl oz/1 cup water
    150ml/¼ pint/⅔ cup crème fraîche
    5ml/1 tsp cornflour (cornstarch)
      mixed with 10ml/2 tsp water
    lemon juice to taste

1 Prepare a steamer. Butter eight 150ml/¼ pint/⅔ cup dariole moulds or ramekins and put a disc of buttered baking parchment on the base of each.

2 Melt 25g/1oz/2 tbsp butter in a frying pan. Add the apples, kumquats and 25g/1oz/2 tbsp sugar and cook over medium heat for 5–8 minutes, or until the apples start to soften and the sugar begins to caramelize. Remove from the heat and leave to cool.

3 Cream the remaining butter with the remaining sugar until pale and fluffy. Add the eggs, one at a time, beating after each addition. Fold in the flour.

4 Evenly divide the apple and kumquat mixture among the prepared moulds. Top with the sponge mixture. Cover the moulds and put into the steamer. Steam for 45 minutes.

5 Meanwhile, make the sauce. Put the kumquats, sugar and water in a pan and bring to the boil, stirring to dissolve the sugar. Simmer for 5 minutes.

6 Stir in the crème fraîche and bring back to the boil, stirring. Remove the pan from the heat and gradually whisk in the cornflour mixture. Return the pan to the heat and simmer very gently for 2 minutes, stirring constantly. Add lemon juice to taste.

7 Turn out the puddings and serve hot, with the sauce.

COLD
DESSERTS

Cold desserts based on citrus fruits are a delightful and refreshing way to end a meal, especially in the summer. The range is extensive, from simple fruit salads to elegant cheesecakes. Rich creamy dishes, such as mousses, are beautifully balanced by the sharp, yet sweet flavour of citrus fruits, while a fresh-tasting home-made jelly is the perfect choice to follow a hot and spicy main course. As well as ever-popular orange and lemon desserts, recipes here feature kumquats, mandarins, limes, clementines and even grapefruit doused in whisky.

GRAPEFRUIT IN HONEY AND WHISKY

CREATE A SIMPLE YET ELEGANT DESSERT BY ARRANGING A COLOURFUL FAN OF PINK, RED AND WHITE GRAPEFRUIT SEGMENTS IN A SWEET WHISKY SAUCE. THIS DESSERT IS PERFECT AFTER A RICH MEAL.

SERVES FOUR

INGREDIENTS
  1 pink grapefruit
  1 red grapefruit
  1 white grapefruit
  50g/2oz/¼ cup sugar
  60ml/4 tbsp clear honey
  45ml/3 tbsp whisky
  mint leaves, to decorate

1 Cut a thin slice of peel and pith from each end of the grapefruit. Place cut side down on a plate and cut off the peel and pith in strips. Remove any remaining pith. Cut out each segment leaving the membrane behind. Put the segments into a shallow bowl.

2 Put the sugar and 150ml/¼ pint/ ⅔ cup water into a heavy pan, bring to the boil, stirring constantly, until the sugar has completely dissolved, then simmer, without stirring, for 10 minutes, until thickened and syrupy.

3 Heat the honey in a pan and boil until it becomes a slightly deeper colour or begins to caramelize. Remove the pan from the heat, add the whisky and, using a match or taper, carefully ignite, if you like, then pour the mixture into the sugar syrup.

VARIATION
The whisky can be replaced with brandy, Cointreau or Grand Marnier.

4 Bring to the boil, and pour over the grapefruit segments. Cover and leave until cold. To serve, put the grapefruit segments on to four serving plates, alternating the colours, pour over some of the syrup and decorate with mint.

ORANGES <u>IN</u> CARAMEL SAUCE

THE APPEAL OF THIS TASTY DESSERT IS THE CONTRAST BETWEEN THE SWEETNESS OF THE CARAMEL AND THE TANGY TARTNESS OF THE ORANGES. MAKE IT IN ADVANCE FOR CONVENIENT ENTERTAINING.

SERVES SIX

INGREDIENTS

   6 large seedless oranges, such
     as Navelina, well-scrubbed
   90g/3½oz/½ cup sugar

1 With a vegetable peeler, remove wide strips of rind from two of the oranges. Stack two or three strips at a time and cut into very thin julienne strips.

2 Using a sharp knife, cut a thin slice of peel and pith from both ends of each orange. Place cut-side down on a plate and cut off the peel and pith in strips. Remove any remaining pith. Slice the peeled fruit crossways into thick rounds about 1cm/½in thick. Put the orange slices in a serving bowl and pour over any juice.

3 Half-fill a large bowl with cold water and set aside. Place the sugar and 45ml/3 tbsp water in a small, heavy pan without a non-stick coating and bring to the boil over a high heat, swirling the pan to dissolve the sugar.

4 Continue to boil, without stirring, until the mixture turns a dark caramel colour. Remove the pan from the heat and, standing well back, dip the base of the pan into the cold water to stop the cooking process.

5 Add about 30ml/2 tbsp water to the caramel, pouring it down the sides of the pan, and swirl to combine.

6 Add the strips of orange rind and return the pan to the heat. Simmer gently over a medium-low heat, stirring occasionally, for 8–10 minutes, or until the strips are slightly translucent. Remove the pan from the heat.

7 Pour the caramel and rind over the oranges, turn gently to mix and chill for at least 1 hour before serving.

FRESH FRUIT SALAD

ORANGES ARE AN ESSENTIAL INGREDIENT FOR A SUCCESSFUL AND REFRESHING FRUIT SALAD, WHICH CAN INCLUDE ANY FRUIT IN SEASON. STRAWBERRIES AND PEACHES ARE USED HERE.

SERVES SIX

INGREDIENTS
  2 apples
  2 oranges
  2 peaches
  16–20 strawberries
  30ml/2 tbsp lemon juice
  15–30ml/1–2 tbsp orange
    flower water
  icing (confectioners') sugar,
    to taste (optional)
  a few sprigs of fresh mint,
    to decorate

COOK'S TIP
There are no rules with this fruit salad, and you could use almost any fruit that you like. Oranges, however, should form the base and apples give a delightful contrast in texture.

1 Peel and core the apples and cut into thin slices. Cut a thin slice of peel and pith from both ends of the oranges, then cut off the remaining peel and pith. Cut out each segment leaving the membrane behind. Squeeze the juice from the membrane and retain.

2 Blanch the peaches for 1 minute in boiling water, then peel off the skin and cut the flesh into thick slices.

3 Hull the strawberries, if you like, and halve or quarter if large. Place all the fruit in a large serving bowl.

4 Blend together the lemon juice, orange flower water and any orange juice. Taste and add a little icing sugar to sweeten, if you like. Pour the fruit juice mixture over the salad and serve decorated with mint leaves.

DRIED FRUIT SALAD

THIS IS A WONDERFUL COMBINATION OF FRESH AND DRIED FRUIT FLAVOURED WITH HONEY AND LEMON, AND MAKES AN EXCELLENT DESSERT THROUGHOUT THE YEAR. YOU CAN USE FROZEN RASPBERRIES OR BLACKBERRIES IN WINTER.

SERVES FOUR

INGREDIENTS
  115g/4oz/½ cup dried apricots
  115g/4oz/½ cup dried peaches
  1 pear
  1 apple
  1 orange
  115g/4oz/1 cup mixed raspberries
    and blackberries
  1 cinnamon stick
  50g/2oz/¼ cup caster
    (superfine) sugar
  15ml/1 tbsp clear honey
  30ml/2 tbsp lemon juice

1 Place the apricots and peaches in a bowl and add water to cover. Set aside to soak for 1–2 hours until plump, then drain and halve or quarter.

2 Peel and core the pear and apple, then dice. Cut a thin slice of peel and pith from each end of the orange. Place cut-side down on a plate and cut off the peel and pith. Remove any remaining pith. Cut the orange into wedges. Place all the fruit in a large pan with the raspberries and blackberries.

3 Add 600ml/1 pint/2½ cups water, the cinnamon, sugar and honey, and bring to the boil. Cover and simmer gently for about 10 minutes, then remove the pan from the heat. Stir in the lemon juice. Leave to cool completely, then transfer the fruit and syrup to a bowl and chill for 1–2 hours before serving.

CLEMENTINES WITH STAR ANISE

CHOOSE THIS FRESH CITRUS DESSERT, DELICATELY FLAVOURED WITH MULLING SPICES, TO COMPLETE A RICH MEAL OVER THE FESTIVE SEASON.

SERVES SIX

INGREDIENTS
rind of 1 lime
350ml/12fl oz/1½ cups sweet
  dessert wine, such as Sauternes
75g/3oz/6 tbsp caster
  (superfine) sugar
6 star anise
1 cinnamon stick
1 vanilla pod (bean)
30ml/2 tbsp Cointreau or other
  orange liqueur
12 clementines

VARIATION
Tangerines or seedless oranges can be used instead of clementines.

1 Thinly pare 1 or 2 strips of rind from the lime. Put in a pan, along with the wine, sugar, star anise and cinnamon. Split the vanilla pod and add it to the pan. Bring to the boil, then lower the heat and simmer for 10 minutes.

2 Remove the pan from the heat and leave to cool, then stir in the liqueur.

3 Peel the clementines. Cut some of them in half and place them all in a dish. Pour over the wine and chill.

CLEMENTINE JELLY

WHEN CLEMENTINES ARE IN SEASON MAKE THIS LIGHT CITRUS JELLY. SERVED WITH WHIPPED CREAM, IT IS SURE TO BE A FAVOURITE WITH ADULTS AND CHILDREN ALIKE.

SERVES FOUR

INGREDIENTS

12 clementines
clear grape juice (see step 1
    for quantity)
15ml/1 tbsp powdered gelatine
30ml/2 tbsp caster (superfine) sugar
whipped cream, to decorate

1 Squeeze the juice from eight of the clementines and pour it into a jug (pitcher). Make up to 600ml/1 pint/ 2½ cups with the grape juice, then strain the mixture through a fine sieve.

2 Pour half the juice mixture into a pan. Sprinkle the gelatine on top, leave for 5 minutes to soften, then heat gently until the gelatine has dissolved. Stir in the sugar, then the remaining juice. Remove from the heat and set aside.

VARIATION
Use four ruby or pink grapefruit instead of the clementines, if you like. Squeeze the juice from half of them and then segment the rest.

3 Pare the rind very thinly from the remaining clementines and set aside. Using a small, sharp knife, cut out each segment leaving the membrane behind. Discard the membrane and white pith.

4 Place half the clementine segments in four dessert glasses and cover with some of the liquid fruit jelly. Place them in the refrigerator and leave to set. This will take about 1 hour.

5 When the jellies are set, arrange the remaining clementine segments on top. Carefully pour over the remaining liquid jelly and chill for a further 1 hour until completely set.

6 Cut the reserved pared clementine rind into fine shreds. Serve the jellies decorated with a generous spoonful of whipped cream sprinkled with clementine rind shreds.

LEMON CHEESE MOUSSE WITH BRANDY SNAP BASKETS

A LIGHT CHEESECAKE-STYLE LEMON MOUSSE WITH A HINT OF GINGER FILLS THESE DAINTY BRANDY SNAP BASKETS. ASSEMBLE THE INDIVIDUAL DESSERTS AT THE LAST MINUTE, SO THAT THEY STAY CRISP.

MAKES SIX TO EIGHT

INGREDIENTS
 45ml/3 tbsp water
 10ml/2 tsp powdered gelatine
 250g/9oz/generous 1 cup curd
  (farmer's) cheese
 150ml/¼ pint/⅔ cup natural
  (plain) yogurt
 juice of 2 lemons
 30ml/2 tbsp clear honey, or to taste
 15ml/1 tbsp grated crystallized
  (candied) ginger
 2 egg whites
 mint sprigs, to decorate
 selection of soft fruit, to serve
For the baskets
 50g/2oz/¼ cup butter
 30ml/2 tbsp golden (light corn) syrup
 50g/2oz/¼ cup granulated sugar
 grated rind of 2 lemons
 50g/2oz/½ cup plain
  (all-purpose) flour
 1 orange, for shaping the baskets

1 To make the baskets, preheat the oven to 190°C/375°F/Gas 5. Line a large baking sheet with baking parchment. Melt the butter, syrup and sugar in a pan, then remove from the heat and stir in half the lemon rind and all the flour. Beat until smooth.

COOK'S TIP
To save time, you can use bought brandy snaps to make the baskets. Simply warm them in a very low oven until they uncurl, then shape them into baskets over the orange.

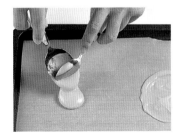

2 Put about 30ml/2 tbsp of mixture on the prepared baking sheet. Using a metal spatula, spread out the mixture to a 13cm/5in circle. Add a second circle, some distance from the first to allow room for spreading. Bake for 5–7 minutes, or until the biscuits (cookies) have spread out and are lacy and light golden brown.

3 Allow the biscuits to cool for about 1 minute so that they firm slightly, but do not harden, then lift each in turn off the baking sheet using a metal spatula. Gently press the biscuits over the orange, carefully fluting the edges, and protecting your hands with a clean dishtowel, if necessary.

4 Remove the baskets when shaped and leave them to cool on a wire rack. Repeat the entire cooking and shaping process with the remaining mixture until you have used it all. If the brandy snaps harden before you have a chance to shape them, simply pop them back in the oven briefly to soften.

5 Make the mousse. Pour the water into a bowl and sprinkle the gelatine over the surface. Leave until spongy, then dissolve over simmering water.

6 Blend the cheese, yogurt, remaining lemon rind, lemon juice, honey and ginger in a food processor. Add the gelatine, blend briefly and pour into a bowl. Chill until just beginning to set.

7 Whisk the egg whites to soft peaks and fold into the mousse. Spoon into the baskets and serve, decorated with mint sprigs, accompanied by soft fruit.

RICH CHOCOLATE MOUSSE
WITH GLAZED KUMQUATS

THE COMBINATION OF CITRUS AND CHOCOLATE HAS ALWAYS BEEN A FAVOURITE. PERFUMED KUMQUATS,
GLAZED IN AN ORANGE LIQUEUR SAUCE, MAKE THIS RICH CHOCOLATE MOUSSE EXTRA SPECIAL.

SERVES SIX

INGREDIENTS
 225g/8oz plain (semisweet)
  chocolate, broken into squares
 4 eggs, separated
 30ml/2 tbsp brandy or orange liqueur
 90ml/6 tbsp double (heavy) cream
For the glazed kumquats
 275g/10oz/2¾ cups kumquats
 115g/4oz/generous ½ cup
  granulated sugar
 15ml/1 tbsp orange liqueur, such as
  Grand Marnier

1 To make the glazed kumquats, halve the fruit lengthways and place cut side up in a shallow serving dish.

2 Place the sugar in a small pan with 150ml/¼ pint/⅔ cup water. Heat gently, stirring constantly, until the sugar has dissolved, then bring to the boil and boil rapidly, without stirring, until a golden-brown caramel forms.

VARIATION
Use peeled and sliced small, seedless oranges in place of the kumquats.

3 Remove the pan from the heat and very carefully stir in 60ml/4 tbsp boiling water. Stir in the orange liqueur, then pour the caramel sauce over the kumquat slices and leave to cool. Once completely cold, cover and chill.

4 Line a shallow 20cm/8in round cake tin (pan) with clear film (plastic wrap). Melt the chocolate in a bowl over a pan of barely simmering water, then remove the bowl from the heat.

5 Beat the egg yolks and brandy or liqueur into the chocolate, then gently fold in the cream. In a separate mixing bowl, whisk the egg whites until stiff, then gently fold them into the chocolate mixture. Pour the mixture into the prepared tin and level the surface. Chill for several hours until set.

6 To serve, turn the mousse out on to a plate and cut into slices or wedges. Serve the chocolate mousse on serving plates and spoon some of the glazed kumquats alongside.

CHOCOLATE MANDARIN TRIFLE

TRIFLE IS ALWAYS A TEMPTING TREAT, BUT WHEN A RICH CHOCOLATE AND MASCARPONE CUSTARD IS COMBINED WITH AMARETTO DI SARONNO AND MANDARIN ORANGES, IT BECOMES SHEER DELIGHT.

SERVES SIX TO EIGHT

INGREDIENTS
    4 trifle sponges
    14 amaretti
    60ml/4 tbsp Amaretto di Saronno or
        sweet sherry
    8 mandarin oranges
For the custard
    200g/7oz plain (semisweet)
        chocolate, broken into squares
    30ml/2 tbsp cornflour (cornstarch)
    25g/1oz/2 tbsp icing
        (confectioners') sugar
    2 egg yolks
    200ml/7fl oz/scant 1 cup milk
    225g/8oz/1 cup mascarpone cheese
For the topping
    225g/8oz/1 cup ricotta cheese
    chocolate shapes
    mandarin orange slices

1 Break up the trifle sponges and place them in a large glass serving dish. Crumble the amaretti evenly over them and then sprinkle with the Amaretto or sweet sherry.

2 Squeeze the juice from two of the mandarins and sprinkle into the dish. Peel the remaining mandarins and remove and discard the pith. Cut out each segment leaving the membrane behind. Squeeze the remaining juice from the membrane and sprinkle into the dish. Add the segments to the dish.

3 Make the custard. Melt the chocolate in a heatproof bowl over a pan of barely simmering water.

4 In a separate bowl, mix the cornflour, sugar and egg yolks to a paste.

5 Heat the milk in a small pan until almost boiling, then pour on to the egg yolk mixture, stirring constantly. Return to the clean pan and stir over a low heat until the custard has thickened slightly and is smooth.

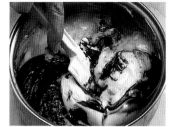

6 Stir in the mascarpone until melted. Add the melted chocolate, mixing it in evenly. Spread over the trifle sponges, cool, then chill.

7 To make the topping, evenly spread the ricotta cheese over the custard. Decorate with chocolate shapes and mandarin slices just before serving.

LEMON COEUR À LA CRÈME WITH ORANGES

THESE CHARMING HEART-SHAPED, CREAMY SWEET CHEESES ARE A TRADITIONAL FRENCH DESSERT.
SURROUNDED BY ORANGES IN A COINTREAU SAUCE, THEY MAKE A DELIGHTFUL AND REFRESHING
FINALE TO A RICH MAIN COURSE.

2 Line four *coeur à la crème* moulds with muslin (cheesecloth), then divide the mixture among them. Level the surface of each, then place the moulds on a plate to catch any liquid that drains from the cheese. Cover with clear film (plastic wrap) and chill overnight.

3 To make the Cointreau oranges, squeeze the juice from two oranges and pour into a measuring jug (cup). Make the juice up to 250ml/8fl oz/1 cup with water, if necessary, then pour the liquid into a small pan. Blend a little of the mixture with the cornflour and then add to the pan with the icing sugar. Gently heat, stirring until thickened.

4 Cut a thin slice of peel and pith from both ends of the remaining oranges. Place cut-side down on a plate and cut off the peel and pith. Remove any bits of remaining pith. Cut out each segment leaving the membrane behind. Add the segments to the pan, stir to coat well then set aside. Cool, then stir in the Cointreau. Cover and chill overnight.

5 Turn the moulds out on to plates and surround the cheeses with the oranges. Decorate with spirals of orange rind and serve immediately.

SERVES FOUR

INGREDIENTS
225g/8oz/1 cup cottage cheese
250g/9oz/generous 1 cup
  mascarpone cheese
50g/2oz/¼ cup caster
  (superfine) sugar
grated rind and juice of 1 lemon
spirals of orange rind, to decorate
  (see Cook's Tip)
For the Cointreau oranges
5 oranges
10ml/2 tsp cornflour (cornstarch)
15ml/1 tbsp icing
  (confectioners') sugar
60ml/4 tbsp Cointreau

1 Put the cottage cheese in a food processor or blender and process until smooth. Add the mascarpone, caster sugar, the grated lemon rind and lemon juice and process briefly to thoroughly mix the ingredients.

COOK'S TIP
To make fine orange rind spirals, use a cannelle knife (zester) and pare long, narrow strips of rind. Twist tightly around cocktail sticks (toothpicks) so that they curl into corkscrews. Slide the sticks out.

CHOCOLATE CONES WITH APRICOT SAUCE

THE SEDUCTIVE COMBINATION OF DARK CHOCOLATE WRAPPED AROUND A CREAMY BRANDY-FLAVOURED FILLING MAKES A DRAMATIC AND DELICIOUS DESSERT THAT IS SURPRISINGLY EASY TO MAKE. LEMON ADDS A SHARP EDGE TO THE SWEET APRICOT SAUCE THAT SURROUNDS THE CONES.

SERVES SIX

INGREDIENTS
  250g/9oz dark (bittersweet)
    chocolate, broken into squares
  350g/12oz/1½ cups ricotta cheese
  45ml/3 tbsp double (heavy) or
    whipping cream
  30ml/2 tbsp brandy
  30ml/2 tbsp icing
    (confectioners') sugar
  finely grated rind of 1 lemon
  strips of thinly pared lemon rind,
    to decorate
For the sauce
  185g/6½oz/⅔ cup apricot jam
  45ml/3 tbsp lemon juice

1 Cut 12 double thickness circles, 10cm/4in in diameter, from baking parchment or paper and shape each into a cone. Secure with masking tape.

3 Stand each cone point downward in a cup or glass, to hold it straight. Leave in a cool place until the chocolate cones are completely set.

4 Make the sauce. Combine the apricot jam and lemon juice in a heavy pan. Melt over a low heat, stirring frequently, then remove the pan from the heat and set aside to cool.

5 Beat the ricotta cheese, cream, brandy and icing sugar in a small bowl. Stir in the lemon rind. Spoon or pipe the ricotta mixture into the cones, then carefully peel off the baking parchment.

6 Serve the chocolate cones in pairs on individual plates, decorated with lemon rind and surrounded with the cooled apricot sauce.

2 Melt the chocolate in a heatproof bowl over a pan of hot water, cool slightly, then spoon a little into each cone, swirling and brushing it to coat the paper in an even layer.

COOK'S TIPS
• When making the paper cones, make sure there is no gap at the pointed end, or the chocolate will run out when you coat them. It is best to let the chocolate cool slightly before use, so that it sets quickly.
• The cones can be made, filled and arranged with the sauce on plates before you start your meal, then chilled.

COLD LEMON SOUFFLÉ WITH ALMONDS

TERRIFIC TO LOOK AT YET EASY TO MAKE, THIS REFRESHING LEMON SOUFFLÉ IS LIGHT AND MOUTHWATERING, IDEAL FOR THE END OF ANY MEAL.

SERVES SIX

INGREDIENTS
  oil, for greasing
  grated rind and juice of
    3 large lemons
  5 large (US extra large)
    eggs, separated
  115g/4oz/generous ½ cup caster
    (superfine) sugar
  25ml/1½ tbsp powdered gelatine
  450ml/¾ pint/scant 2 cups double
    (heavy) cream
For the topping
  75g/3oz/¾ cup flaked
    (sliced) almonds
  75g/3oz/¾ cup icing
    (confectioners') sugar

1 Cut a strip of baking parchment long enough to fit around a 900ml/1½ pint/ 3¾ cup soufflé dish and wide enough to extend 7.5cm/3in above the rim. Fit the strip around the dish, tape, then tie it around the top of the dish with string.

2 Using a pastry brush, lightly coat the inside of the paper collar with oil.

3 Put the lemon rind and egg yolks in a bowl. Add 75g/3oz/6 tbsp of the caster sugar and whisk thoroughly until the mixture becomes light and creamy.

COOK'S TIP
To dissolve the gelatine more quickly, heat the lemon juice and gelatine in a microwave, on full power, in 30-second bursts, stirring between each burst, until it is fully dissolved.

4 Place the lemon juice in a heatproof bowl and sprinkle over the gelatine. Set aside for 5 minutes, then place the bowl in a pan of simmering water. Heat, stirring occasionally, until the gelatine has dissolved. Cool slightly, then stir into the egg yolk mixture.

5 Whip the cream to soft peaks. Fold into the egg yolk mixture and set aside.

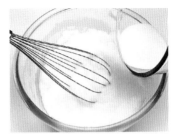

6 Whisk the egg whites to stiff peaks, then whisk in the remaining caster sugar until stiff. Fold the whites into the yolk mixture. Pour into the dish, smooth the surface and chill for 4–5 hours.

7 To make the topping, brush a baking sheet lightly with oil. Preheat the grill (broiler). Sprinkle the almonds over the baking sheet and sift the icing sugar over them. Grill (broil) until the nuts have turned a rich golden colour and the sugar has caramelized.

8 Leave to cool, then remove the almond mixture from the tray with a metal spatula and break it into pieces.

9 When the soufflé has set, peel off the paper. If the paper does not come away easily, hold the flat blade of a knife against the set soufflé as you peel the paper away – this will help the soufflé keep its shape. Sprinkle the caramelized almonds on top of the lemon soufflé, and serve immediately.

VARIATION
This soufflé is wonderfully refreshing when served semi-frozen. Place the undecorated, set soufflé in the freezer for about an hour. Just before serving, remove from the freezer and decorate with the caramelized almonds.

LEMON AND LIME CHEESECAKE

HERE IS A LEMON AND LIME CHEESECAKE THAT IS A CUT ABOVE THE REST. TOPPED WITH A ZESTY
LIME SYRUP, IT IS TRULY A CITRUS SENSATION.

SERVES EIGHT

INGREDIENTS
  150g/5oz digestive biscuits
  (graham crackers)
  40g/1½oz/3 tbsp butter
For the topping
  grated rind and juice of 2 lemons
  10ml/2 tsp powdered gelatine
  250g/9oz/generous 1 cup
  ricotta cheese
  75g/3oz/⅓ cup caster
  (superfine) sugar
  150ml/¼ pint/⅔ cup double
  (heavy) cream
  2 eggs, separated
For the lime syrup
  finely pared rind and juice of 3 limes
  75g/3oz/⅓ cup caster
  (superfine) sugar
  5ml/1 tsp arrowroot mixed with
  30ml/2 tbsp water
  a little green food
  colouring (optional)

1 Grease a 20cm/8in round springform
cake tin (pan). Process the biscuits in
a food processor to fine crumbs. Melt
the butter in a pan, then stir in the
crumbs. Spoon into the cake tin, press
the crumbs down well in an even layer,
then cover and chill.

2 Make the topping. Put the lemon rind
and juice in a pan and sprinkle over the
gelatine. Leave for 5 minutes, then heat
until the gelatine has dissolved. Set
aside to cool slightly. Beat the ricotta
and sugar. Stir in the cream and egg
yolks. Whisk in the gelatine mixture.

3 Whisk the egg whites in a grease-free
bowl until they form soft peaks. Fold
them into the cheese mixture. Spoon on
to the biscuit base, level the surface
and chill for 2–3 hours.

4 Meanwhile, make the lime syrup.
Cut the lime rind into very fine shreds.
Place the lime shreds, juice and caster
sugar in a small pan. Bring to the boil,
stirring constantly, then boil the syrup
for 5 minutes, without stirring.

5 Stir in the arrowroot mixture and
continue to stir over a low heat until the
syrup boils again and thickens slightly.
Tint the syrup pale green with a little
food colouring, if you like. Cool, then
chill until required.

6 Spoon the lime syrup over the set
cheesecake. Remove from the tin and
cut into slices to serve.

LEMON CHEESECAKE WITH FOREST FRUITS

NO COLLECTION OF CITRUS RECIPES WOULD BE COMPLETE WITHOUT A CREAMY LEMON CHEESECAKE.
THIS ONE HAS A LIGHT CORNFLAKE BASE AND IS SERVED TOPPED WITH LUSCIOUS, FOREST FRUITS.

SERVES EIGHT

INGREDIENTS
  50g/2oz/¼ cup unsalted
    (sweet) butter
  25g/1oz/2 tbsp light soft brown sugar
  45ml/3 tbsp golden (light corn) syrup
  115g/4oz/generous 1 cup cornflakes
  11g/¼oz sachet powdered gelatine
  225g/8oz/1 cup soft cheese
  150g/5oz/generous ½ cup Greek (US
    strained plain) yogurt
  150ml/¼ pint/⅔ cup single
    (light) cream
  finely grated rind and juice of
    2 lemons
  75g/3oz/6 tbsp caster
    (superfine) sugar
  2 eggs, separated
  225g/8oz/2 cups mixed, prepared
    fresh forest fruits, such as
    blackberries, raspberries and
    redcurrants, to decorate
  icing (confectioners') sugar,
    for dusting

1 Place the butter, brown sugar and syrup in a pan and heat over a low heat, stirring, until the mixture has melted and is well blended. Remove from the heat and stir in the cornflakes.

2 Press the mixture over the base of a deep 20cm/8in loose-based round cake tin (pan). Chill for 30 minutes.

VARIATION
Use unsweetened puffed rice cereal or rice crispies in place of the cornflakes.

3 Sprinkle the gelatine over 45ml/ 3 tbsp water in a bowl and leave to soak for a few minutes. Place the bowl over a pan of simmering water and stir until the gelatine has dissolved. Place the cheese, yogurt, cream, lemon rind and juice, caster sugar and egg yolks in a large bowl and beat until smooth and thoroughly mixed.

4 Add the hot gelatine to the cheese and lemon mixture and beat well.

5 Whisk the egg whites until stiff, then fold into the cheese mixture.

6 Pour the cheese mixture over the cornflake base and level the surface. Chill for 4–5 hours, or until the filling has set.

7 Carefully remove the cheesecake from the tin and place on a serving plate. Decorate with the mixed fresh fruits, dust with icing sugar and serve.

BAKLAVA

The origins of this recipe are in Greece and Turkey, but it has been willingly adopted throughout south-eastern Europe. Nuts and cinnamon are encased in light pastry and soaked in a sweet honey and lemon syrup, making this an extra sweet dessert.

MAKES TWENTY-FOUR PIECES

INGREDIENTS
175g/6oz/¾ cup butter, melted
400g/14oz packet filo pastry, thawed
   if frozen
30ml/2 tbsp lemon juice
60ml/4 tbsp set
   (crystallized) honey
50g/2oz/¼ cup caster
   (superfine) sugar
finely grated rind of 2 lemons
10ml/2 tsp cinnamon
200g/7oz/1¾ cups blanched
   almonds, chopped
200g/7oz/1¾ cups walnuts, chopped
75g/3oz/¾ cup pistachio nuts or
   hazelnuts, chopped
chopped pistachio nuts, to decorate
For the syrup
350g/12oz/1¾ cups caster
   (superfine) sugar
115g/4oz/½ cup clear honey
600ml/1 pint/2½ cups water
2 strips of thinly pared lemon rind

1 Preheat the oven to 160°C/325°F/
Gas 3. Lightly brush the base of a
shallow, rectangular 30 × 20cm/12 ×
8in loose-based tin (pan) with a little of
the melted butter.

2 Using the tin as a guide cut the
sheets of filo pastry with a sharp knife
to fit the tin exactly.

COOK'S TIP
Keep spare sheets of filo covered with a
damp dishtowel so that it doesn't dry out.

3 Place one sheet of pastry in the base
of the tin, brush with melted butter,
then repeat until you have used half of
the pastry sheets. Cover the remainder
with a clean, damp dishtowel.

4 Place the lemon juice, honey and
sugar in a pan and heat gently until
dissolved. Stir in the lemon rind,
cinnamon and chopped nuts. Mix well.

5 Spread half the filling over the pastry,
cover with three filo sheets, brush with
a little melted butter, then spread the
remaining filling over the pastry.

6 Finish by covering the filling with the
remaining sheets of pastry and brushing
the top of the pastry liberally with the
melted butter.

7 Using a sharp knife, carefully mark
the pastry into squares or diamonds,
almost cutting through the filling. Bake
the baklava in the preheated oven for
1 hour, or until crisp and golden brown.

8 Meanwhile, make the syrup. Place
the caster sugar, honey, water and
lemon rind in a pan and stir over a low
heat until the sugar and honey have
dissolved. Bring to the boil, then boil
for a further 10 minutes, or until the
mixture has thickened slightly.

9 Take the syrup off the heat and leave
to cool slightly. Remove the baklava
from the oven. Remove and discard the
lemon rind from the syrup, then pour
over the pastry. Set aside to soak for
6 hours or overnight. Cut into diamonds
or squares and serve, decorated with
chopped pistachio nuts.

ICES AND ICED DESSERTS

Home-made ice cream is truly a special treat and, when flavoured with citrus fruits, nothing is more cooling and refreshing on a hot summer day — except, perhaps, a lemon sorbet or orange granita. Recipes range from straightforward, easy-to-prepare iced desserts for family meals to elaborate and sophisticated confections to crown a formal dinner party. Oranges, lemons, grapefruit and limes can be partnered with a vast array of other ingredients, from nuts to liqueurs and from ginger to basil, to create an iced flavour sensation that literally melts in the mouth.

LEMON SORBET

THIS HAS TO BE THE CLASSIC SORBET. REFRESHINGLY TANGY AND YET DELICIOUSLY SMOOTH, IT IS WELCOME ALL YEAR ROUND, NOT JUST DURING THE WARMER MONTHS.

SERVES SIX

INGREDIENTS
200g/7oz/1 cup caster
  (superfine) sugar
300ml/½ pint/1¼ cups water
4 lemons, well scrubbed
1 egg white
sugared lemon rind, to decorate (see
  Cook's Tip)

1 Put the sugar and water into a pan and bring to the boil over a low heat, stirring occasionally until the sugar has just dissolved.

COOK'S TIP
To make sugared lemon rind, thinly pare the rind with a zester. Dust with a little caster (superfine) sugar.

2 Using a vegetable peeler pare the rind thinly from two of the lemons so that it falls straight into the pan.

VARIATION
Substitute four oranges for the lemons or use two oranges and two lemons for a mixed citrus sorbet.

3 Simmer for about 2 minutes without stirring, then take the pan off the heat. Leave to cool, then chill.

4 Squeeze the juice from all the lemons and add it to the syrup. Strain the syrup into a shallow freezerproof container, reserving the rind. Freeze the mixture for 4 hours, until it is mushy. If you are using an ice cream maker, strain the syrup and lemon juice and then churn the mixture until thick.

5 Scoop the sorbet (sherbet) into a food processor and beat it until smooth. Lightly whisk the egg white with a fork until it is just frothy. Spoon the sorbet back into the container, beat in the egg white and return the mixture to the freezer for 4 hours. If you are using an ice cream maker, add the egg white to the mixture and continue to churn for 10–15 minutes, or until the sorbet is firm enough to scoop.

6 Scoop the sorbet into bowls or sundae glasses, decorate with sugared lemon rind and serve.

LEMON AND CARDAMOM ICE CREAM

THE CLASSIC PARTNERSHIP OF LEMON AND CARDAMOM GIVES THIS RICH ICE CREAM A LOVELY CLEAN TANG. IT IS THE PERFECT CHOICE FOR SERVING AFTER A SPICY MAIN COURSE.

SERVES SIX

INGREDIENTS

15ml/1 tbsp cardamom pods
4 egg yolks
115g/4oz/generous ½ cup caster
   (superfine) sugar
10ml/2 tsp cornflour (cornstarch)
grated rind and juice of 3 lemons
300ml/½ pint/1¼ cups milk
300ml/½ pint/1¼ cups
   whipping cream
fresh lemon balm sprigs and
   icing (confectioners') sugar,
   to decorate

1 Put the cardamom pods in a mortar and crush them with a pestle to release the seeds. Pick out and discard the shells, then grind the seeds to break them up slightly.

2 Put the egg yolks, sugar, cornflour, lemon rind and juice in a bowl. Add the cardamom seeds and whisk well.

COOK'S TIPS
• Lemon balm, which has a pronounced lemony flavour and fragrance, is an easy herb to grow. The leaves are best picked before the flowering period, when they are at their most fragrant. Lemon balm does not dry successfully.
• Transfer the ice cream from the freezer to the refrigerator about 30 minutes before serving so that it softens slightly.
• Always buy cardamom whole, in the pod, and grind the seeds as you require them. Once ground, cardamom quickly loses its flavour.

3 Bring the milk to the boil in a pan, then pour over the egg yolk mixture, stirring well. Return the mixture to the pan and cook over a very low heat, stirring constantly until thickened.

4 Pour the custard into a bowl, cover the surface with baking parchment and leave to cool. Chill until very cold.

5 Whip the cream lightly and fold into the custard. Pour into a container and freeze for 3–4 hours, beating twice to break up the ice crystals. If you are using an ice cream maker, whisk the cream lightly into the custard and churn the mixture until it holds its shape. Scoop into glasses and decorate with the lemon balm and icing sugar.

TEQUILA AND ORANGE GRANITA

FULL OF CITRUS FLAVOUR ENLIVENED WITH TEQUILA, THIS DISTINCTIVE MEXICAN-STYLE GRANITA WILL HAVE GUESTS CLAMOURING FOR MORE. SERVE SIMPLY WITH WEDGES OF CITRUS FRUIT OR SPOON OVER A LITTLE GRENADINE FOR EXTRA COLOUR.

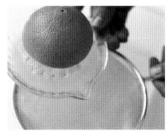

2 Strain the syrup into a shallow, freezer-proof plastic container. Squeeze all the oranges, strain the juice into the syrup and then stir in the tequila. Check that the mixture is no more than about 2.5cm/1in deep; transfer to a larger container if needed.

3 Cover and freeze for about 2 hours, or until the mixture around the sides of the container is mushy. Mash well with a fork to break up the ice crystals and return the granita to the freezer.

SERVES SIX

INGREDIENTS
  115g/4oz/generous ½ cup caster
    (superfine) sugar
  300ml/½ pint/1¼ cups water
  6 oranges, well scrubbed
  90ml/6 tbsp tequila
  orange and lime wedges,
    to serve

4 Freeze for a further 2 hours, mashing the mixture with a fork to break up the crystals every 30 minutes or so, or until the granita has a slushy consistency. Scoop it into dishes and serve with orange and lime wedges.

VARIATION
If you don't have any tequila, make the granita with vodka, Cointreau, or even white rum. Do not be tempted to add more than the recommended amount; too much alcohol will prevent the granita from freezing.

1 Put the sugar and water into a pan. Using a vegetable peeler, thinly pare the rind from three of the oranges, letting it fall into the pan. Bring to the boil, stirring to dissolve the sugar. Pour the syrup into a bowl, cool, then chill.

COOK'S TIP
There are two types of tequila – white and golden. The latter is aged, has a more subtle flavour and, therefore, is a little more expensive. Both types are quite suitable for this granita.

RUBY GRAPEFRUIT GRANITA

THE GRAINY, SNOW-LIKE FLAKES OF ICE OF THIS GRANITA ARE GIVEN A BEAUTIFUL, SOFT ROSE-PINK COLOUR AND A SLIGHTLY SHARP, REFRESHING TASTE THROUGH THE ADDITION OF RUBY GRAPEFRUIT. IT IS IDEAL TO SERVE AFTER A RICH MAIN COURSE.

SERVES SIX

INGREDIENTS

200g/7oz/1 cup caster
(superfine) sugar
300ml/½ pint/1¼ cups water
4 ruby grapefruit
tiny mint leaves, to decorate

1 Put the sugar and water into a pan. Bring the water to the boil, stirring until the sugar has dissolved. Pour the syrup into a bowl, cool, then chill.

2 Cut the grapefruit in half. Squeeze the juice, taking care not to damage the grapefruit shells. Set these aside. Strain the juice into a large plastic container. Stir in the chilled syrup, making sure that the depth of the mixture does not exceed 2.5cm/1in.

3 Cover and freeze for 2 hours, or until the mixture around the sides of the container is mushy. Using a fork, break up the ice crystals and then mash the granita finely.

4 Freeze for about 2 hours more, mashing the mixture with a fork every 30 minutes, or until the granita consists of fine, even crystals.

VARIATION
You could also use Sweetie grapefruits to make this granita. Although this variety does not have pink flesh, it is naturally very sweet and the shells will make attractive bright green "dishes".

5 Select the six best grapefruit shells for use as the serving dishes. Using a sharp knife, remove the grapefruit pulp, leaving the shells as clean as possible.

6 Evenly divide the granita among the grapefruit shells and place on serving plates. Decorate with the tiny mint leaves and serve.

COOK'S TIP
Grapefruit shells make very good serving dishes. For a rather more contemporary treatment, consider the effect you would like to achieve when you are halving the grapefruit. They look great when they are tilted at an angle. Having squeezed the juice and removed the membrane, trim a little off the base of each shell so that they will remain stable when filled with the granita.

BASIL AND ORANGE GRANITA

MORE OFTEN ASSOCIATED WITH SAVOURY DISHES, BASIL HAS A SWEET, AROMATIC FLAVOUR THAT COMPLEMENTS TANGY ORANGES BEAUTIFULLY.

SERVES SIX

INGREDIENTS
  5 large oranges
  175g/6oz/scant 1 cup caster
    (superfine) sugar
  450ml/¾ pint/scant 2 cups water
  orange juice (if necessary)
  15g/½oz/½ cup fresh basil leaves
  a few tiny fresh basil leaves,
    to decorate

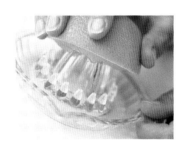

1 Pare the rind thinly from three of the oranges and place the rind in a pan.

2 Add the caster sugar and water. Heat gently, stirring constantly until the sugar has completely dissolved. Remove from the heat and leave to cool, then pour into a bowl and chill.

3 Squeeze the juice from the oranges and pour it into a large measuring jug (cup). You should have about 600ml/17fl oz/scant 2¼ cups. If there is not enough, make it up to the required quantity with more fresh orange juice.

4 Pour the juice into a food processor or blender and add the basil leaves. Process the mixture until the basil has been chopped into very small pieces.

5 Using a slotted spoon, remove the orange rind from the chilled syrup. Stir in the orange juice and basil mixture, then pour into a large plastic tub or similar freezerproof container. Cover and freeze for about 2 hours, or until the mixture around the edges is just turning mushy.

6 Break up the ice crystals with a fork and stir well. Freeze for 30 minutes more until once again frozen around the edges. Break up with a fork and return to the freezer. Repeat the procedure until the ice forms fine crystals.

7 To serve, spoon the granita into chilled tall glasses and decorate with the tiny basil leaves.

COOK'S TIP
Ruby grapefruit could be used in place of the orange, if you wish.

STAR ANISE AND GRAPEFRUIT GRANITA

WITH ITS ANISEED FLAVOUR, STAR ANISE MAKES AN INTERESTING ADDITION TO CITRUS FRUIT DESSERTS, AND ITS DRAMATIC APPEARANCE MAKES IT THE IDEAL DECORATION. THIS REFRESHING AND UNUSUAL GRANITA IS BOTH TANGY AND SWEET.

SERVES SIX

INGREDIENTS
  200g/7oz/1 cup caster
    (superfine) sugar
  450ml/¾ pint/scant 2 cups water
  6 whole star anise
  4 grapefruit

1 Put the caster sugar and water in a small, heavy pan and heat gently, stirring occasionally, until the sugar has completely dissolved.

2 Stir in the star anise and heat the syrup gently, without stirring, for about 2 minutes, until slightly thickened and syrupy. Remove the pan from the heat and leave to cool.

3 Using a sharp knife, take a slice off the top and bottom of each grapefruit, then slice off the skin and all the pith. Chop the flesh coarsely and place it in a food processor. Process until almost smooth, then press the pulp through a sieve into a bowl.

4 Strain the syrup into the bowl of grapefruit purée, reserving the star anise. Mix well, then pour the mixture into a shallow freezerproof container. Cover and freeze for about 2 hours, or until the mixture starts to freeze and forms ice crystals around the edges of the container.

5 Using a fork, break up the ice crystals, then return the mixture to the freezer. Freeze for 30 minutes more, mash with a fork again, then return to the freezer. Repeat the process until the mixture forms fine ice crystals.

6 To serve, spoon the granita into glasses and decorate with the reserved star anise.

ORANGE FLOWER WATER ICE CREAM

DELICATELY PERFUMED WITH ORANGE FLOWER WATER AND A LITTLE GRATED ORANGE RIND
THIS NUTTY, LIGHTLY SWEETENED ICE CREAM TAKES IT'S INSPIRATION FROM DESSERTS THAT ARE
POPULAR THROUGHOUT THE MIDDLE EAST.

SERVES FOUR TO SIX

INGREDIENTS
 4 egg yolks
 75g/3oz/6 tbsp caster
  (superfine) sugar
 5ml/1 tsp cornflour (cornstarch)
 300ml/½ pint/1¼ cups
  semi-skimmed (low-fat) milk
 300ml/½ pint/1¼ cups
  whipping cream
 150g/5oz/ 1¼ cups cashew nuts,
  finely chopped
 15ml/1 tbsp orange flower water
 grated rind of ½ orange, plus spirals
  of orange rind, to decorate

1 Whisk the egg yolks, caster sugar and cornflour in a bowl until thick. Pour the milk into a pan and bring it to the boil. Whisk it into the egg yolk mixture.

2 Return to the pan and cook over a low heat, stirring constantly, until very smooth. Pour back into the bowl. Leave to cool, then chill.

3 Heat the cream in a pan. When it boils, stir in the chopped cashew nuts. Leave to cool.

4 Stir the orange flower water and grated orange rind into the chilled custard. Process the cashew nut cream in a food processor or blender until it forms a fine paste, then stir it into the custard mixture.

5 Pour the mixture into a plastic tub or similar freezerproof container and freeze for 6 hours, beating twice with a fork or whisking briefly with an electric mixer to break up the ice crystals until smooth. If you are using an ice cream maker, churn the mixture until it is firm enough to scoop.

6 To serve, scoop into dishes and decorate with orange rind curls.

LIME SABAYON WITH CHOCOLATE ICE CREAM

SABAYON SAUCE HAS A LIGHT, FOAMY TEXTURE THAT PERFECTLY COMPLEMENTS THE RICH, SMOOTH
FLAVOUR OF ICE CREAM. THIS TANGY LIME VERSION IS DELICIOUS WITH CHOCOLATE ICE CREAM, BUT
CAN ALSO BE SERVED WITH TROPICAL FRUIT, SOFT FRUIT OR VANILLA ICE CREAM.

SERVES FOUR

INGREDIENTS
  2 egg yolks
  65g/2½oz/5 tbsp caster
    (superfine) sugar
  finely grated rind and juice of
    2 limes
  60ml/4 tbsp white wine or
    apple juice
  45ml/3 tbsp single (light) cream
  500ml/17fl oz/2¼ cups chocolate
    ice cream
  thinly pared strips of lime rind,
    to decorate

1 Put the egg yolks and caster sugar
in a heatproof bowl and beat well until
thoroughly combined. Beat in the lime
rind and juice, then the white wine or
apple juice.

2 Whisk the mixture over a pan of
simmering water until the sabayon
is smooth and thick, and the mixture
leaves a ribbon trail when the whisk is
lifted from the bowl.

3 Lightly whisk in the cream. Remove
the bowl from the pan and cover with a
lid or plate.

4 Working quickly, place scoops of the
chocolate ice cream into four chilled
sundae glasses or individual serving
dishes. Spoon the warm lime sabayon
sauce over the ice cream, sprinkle with
the strips of lime rind to decorate and
serve immediately.

VARIATIONS
You can substitute other citrus fruit for
the limes in the sabayon sauce. Orange
sabayon, using the rind and juice of one
orange, would also go well with chocolate
ice cream, while lemon sabayon sauce
complements peach sorbet (sherbet).

COOK'S TIP
For a special occasion, serve the ice
cream in frosted glass. Rub the rim of
the glasses with a lime wedge, then dip
in a saucer of caster (superfine) sugar.
Leave to dry before carefully adding the
scoops of ice cream.

LEMON SORBET CUPS WITH SUMMER FRUITS

IN THIS STUNNING DESSERT, LEMON SORBET IS MOULDED INTO CUP SHAPES TO MAKE PRETTY CONTAINERS FOR A SELECTION OF SUMMER FRUITS. THEY ARE IDEAL FOR ENTERTAINING, AS YOU CAN PREPARE THE CUPS MANY DAYS IN ADVANCE AND JUST FILL THEM WHEN READY TO SERVE.

3 Cut the strawberries in half and place in a bowl with the raspberries and red, black or white currants. Add the sugar and liqueur and toss the ingredients together lightly. Cover and chill for at least 2 hours.

4 Once the sorbet in the moulds has frozen completely, loosen the edges with a knife, then dip in a bowl of very hot water for 2 seconds. Invert the sorbet cups on a small tray, using a fork to twist and loosen the cups if necessary.

5 If you need to, dip the moulds very briefly in the hot water again. Turn out the sorbet cups and turn them over so they are ready to fill. Return them to the freezer until required.

6 To serve, place the cups on serving plates and fill with the fruits, spooning over any juices.

COOK'S TIP
When lining the moulds with the sorbet (sherbet), wrap your hand in a dishtowel.

SERVES SIX

INGREDIENTS
    500ml/17fl oz/2¼ cups lemon
      sorbet (sherbet)
    225g/8oz/2 cups small strawberries
    150g/5oz/scant 1 cup raspberries
    75g/3oz/¾ cup redcurrants,
      blackcurrants or white currants
    15ml/1 tbsp caster
      (superfine) sugar
    45ml/3 tbsp Cointreau or other
      orange-flavoured liqueur

1 Put six 150ml/¼ pint/⅔ cup metal moulds in the freezer for 15 minutes to chill. At the same time, remove the sorbet from the freezer to soften slightly.

2 Using a teaspoon, pack the sorbet into the moulds, building up a layer about 1cm/½in thick around the base and sides, and leaving a deep cavity in the centre. Return each mould to the freezer when it is lined.

ICED ORANGES

THESE TANGY LITTLE ICES, SERVED IN THE ORANGE SHELLS, WERE ORIGINALLY SOLD IN BEACH CAFÉS IN THE SOUTH OF FRANCE. THEY ARE PRETTY AND EASY TO EAT — EQUALLY AT HOME AT A DINNER PARTY, OR PREPARED AS A PICNIC TREAT TO STORE IN THE COLD BOX.

SERVES EIGHT

INGREDIENTS
about 150g/5oz/¾ cup
 granulated sugar
juice of 1 lemon
14 medium oranges
fresh orange juice, if needed
8 fresh bay leaves, to decorate

1 Put the sugar in a heavy pan. Add half the lemon juice, and 120ml/4fl oz/½ cup water. Cook over a low heat, stirring constantly until the sugar has dissolved. Bring to the boil, and boil, without stirring, for 2–3 minutes, or until the syrup is clear. Remove the pan from the heat and leave to cool.

2 Slice off the tops off eight of the oranges, to make "hats". Scoop out the flesh of the oranges, and reserve. Put the empty orange shells and hats on a tray and place in the freezer.

3 Grate the rind of the remaining oranges and add to the cooled syrup.

4 Squeeze the juice from the oranges, and from the reserved flesh. There should be about 750ml/1¼ pint/3 cups. Squeeze another orange or add bought orange juice, if necessary to make up to the required quantity.

5 Stir the orange juice and remaining lemon juice, with 90ml/6 tbsp water into the syrup. Pour into a freezerproof container, cover and freeze for 3 hours.

6 Turn the mixture into a large bowl, and quickly whisk with a small balloon whisk or electric mixer to break down the ice crystals.

7 Return the citrus mixture to the freezerproof container and freeze for about 4 hours more, until just firm, but not solid.

8 Pack the mixture into the orange shells, mounding it up, and set the hats on top. Freeze until ready to serve. Just before serving, push a skewer into the tops of the hats and push in a bay leaf for decoration.

COOK'S TIP
Use crumpled kitchen paper between the shells to keep them upright.

RUBY ORANGE SHERBET IN GINGER BASKETS

THIS SUPERB FROZEN DESSERT IS PERFECT FOR PEOPLE WITHOUT ICE CREAM MAKERS WHO CANNOT BE BOTHERED WITH THE FREEZING AND STIRRING THAT HOME-MADE ICES NORMALLY REQUIRE. IT IS ALSO IDEAL FOR SERVING AT A SPECIAL DINNER PARTY AS BOTH THE SHERBET AND GINGER BASKETS CAN BE MADE IN ADVANCE AND THE DESSERT SIMPLY ASSEMBLED BETWEEN COURSES.

SERVES SIX

INGREDIENTS
grated rind and juice of
2 blood oranges
175g/6oz/1½ cups icing
(confectioners') sugar
300ml/½ pint/1¼ cups double
(heavy) cream
200g/7oz/scant 1 cup Greek
(US strained plain) yogurt
blood orange segments, to
decorate (optional)
For the ginger baskets
25g/1oz/2 tbsp unsalted
(sweet) butter
15ml/1 tbsp golden (light
corn) syrup
30ml/2 tbsp caster (superfine) sugar
1.5ml/¼ tsp ground ginger
15ml/1 tbsp finely chopped mixed
citrus peel
15ml/1 tbsp plain (all-purpose) flour
butter, for greasing

1 Place the orange rind and juice in a bowl. Sift the icing sugar over the top and set aside for 30 minutes, then stir until smooth.

COOK'S TIP
When making the ginger baskets it is essential to work quickly. Have the greased tins (pans) or cups ready before you start. If the biscuits (cookies) cool and firm up before you have time to drape them all, return them to the oven for a few seconds to soften them again.

2 Whisk the double cream in a large bowl until the mixture forms soft peaks, then fold in the yogurt.

3 Gently stir in the orange juice mixture, then pour into a freezerproof container. Cover and freeze for about 3 hours, until firm.

4 Make the baskets. Preheat the oven to 180°C/350°F/Gas 4. Place the butter, syrup and sugar in a heavy pan and heat gently until melted.

5 Add the ground ginger, mixed citrus peel and flour and stir until the mixture is smooth.

VARIATION
For a simpler dish, you can also roll the freshly cooked ginger biscuits (cookies) around the well-greased handles of wooden spoons, in the same way as you would when making brandy snaps. Scoop the sherbet into glasses and serve it accompanied by the ginger biscuits.

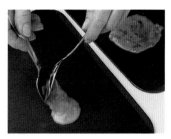

6 Lightly grease two baking sheets. Using about 10ml/2 tsp of the mixture at a time, drop three portions of the ginger dough on to each baking sheet, spacing them well apart. Spread each one to a 5cm/2in circle, then bake for 12–14 minutes, or until the biscuits (cookies) are dark golden in colour.

7 Remove the biscuits from the oven and leave to stand on the baking sheets for 1 minute to firm slightly. Carefully lift them off with a metal spatula and drape over six well-greased mini pudding tins (pans) or upturned cups; flatten the top of the biscuits (which will become the base) and flute the edges to form a decorative basket shape.

8 Once they are cool and set, lift the baskets off the tins or cups and place on individual dessert plates. Arrange small scoops of the frozen orange sherbet in each basket. Decorate each portion with a few orange segments, if you like.

ICED LIME CHEESECAKE

This cheesecake has a deliciously tangy, sweet lime flavour, but needs no gelatine to set the filling, unlike most unbaked cheesecakes. It is not difficult to prepare and looks pleasantly summery with its fresh citrus decoration.

SERVES TEN

INGREDIENTS
175g/6oz almond biscuits (cookies)
65g/2½oz/5 tbsp unsalted
   (sweet) butter
8 limes
115g/4oz/generous ½ cup caster
   (superfine) sugar
90ml/6 tbsp water
200g/7oz/scant 1 cup
   cottage cheese
250g/9oz/generous 1 cup
   mascarpone cheese
300ml/½ pint/1¼ cups double
   (heavy) cream

1 Lightly grease the base and sides of a 20cm/8in springform cake tin (pan) and line with baking parchment. Break up the almond biscuits slightly, then put them in a strong plastic bag and crush them completely with the side of a rolling pin.

2 Melt the butter in a small pan and stir in the biscuit crumbs until evenly combined. Spoon the mixture into the tin and pack it down with the back of a spoon. Freeze the biscuit mixture while you make the filling.

3 Finely grate the rind and squeeze the juice from five of the limes. Heat the sugar and water in a small, heavy pan, stirring constantly until the sugar has completely dissolved. Bring to the boil and boil for 2 minutes, without stirring, then remove the pan from the heat, stir in the lime juice and rind and leave the syrup to cool.

4 Press the cottage cheese through a sieve into a large bowl. Beat in the mascarpone, then the lime syrup. Lightly whip the cream and fold into the cheese mixture. Pour into a shallow container, cover and freeze until thick. If you are using an ice cream maker, add the cream and churn in the ice cream maker until thick.

5 Meanwhile, using a sharp knife, cut a thin slice of peel and pith from both ends of the each of the remaining limes. Place cut side down on a plate and cut off the peel and pith in strips. Remove any remaining pith. Cut the limes into thin slices.

6 Arrange the lime slices around the sides of the tin, against the parchment.

7 Carefully pour the cheese mixture over the biscuit base in the tin and level the surface with a round-bladed knife. Cover with clear film (plastic wrap) and freeze the cheesecake overnight.

8 About 1 hour before you are going to serve the cheesecake, carefully transfer it to a serving plate and put it in the refrigerator to soften slightly.

STRATEGY STRAWBERRY AND LEMON CURD GÂTEAU

IN THIS FROZEN DESSERT, STRAWBERRY ICE CREAM AND A LAYER OF LEMON CURD CREAM TOP A LIGHT SPONGE CAKE. FRESH, JUICY STRAWBERRIES COMPLETE THIS GATEAU MAKING IT PERFECT FOR SUMMER ENTERTAINING OR A FAMILY CELEBRATION.

SERVES EIGHT

INGREDIENTS
115g/4oz/½ cup unsalted (sweet) butter, softened, plus extra for greasing
115g/4oz/generous ½ cup caster (superfine) sugar
2 eggs
115g/4oz/1 cup self-raising (self-rising) flour
2.5ml/½ tsp baking powder
500ml/17fl oz/2¼ cups strawberry ice cream, softened
300ml/½ pint/1¼ cups double (heavy) cream
200g/7oz/¾ cup good quality lemon curd
30ml/2 tbsp lemon juice
For the topping
500g/1¼ lb/5 cups fresh strawberries, hulled
25g/1oz/2 tbsp caster (superfine) sugar
45ml/3 tbsp Cointreau or other orange-flavoured liqueur

1 Preheat the oven to 180°C/350°F/ Gas 4. Grease and line a 23cm/9in springform cake tin (pan) with baking parchment. In a large mixing bowl, beat the butter with the sugar, eggs, flour and baking powder until creamy, pale and fluffy.

2 Spoon the mixture into the prepared tin and bake for about 20 minutes, or until just firm. Leave to cool for about 5 minutes, then turn the cake out on a wire rack. Leave to cool completely.

3 Wash and thoroughly dry the cake tin, ready to use again. Line the sides of the clean cake tin with a strip of baking parchment.

VARIATION
Use raspberry ice cream and fresh raspberries instead of strawberry ice cream and strawberries.

4 Using a sharp knife, carefully slice off the top of the cake where it has formed a crust. Save this for another purpose. Fit the cake in the tin, cut side down. Freeze for 10 minutes, then spread the ice cream evenly over the sponge and freeze until firm.

5 Pour the cream into a bowl, whip it until it forms soft peaks, then gently fold in the lemon curd and lemon juice. Spoon the mixture over the strawberry ice cream. Cover with clear film (plastic wrap) and freeze overnight.

6 About 45 minutes before you intend to serve the dessert, make the topping. Cut half the strawberries into thin slices. Put the remainder in a food processor or blender and add the caster sugar and Cointreau or other liqueur. Process the mixture to make a smooth purée.

7 Arrange the sliced strawberries over the top of the frozen gâteau and place in the refrigerator to soften. Serve with the sauce spooned over the top.

ICED PUMPKIN AND ORANGE BOMBE

PUMPKIN HAS A SUBTLE FLAVOUR THAT IS TRULY TRANSFORMED WITH THE ADDITION OF CITRUS FRUITS AND SPICES. HERE, THE DELICIOUS MIXTURE IS ENCASED IN SYRUPY SPONGE AND SERVED WITH AN ORANGE AND WHOLE SPICE SYRUP.

SERVES EIGHT

INGREDIENTS
  115g/4oz/½ cup unsalted (sweet)
    butter, softened, plus extra
    for greasing
  115g/4oz/generous ½ cup caster
    (superfine) sugar
  115g/4oz/1 cup self-raising
    (self-rising) flour
  2.5ml/½ tsp baking powder
  2 eggs
For the ice cream
  1 orange, well-scrubbed
  300g/11oz/scant 1½ cups golden
    granulated sugar
  300ml/½ pint/1¼ cups water
  2 cinnamon sticks, halved
  10ml/2 tsp whole cloves
  30ml/2 tbsp orange flower water
  400g/14oz can unsweetened
    pumpkin purée
  300ml/½ pint/1¼ cups extra thick
    double (heavy) cream
  2 pieces preserved stem
    ginger, grated
  icing (confectioners') sugar,
    for dusting

1 Preheat the oven to 180°C/350°F/
Gas 4. Grease and line a 450g/1lb loaf
tin (pan). Beat the softened butter,
caster sugar, flour, baking powder and
eggs in a bowl until creamy.

2 Spoon the mixture into the prepared
tin, level the surface and bake for about
30 minutes, or until firm in the centre.
Leave to cool.

3 To make the ice cream, pare thin
strips of rind from the orange, then cut
the strips into fine shreds. Squeeze the
orange and set the juice aside. Heat
the sugar and water in a small, heavy
pan, stirring constantly, until the sugar
dissolves. Bring to the boil and boil
rapidly, without stirring, for 3 minutes.

4 Stir in the orange shreds, juice,
cinnamon and cloves and heat for about
5 minutes. Strain the syrup, reserving
the orange shreds and spices. Measure
300ml/½ pint/1¼ cups of the syrup
and reserve. Return the spices to the
remaining syrup and stir in the orange
flower water. Pour into a jug (pitcher)
and set aside to cool.

5 Beat the pumpkin purée with 175ml/
6fl oz/¾ cup of the measured strained
syrup until evenly combined. Stir in the
cream and ginger. Cut the cake into
1cm/½in slices. Dampen a 1.5 litre/
2½ pint/6¼ cup pudding bowl and line
it with clear film (plastic wrap). Pour the
remaining strained syrup into a dish.

6 Dip the slices of cake briefly in the
syrup and use to line the prepared
bowl, placing the syrupy coated sides
against the side of the bowl. Trim the
pieces to fit where necessary, so that
the lining is even and any gaps are
filled. Place the bowl in the refrigerator
or freezer to chill.

7 Pour the pumpkin mixture into a
shallow container, cover and freeze
until firm. Spoon the ice cream into the
sponge-lined bowl, level the surface and
freeze until firm, preferably overnight.
If you are using an ice cream maker,
churn the pumpkin mixture until very
thick, then spoon it into the sponge-
lined bowl. Level the surface and freeze
until firm, preferably overnight.

8 To serve, remove the bombe from the
freezer about 30 minutes in advance to
allow it to soften slightly. Invert the ice
cream on to a serving plate. Carefully
lift off the bowl and peel away the clear
film. Dust with a little icing sugar and
serve in wedges with the spiced syrup
spooned over.

COOK'S TIP
If you prefer a smooth syrup, strain to
remove the cinnamon sticks and cloves
before spooning it over the bombe.

INDEX

Bibliography
The Oxford Companion to Food by Alan Davidson, Oxford University Press, Oxford, 1999

Jane Grigson's Fruit Book by Jane Grigson, Penguin Books, London, 1982

Citrus Varieties of the World by James Saunt, Sinclair International, revised and updated, Norwich, 2000

Picture Acknowledgements
The publishers would like to thank the following companies for the loan of their pictures: The Art Archive p6tr, p9bl; The Bridgeman Art Library Still life of grapes, oranges and a peeled lemon by Gillemans, Jan Pauwel the Elder (1618–75) Johnny van Haeften Gallery, London, UK p 6bl; Garden Picture Library p20, 21, 23, 29; Garden Wildlife Matters p14, 22 tr; Mary Evans Picture Library p7tr and b, p9tr; and V & A Picture Library p8.